Shooting Up

Shooting Up

A Memoir of Love, Loss and Addiction

JONATHAN TEPPER

CONSTABLE

CONSTABLE

First published in Great Britain in 2026 by Constable

1 3 5 7 9 10 8 6 4 2

Copyright © Jonathan Tepper, 2026

The moral right of the author has been asserted.

All rights reserved.
No part of this publication may be reproduced, stored in a retrieval system, or transmitted, in any form or by any means, without the prior permission in writing of the publisher, nor be otherwise circulated in any form of binding or cover other than that in which it is published and without a similar condition including this condition being imposed on the subsequent publisher.

A CIP catalogue record for this book is available from the British Library.

ISBN 978-1-40872-495-8 (hardback)
ISBN 978-1-40872-496-5 (trade paperback)

Typeset in Janson Text by Hewer Text UK Ltd, Edinburgh
Printed and bound in Great Britain by Clays Ltd, Elcograf S.p.A

Papers used by Constable are from well-managed forests and other responsible sources.

Constable
An imprint of
Little, Brown Book Group
Carmelite House
50 Victoria Embankment
London EC4Y 0DZ

The authorised representative
in the EEA is
Hachette Ireland
8 Castlecourt Centre,
Dublin 15, D15 YF6A, Ireland
(email: info@hbgi.ie)

An Hachette UK Company
www.hachette.co.uk

www.littlebrown.co.uk

To my parents, Elliott and Mary,
and brothers, David, Peter and Timothy, with love

Shooting Up is a memoir, a work of non-fiction. To protect people's privacy, I have changed some names. Many quotes from characters come straight from letters, diaries, news articles, emails, interviews and recordings. I have recreated some dialogues imperfectly, but I have tried to capture the spirit of the conversations as I remember them. Human memory works imperfectly, yet there are some things that you can never forget.

How natural it all seemed then; how remote and improbable now!

George Orwell, *Homage to Catalonia*

Chutando

Shooting Up

WE WERE ON the lookout for *yonkis*. My brothers and I shuffled our piles of pamphlets, hoping to get rid of them.

My father had been very clear. Before we headed out from our apartment, he called the family together in the living room, and we put our toy soldiers aside. Dad took a small mountain of religious tracts in his hands. He divided it into small piles, and we folded them neatly. It took for ever, and we started aligning the edges one by one, but we soon learned to fold them ten by ten by pushing all our weight onto them. They covered our coffee table, and when we were done, the pile rose thicker than a phone book.

'Give them to anyone who looks like a heroin addict. Come back empty-handed,' he told us. 'You will get an ice cream of whatever flavour you want if you do.'

I would definitely have a chocolate ice cream.

'Do you hear me, Jonathan?'

I nodded.

Dad prayed to bless our endeavour, and we headed out to find junkies.

One of the best places to find the addicts was by the Metro near Parque El Paraíso. Little Timothy, who was only two, played at my mother's feet, as she stood by my father. David, Peter and I moved through the sand and patches of green in El Paraíso, glancing from side to side for anyone who might look like a *yonki*. I had watched the junkies shoot up near our apartment, so it wouldn't be hard to recognise them.

My older brother, David, took off, determined to give everyone a copy of the pamphlet. He sprinted into the distance and chased a frightened Spanish kid as he forced the tract into his hand. In his excitement, David forgot the pamphlets were only for junkies. My younger brother Peter stayed close to me.

The pamphlet said 'VEN', which means 'Come' in Spanish. Our phone number appeared on the back, if they wanted to call us and get off drugs. It served as an unusual invitation to our home.

Under the headline 'I AM DRUGS', a smiling skeleton reached out his claw-like fingers towards the reader as he introduced himself:

It's me who in the beginning makes you live beyond the present world full of problems. But with time I am the very thing you cannot live without. After you have tried me, you're mine for the rest of your life.

I am destroying your life in every area – physically, morally and spiritually. It's me who has destroyed your family. It's me that caused you to go to prison.

I have you trapped.

You are in love with me. There is nothing in the world that can break our love affair.

The skeleton scared me a little; that was the point.

I gave my first pamphlet to a young man drinking a *litrona* of beer and eating sunflower seeds. He examined the paper and mouthed the words as he read them.

By the grass I spotted a man leaning against a park bench. His skull tilted to one side, his eyes staring into nowhere. His hair appeared oily and matted with dirt. I squatted and pushed the piece of paper into his hand, but he did not respond. I slid it into his shirt pocket.

'Keep it. It's got a phone number. Dial it if you want to get off drugs,' my small voice barely rising more than a whisper.

He looked up, his eyelids moving as if time proceeded more slowly for him than for me. I stared at him, and he stared back at me.

'You're a *guiri*. You look Swedish but sound Mexican.'

'I'm not Swedish. I'm American. My parents are missionaries.'

'If I were you, I'd lose that fucking accent.'

I was only seven, and I had spent almost all my life speaking Spanish the wrong way.

I nodded.

'You've got the pamphlet. Don't lose it, OK?'

Having escaped that encounter, I walked further ahead and found two men lying on a patch of grass. They were smoking cigarettes, but their sunken cheeks and rotting teeth told me they were junkies.

One man used the hollow of the bottoms of Coke cans to cook heroin powder with lemon juice before he drew it into the syringe. He shot up and blood speckled the syringe, and then he passed on the needle. My heart thumped as I approached. When they finished, they lay back, their eyes drifting into a hollow stare before closing and shutting out the world around them.

But I persisted, tapping the first guy on the shoulder and offering him a pamphlet.

'*Déjame en paz, chaval, o te rajo.*' – Leave me alone, kid, or I'll slit you.

I smiled nervously and backed away, relieved they did not get up to follow me.

Most of the addicts, though, took the pamphlets and put them in their pocket without saying a word. Others read the pamphlets as they drifted away. I hoped we would see them again.

As I walked up to *yonkis*, I studied them from a distance and learned to read their moods. Were they on edge and out to get money to buy drugs? Were they already high? My father said addicts might hurt each other, but they'd leave us alone. Bullies who bark are scared animals who almost never bite, he said.

David, Peter and I obeyed with unquestioning enthusiasm. Perhaps it was my parents' belief that God Himself would protect us that gave my brothers and me safe passage. Maybe it was the innocence of childhood. We were too small, too blond and too odd to be a threat to anyone.

I stepped among the broken syringes, their needles glistening before me. They were everywhere in San Blas. I had seen them in the dump behind our apartment and by the buildings down the street. They blanketed the entrance to the Gypsy camp. The junkies scavenged for used syringes and rebuilt them, mixing a needle from one and the body of another if the blood inside had not dried. Then they shared them.

As the sun set, the distant orange glow of cigarette ends guided me like faint beacons. My pile was thinning out, and one by one I gave out the leaflets until none remained.

We returned home empty-handed. No leaflets. But no addicts either. That was OK, though. My father told us we had planted seeds in men's hearts. Soon the harvest time would come.

My father was happy. I was too as I licked the chocolate ice cream.

When we arrived in Madrid, my three brothers and I – all blond-haired, blue-eyed American boys – did not look at all like the Spaniards around us. We were the only foreigners I knew in the neighbourhood.

We had gone from being Christian missionaries in Mexico to missionaries in Spain. I had lived almost all my life abroad, as we marched wherever God ordered. We were to be His shining witnesses, following His call to preach the gospel to the ends of the earth. Madrid wasn't a jungle in Africa, but our neighbourhood of San Blas might as well have been the edge of the world.

The umbilical cord back to our homeland was a microscopic black-and-white TV that we had to crowd around to watch. My parents thought television corrupted, not only morally, but intellectually. They relented and bought one for the 1984 Olympics in Los Angeles. Spain only had two TV channels, but they showed Carl Lewis win his gold medals in track and field, and Michael Jordan crush the Spaniards 96–65 in the basketball final.

When America won, we danced and chanted, 'USA, USA, USA!'

'Keep your voices down!' my mother scolded. 'Our neighbours won't be happy tonight.'

It wasn't only on the field and court that we beheld America's might. We felt it too when the F-16s streaked across the sky towards the NATO airbase in Torrejón. We had never visited, but the rumour was you could buy A&W Root Beer and M&Ms at the commissary. And I connected with American culture when I coaxed the radio dial. The Armed Forces Network station played Chuck Berry, Miles Davis and John Coltrane. But America remained far away: a place to which we only retreated on our missionary furlough every four years. Meanwhile, my mother's beautiful, handwritten letters to America took weeks to arrive, and transatlantic phone calls were a rare, expensive treat. We were adrift, on our own.

Millions of Americans lived scattered abroad, and Dad said we could be proud Americans and at home anywhere in the world. American expats had a long tradition going back to Thomas Jefferson and President John Quincy Adams, who spoke eight languages. Great writers like Henry James, Ernest Hemingway and T. S. Eliot had lived in other countries. Some Americans served in the armed forces, while others went to distant lands with Coca-Cola or the Peace Corps, and some were even missionary kids like me. Americans spread out, sprinkled about like specks of light in the night sky, brightening the world.

Our walls at home were sparse, even monastic. Not monastic like we were Catholics, because we were Protestants, even though my parents said God loved Catholics too. My father said many only went to church for the photographs of the first communion. The only things that adorned the walls by our dinner table in San Blas were small plaques and two posters – nothing fancy and not even framed, because it was the message that counted.

In the entrance, a small plaque hung with a quote from C. T. Studd, the founder of our mission: 'Some want to live within the sound of church or chapel bell; I want to run a rescue shop, within a yard of hell.'

In the sitting room, on one side hung *Freedom from Want*, a Norman Rockwell print of a perfect American family eating Thanksgiving dinner. America was a land we had left behind. The precision of the painting made it look like a photo. It reminded me of home, even though as a missionary kid, I never had a home – not that I particularly minded. In the picture the grandparents looked like my mom's parents back in the US, just a little shorter and chubbier. Or I may have been confusing things; my ideas of the place came from faded family photos and *Time* magazine covers.

On the other wall was a poster of a shepherd clinging to the edge of a cliff, his arm outstretched towards his lost sheep. An eagle swooped in the distance to seize the sheep with its sharp, giant claws. The way it looked to me, the shepherd was about to fall into the ravine with his sheep. He was barely holding on. Dad said the good shepherd lays down his life for his sheep. I just hoped he made it back up.

The images overlooked our family meals.

Dad quoted the Bible, as usual, 'Which of you men, if you had one hundred sheep, and lost one of them, wouldn't leave the ninety-nine in the wilderness, and go after the one that was lost, until he found it?'

He said that's what missionaries do, leaving behind the flock in America in search of the lost sheep. 'Pastor' meant 'shepherd' in Latin, after all . . .

We didn't have a church yet. In fact, we didn't have any sheep. We would have to find them. That was our mission.

Dad even placed The Great Commission with our family photo above his desk. It said, 'Elliott and Mary Tepper, missionaries to Spain', and below that Mark 16:15: 'And He said to them, "Go into all the world and preach the gospel to every creature."' He had copies printed so American churchgoers could hang it on their refrigerators and wouldn't forget we existed as the years passed.

Dad explained to us in our usual morning devotional – our interminable daily Bible-reading and prayer session – that God loves sinners, and we would bring them to Him. 'I tell you that even so there will be more joy in heaven over one sinner who repents, than over ninety-nine righteous people who need no repentance.'

I thought Dad said that because he'd been a sinner and God saved him like the little sheep. Even though he grew up Jewish in Long Island, he found Jesus after doing LSD at Harvard Business School. Make money, not war, and avoid the draft, his friends said, but he yearned for something else. That was when he and the hippies used mescaline and listened to Dylan and Baez. Their words lit the steps on the path to truth. He lived on a commune, but not a seedy one, he said, more like one for people from Harvard and MIT. That was before he met God.

Dad's arms grew hard from college wrestling, and he only spanked us with a reluctant resolve when we did not do exactly as he and Mom said. He was a clown who could walk up three flights of stairs doing handstands, do thirty one-handed push-ups, and wrestled my brothers and me on the carpet all at once until we were sweaty and stinky before dinner, which Mom did not like. But he was soft too. Words tugged at his soul, and he cried at the dinner table when he read stories to us.

'My body is broken. I go to my fathers. And even in their mighty company I shall not now be ashamed.' That's what Théoden said in Tolkien's *Lord of the Rings* before he died. And it made my father sad.

My father told us we needed to be wise and brave, but above all noble like Théoden, 'True nobility is in our hearts.'

Dad had grand visions of rescuing the lost sheep. He said he saw things beyond the veil that others did not. He told us at morning devotionals that when he died, we must put the words of Genesis 37:19 on his tombstone: 'Look, here comes the dreamer.'

We would find the sheep, he reassured us, even if I couldn't see them yet.

My mother didn't need to be rescued by God. She had known Him since she was a young girl in Sunday school. If she hadn't been born a Southern Baptist in Wilmington, North Carolina, she would have been a grand dame with a portrait in a museum. She stood tall and serene and always looked at ease. She spoke with no Southern accent like her parents, and when she talked in Spanish, she did so without fault. Even though she had never been outside of the US before becoming a missionary, she had poise, never looked out of place, and always had the right thing to say.

My mother was the Sancho Panza to Dad's quixotic dreams and the only one who could bend his plans and moderate his visions. Although she was tall and he was shorter, which was not like in my Don Quixote comic book. She was the one we went to if Dad wanted to spank us. She read my thoughts and looked after my brothers and me, yet not once did I wonder or ask how she felt about caring for four boys and a dreamer. She held little Timothy and smiled when we said goodbye to her parents in Wilmington, but she turned away to hide her tears and follow my father's visions into the distant unknown.

My mother packed our bags neatly and tightly; she fitted everything into the smallest number of suitcases possible. She had labelled and ordered everything. My father may have been the ringleader of the Tepper circus, but my mother kept the show on the road.

My aunt said they married first and fell in love later. They had a shared mission when they married, but had to figure out how to live with each other.

Mom and Dad were on a mission. Everything else, they told us, pales in the light of eternity. We had to abandon it all for the sake of the call.

C. S. Lewis wrote, 'Everything that is not eternal is eternally out of date.' That was why we had few earthly belongings.

Next to our dinner table sat a bookcase Dad had made by hand from cheap wood to house our *World Book* encyclopedias and *National Geographic* magazines. David was ten and had read them all. He remembered how many pages were in each volume, and he knew which numbers were primes and therefore more beautiful. But I didn't see what he saw in numbers. I advanced more slowly as my curiosity flitted back and forth like a butterfly alighting on pages. I lingered at the letter S, lost somewhere between Somalia and Suriname.

The encyclopedias were my favourite things in the world, even more than my green World War II toy soldiers and Matchbox cars. I burned with desire to know everything, and in the *National Geographic*s and encyclopedias, it was mine for the taking.

If your parents are engineers, plumbers or lawyers, it doesn't matter one bit to your life, but if your parents are missionaries, it changes everything. You can't pick your parents, but they get to pick your life. They decide where you'll live, when you'll pack your bags and go, and you'll get roped into their work saving the lost.

I couldn't decide almost anything about my life, but with my books and encyclopedias, my mind was free to roam where it wanted. Books could fit in any backpack, yet they contained entire worlds. They were my magic carpet to change reality and take me wherever I wanted.

Books filled every corner of our small apartment. My parents had made a study with bookcases that lined the walls from the floor to the ceiling, as my father had when he was growing up. Books were stacked randomly in piles on the carpet like stalagmites. My parents said books had the power to transport and transform you.

David shared a room with Timmy, and I bunked with Peter, who was only one year two months and one day younger than me. But my parents' books had a room all to themselves.

Theology, history and poetry books were the only thing we brought with us to Spain. Forget Betty Crocker cake mixes, American candy and other things that useless missionaries bring.

'They'll never cut it on the mission field,' my father said of the weak missionaries who had heard God's call but were not prepared to pay the price. 'They're chocolate soldiers who will melt when they face the heat.'

No. Real missionaries were like the Olympic gold medallist Eric Liddell. He was our hero, and when we ran, we held our heads high just as he did. Like me, Liddell grew up in a missionary family. The film *Chariots of Fire* ends with the words: 'Eric Liddell, missionary, died in occupied China at the end of World War II. All of Scotland mourned.' He taught classes to the children in the Japanese internment camp until his dying day.

My parents wanted to start a church among university students – the sort of people who liked books and learning as much as we did, the sort of people you could have conversations with and argue with at the dinner table late into the night.

That was how my father visited universities in Madrid in search of converts, but he returned home downcast and empty-handed. He shut the front door, took off his tweed jacket, made a cup of tea and retreated to his study to read the Bible and pray. The students did not want eternal salvation, even if it was free.

Every day he ventured out to the universities to speak to students about Jesus, and every day he returned alone. This continued for months, but their response was always the same. I felt sorry for him that his job was not easier.

'Their hearts are hard,' Dad said.

My father strained a smile and promised that soon God would send us sheep, but he retreated to the study where his cups of tea and small lithographs of Cambridge University consoled him. They reminded him of the year he spent studying economics at Selwyn College and how he stepped into its chapel and heard the voice of God when the choir sang. But like the university students in Madrid, he did not heed the call the first time God came to him. That only happened later after Harvard Business School when he had a vision of heaven and hell, and God told him to give his life to Him. My father obeyed and threw himself through a storefront window close to Harvard Yard.

The doctors who sewed him up thought it was LSD. My father said it was God.

His story sounded weird even to me. 'Why did God make you jump through a window?' I asked.

'Milton and Dante had visions of heaven and hell. The Apostle Paul's vision on the way to Damascus was strange, but Paul changed the world. Sometimes you've got to be a little strange to change the world.'

Dad stared off into the distance, enraptured in thought. He played Joan Baez's 'Forever Young' again. I pulled at his arm and twirled the hair on his forearms into curls to get his attention, but he put his finger to his lips. The music, he told me, was from a time when righteousness, truth and beauty mattered. Today, no one cared. But we would bring light to the lost.

Eres valiente . . .
o muy estúpido

You must be brave . . . or very stupid

A FEW WEEKS LATER, David, Peter, Timothy and I were getting ready for bed. Dressed in our Superman Underoos, we smelled of Johnson & Johnson children's shampoo, and our hair was wet and neatly combed. I clutched my copy of Kipling's *Just So Stories for Little Children*, waiting to go back to bed and read about snakes and mongooses. We sat on the edge of the sofa with our legs dangling, waiting to hear from my father.

My father spoke to us in the voice he always used to explain things. Planting a church among university students had not worked. Working with students was a dream that had to die. We would have to do something much bolder if we were going to succeed.

Fortunately, my parents told us that God had spoken. They said it as if He were our next-door neighbour.

I lived in a household where God talked back. My parents and God spoke to each other often. They chatted in the study among the books where they found peace and quiet, early in the morning before my brothers and I woke up. Perhaps that was why I had never seen God.

God sometimes sounded like a friend you could tell your problems to, and He would solve them if He wanted to. But other times, I imagined Him like a boss who told people where to go and what to do. It probably depended on God's mood. And if you rebelled, you might end up in the belly of a whale, like Jonah.

One morning, during one of these conversations, God summoned my parents to start a church for the *yonkis* in San Blas. From then on, we were going to work with heroin addicts.

My mother and father had not been interested in the Gypsies or dope addicts. Their dream had been to work with students in a world of letters. Our home stood as a temple of learning and culture, and the heroin addicts did not understand our life or appreciate good books. Our worlds could never meet.

My parents had resisted His call. And though you can argue with God, you can't ignore His voice for ever, they told us. They would have to sacrifice their dream of working with university students.

As Jesus said, 'To whom much is given, much is required.' We had a duty to help others.

If we strived, my father told us that one day we would be like William and Catherine Booth, who founded the Salvation Army. We were going to reach poor people in slums, bars, jails, brothels and factories, like the Booths did in the East End of London.

My father made it sound simple, and I believed it was. We would hold devotionals and speak to them about God. The junkies would be our flock, and we'd go out to the streets and invite them to our home for meetings. My father said with great certainty – the kind that comes from convening with the Almighty on a regular basis – that we would establish a church and that we were going to fill it.

'If we're willing to work with drug addicts, prostitutes and alcoholics, God is going to give us a church, a great church,' my father said. And unlike the students, the addicts would be desperate enough to listen.

If we did nothing to help the *yonkis*, we would be no better than the Pharisee strolling by the suffering man in the parable of the Good Samaritan. The addicts may have wrecked their own lives, but it was our duty to show them unconditional love. God would protect us and guide us in our task, my parents said.

We would live by the words of Saint Francis of Assisi, 'Preach the gospel at all times, use words if necessary.'

The next day David held Timmy in his arms and pressed his cheek against the glass to get a better view. From our enclosed balcony we looked out at the *barrio* from our small second-floor apartment. The neighbourhood's red-tiled rooftops waved and merged in the dry summer heat.

'Look at them,' David said. 'Those are *yonkis*. They could kidnap you.'

Timothy started crying, and my mother dived in and took him away.

'Do not tease him like that again.'

'Mommy's boy! Mommy's boy!' Peter squealed.

Thousands of heroin addicts came from all over Madrid to buy drugs, forming long uneven lines as they made their way towards the Gypsy camp. It did not matter if the sun was throbbing on summer days when Spaniards took their *siestas*, or if the ditches iced over in the dead of a Madrid winter; the addicts came and departed, like ants, forming a long line of pedestrians and vehicles. Their ashen outlines were a blur from a distance, only becoming clearer as they came closer.

Our neighbourhood was the biggest drug supermarket not only in Spain but in all of Europe, and it was happening right on our doorstep.

My mother wouldn't have picked the neighbourhood if given a choice, but San Blas was home because rent was cheap, and it was all penniless missionaries could afford.

Open fields bordered San Blas, but the red-brick apartment buildings within the neighbourhood sat squat and packed together. In the *barrio* three generations often lived in the same apartment. The dirt lots between the buildings collected garbage and the air was filled with the smell of burnt-out cars.

Our apartment on Calle Butrón stood back as a lonely sentry on a steep hill. Garbage accumulated in the dump behind it. Brick-masons came from all over Madrid to discard their rubbish late at night, driving down the dirt roads at the far end with their lights turned off. Chunks of cement and cardboard boxes mixed with used needles.

Beyond the dump, a Gypsy village teemed with life. The Gypsy camp sat on the edge of Avenida de Guadalajara and Carretera de Vicálvaro, a busy two-lane highway that connected San Blas with the town of Vicálvaro. The *gitanos* lived on the periphery of Spanish society. The camp had electricity, stolen from the municipal grid. They built huts with odd pieces of wood and plastic sheets held down by tyres. The small huts were like skulls; the glassless panes were sockets where dark children peered out at me like eyes.

The Spanish government set aside a few prefabricated houses on one side of the camp for the *gitanos*, but many sat uninhabited, the copper pipes torn out and the doors taken off their hinges. These prefabs were *Los Focos*, and they were the centre of the heroin trade in Madrid.

My brothers and I stood at a distance from the camp entrance to watch the spectacle.

The Gypsies' mysterious presence intrigued me. They sold heroin but almost never consumed it, as if following some unwritten code. The Gypsies dealt for the same reason they sold tubs and pipes: there were buyers and the money was better. The Gypsies drove new Mercedes vans large enough to carry their meagre belongings yet lived in dilapidated houses. They migrated from city to city and the Spaniards encouraged them not to settle anywhere too long.

At the entrance to the Gypsy camp someone had spray-painted a graffito in Spanish on a wall, 'Abandon all hope, you who enter.' The Gypsies didn't care what others thought of them, and I admired that.

I asked my father about the quotation.

'It's from Dante. One day you'll be old enough to read him.'

Every Friday night we ventured out to the streets of San Blas to invite the addicts into our home. We went out to the camp, to El Paraíso park, and to bars. My mother accompanied us and carried Timothy in her arms. He was still too young to hand out VENs, but he often played at my father's feet while David, Peter and I handed out tracts. I felt a quiver of excitement every time we headed out to meet the *yonkis*.

Some junkies wanted us to send them to a rehab centre. Others asked for money; perhaps they thought of us as marks to be conned, ready to support their habit. They weren't counting on my mother, who reminded us of Jesus's words from the book of Matthew, 'Behold, I send you forth as sheep in the midst of wolves: be ye therefore wise as serpents, and harmless as doves.' She hugged and kissed addicts no matter how much grime they had under their fingernails or if they had gone days without bathing. She treated princes and paupers alike, but she had a sixth sense of who needed help and who was conning us. I envied her skill – I had given too many hundred-*peseta* allowances to junkies who told me they were hungry.

Yonkis had no jobs. Instead, they spent their days wandering around the neighbourhood looking for things to steal. Once they had succeeded, they sold the loot and bought drugs. Rest only came once they had shot up.

My parents worked with Lindsay, a young Australian fellow missionary who lived a few blocks away from our house, and Myk, a missionary nurse from New Zealand. Lindsay was a clean-cut man in his late twenties. He parted his brown hair down the middle and he wore a short, well-groomed moustache. Myk always brought her guitar along to play in the park. If nothing else, people gathered around to hear her sing.

After every song, my father and Lindsay invited people to come to our home for a Bible study, but almost no one came. Sometimes David, Peter, Timothy and I found ourselves the only people in attendance besides Lindsay and Myk.

While my father spoke about how we all have a hole in our hearts and an emptiness that only God can fill, I squirmed on the living-room rug with my brothers and thought of other things. Could my toy Tyrannosaurus Rex beat my Triceratops in a fight, even if the Triceratops was quick and used his horns? If a Siberian snow tiger met a regular one, would they get along or fight? And what time was it anyway? I was hungry.

The talk went on, so I opened my *A Child's History of the World* by V. M. Hillyer that I hid under my Bible. With my crayons I coloured in the faces of Xerxes, Henry VIII and Anne Boleyn, as well as Abraham Lincoln. When I became somebody – a great man one day – would a young boy crayon my face a hundred years later? I trusted that with a little luck, he would make me look sharp and stay inside the lines.

The empty meetings did not dissuade my parents. Hadn't Moses and Jesus ignored rejection when they first brought their message? The sheep would come. So my brothers and I continued in our children's crusade to hand out tracts and bring *yonkis* back to our apartment.

Camellos worked everywhere in San Blas, and many of them did their deals in bars like El Nilo, Torre del Campo and El Sila. The closest to our home was Torre del Campo on Calle de la Masilla. It was by the police station and would have been an unremarkable place if its clientele weren't dealers and *yonkis*.

The bar was in the middle of a maze of compact red-brick buildings. The passageways between them were covered so that you moved from one to the other without seeing the sun. Nearly every family living near the bar had a child who was a heroin addict, and many had lost a son to an overdose.

I stayed outside Torre del Campo with my brothers while my father and Lindsay entered. They talked to the *yonkis* there, sometimes interrupting the purchase of tinfoil *papelinas*. Torre del Campo had wrought-iron doors, and a large striped awning kept it in the shade. From a distance I could hear Michael Jackson's 'Beat It' playing, and it was impossible to see where the black doors ended and the darkness inside began.

One day while my father and Lindsay stood at the bar, a man introduced himself, 'You're looking for *yonkis*, I hear. I'm Ángel. Everyone calls me *Veneno*, but I don't mind.'

He lifted his sleeve and showed a crudely inked tattoo on his right arm that read in bold letters *VENENO*, 'poison' in Spanish.

Veneno was short and had brown hair that covered his eyes and ears. His green eyes darted and flickered as he peered through his long bangs, only relaxing when my father listened.

Without much persuading, he unburdened himself of his own story. He spoke with a *rat-tat-tat* of facts and anecdotes that he juggled in his mind. *Veneno* did not know who his father was, and his mother was a prostitute who had left him to be raised by her father in his cramped one-bedroom apartment. His grandfather suffered from wounds inflicted in the Spanish Civil War and the indignities of age. Once a month *Veneno* carried him on his back to collect his pension. After they collected it, *Veneno* borrowed a quarter of it to buy heroin. He always promised to repay the money, and he convinced himself he would.

Veneno was the man my father had been waiting for. He knew everything about everyone and promised he would bring many people to my father. He would point to someone, 'See that guy . . .' and the stories would flow. Like a Russian doll, each story contained more stories nestled inside.

At the bar, my father learned dealers slashed *yonkis* in the chin when they failed to pay; the scars marked them as thieves. Others suffered from the impurities used to dilute the dope. Enrique, an addict my father met, went blind after shooting up. A dealer had cut his heroin with strychnine, a rat poison.

As my father looked around the neighbourhood, I always caught *Veneno* glancing back, waiting for a smile or a nod. Information served as his currency, exchanging it only for rapt attention. He put his hand on my father's shoulder, guiding his audience, and took him over to meet his targets. He swooped on long cigarette butts by the bus stop, even as he told his stories. David, Peter and I stuck close behind like remoras to a shark, attaching ourselves to the conversation, hoping some of the juicier bits would fall our way.

Often the men wore Rolling Stones and Iron Maiden T-shirts, but in the summer they walked around with their shirts off, their skin deeply tanned and adorned with tattoos. When they wore shorts, I saw the marks of their addiction on the veins in their legs. The *yonkis* all looked the same to me. But *Veneno* knew them by name and was the keeper of their stories.

What addicts wanted was to shoot up, to chase the high. When they weren't using, they hunted for anything to make some cash to score. Not having the drug made them anxious, pulsing with a nervous energy. To keep themselves going they devoured sweets and Cokes. The sugar gave them a burst of energy, but that was about it. If they were lucky, nicotine helped a little.

The *yonkis* took all kinds of drugs, but heroin was their daily bread. They were always desperate for money to score one more gram. Some addicts hawked Kleenex boxes at traffic lights, standing for hours in the sun as they competed against groups of Gypsy children who threw water on the windscreens. Other *yonkis* stole from shops at knifepoint or broke into cars to take the radios. They would not rest until they had scored.

Veneno introduced my father to the VIPs '*los que importan*' like Manolo, whose nickname was *Majara*, Crazy. He had been called that ever since a dealer stuck a gun in his face and Manolo grabbed the barrel, stuck it in his mouth and dared the dealer to pull the trigger. *Majara* was short but strong, with large, rough hands, and I liked to see the muscles in his jaw bulge and ripple when he gritted his teeth. The first time my father tried to talk to him, *Majara* threatened to slit my father's neck if he ever spoke to him again. *Majara* always carried a knife in his boot and brandished it, enjoying the dance of light on the blade, but it was not an idle threat.

'What kind of God permits all the hunger and suffering and misery that surrounds us?' *Majara* said. 'He has a lot to answer for.'

My father said something about God's love and grace and all that kind of stuff, but I stopped listening when *Majara* pulled out a gun and stuck it in my father's face. I was too excited to be afraid.

'I could shoot you if I wanted.'

'I'm sure you could.'

'You must be brave . . . or very stupid,' *Majara* said.

Veneno was true to his word: every meeting he introduced my father to more addicts and brought them to our living room. Some appeared deranged, others too high to be coherent. Many fell asleep in the meetings, and others came and left without paying much attention to what was happening – to the irritation of our neighbours. But the *yonkis* kept on coming for help.

My father hoped he'd find his Apostle Peter. He was one of Jesus's first disciples and the great fisher of men. Although Peter wasn't high most of the time.

'You have to meet Raúl, but everyone calls him *El Tocho*,' *Veneno* said like it was news of great weight. It was Christmas, and *Veneno* offered him as a gift to us.

Veneno said that if you had no nickname, you weren't worth meeting. Most addicts had a telltale gaunt and weak look. Food came a distant second behind scoring a gram. But, somehow, despite his heroin addiction, Raúl never lost much weight or strength and earned the nickname *El Tocho*, Stocky.

Raúl teetered in, sweaty and wafting an aroma telling me he hadn't showered for a few days. Bandages covered his left arm.

My father's mother was visiting us from America. She thought my father displayed signs of insanity – hearing from God, wasting his life as a missionary. Raúl's gin-soaked kisses on both cheeks only confirmed her views.

'Elliott, keep him away from me!' she said as she retreated and firmly held her handbag close to her body. 'What kind of life is this for your kids, exposing them to this? You will ruin their lives. They will never forgive you.'

I felt relieved no one understood her English.

'What's wrong with your arm? Did it get infected shooting up?' I said as I poked at Raúl's bandage.

'You shouldn't ask questions like that at your age, kid. It's not polite,' Raúl said.

'Does it hurt when the needle goes in?'

'You ask too many questions. You sound like a cop. *Tranqui*. Take it easy.'

I considered myself a bit of an expert on track marks. I had watched my mother clean the bleeding, infected arm of an addict in the kitchen, between her duty serving lemonade and cookies and looking after little Timothy.

Track marks lined the arms of the *yonkis*. If they found a vein in the forearm, they shot up in the same place until they developed scabs. Their veins eventually collapsed. Addicts could shoot old veins, but they were liable to shoot the skin instead. They started with their left arm and then turned to the right when the left had wasted. Then they injected in the arteries behind the knees or on the back of the hands, and they moved on to the groin, the neck, or under the tongue.

Where was Raúl shooting up now? I'd ask him when he was in a better mood.

As I looked more closely at his hands, I saw the burn marks. After shooting up *yonkis* appeared to fall asleep, and sometimes while smoking a cigarette they burned their fingers. My brothers and I learned to identify addicts by the marks of their addiction – the track marks and the burns on their fingers.

I took Ángel and *Majara* back to the room I shared with Peter to play with our Matchbox cars. *Majara* displayed little interest in the toys and pinched my arms for amusement. When he shook my hand, his strong grip crushed my fingers.

He squeezed and I winced in pain. Certain that my knuckles would break, I waited for the crack.

'Stop! Please, please stop!'

I tried not to scream.

I knew that if I called out for my father, he would ask me why I was fighting and not setting a proper example. *Be kind. Be Christian.* That's what my parents always said.

Majara only offered a pitying laugh. With my free hand I punched his arm, but he punched me back, hurting me far more than I'd hurt him.

'Leave the kid alone.'

I turned around to see Raúl standing in the doorway with his bandaged arm.

'What are you going to do? You've only got one good arm,' *Majara* taunted.

'My right's OK and that's all I need to knock you out. Leave the kid alone.'

Majara held my hand as he glared at Raúl. He slowly let go and smirked as he left the room.

I rubbed my hand, trying to coax blood back into my fingers.

Raúl came over, kneeled by my side and gave me a playful punch on the shoulder. 'Don't take it too hard, kid. It's got nothing to do with you. His dad used to beat him. Well . . . he did until his mother punched the old man down a stairwell.'

'Thanks. Want to play?'

'You heard it. I've only got one good arm.' He smiled. 'And I've got to go.'

'Will you come back and play sometime?'

'We'll see each other again.'

I hoped he would be true to his word and stay around to protect me.

Mejor solo que mal acompañado

Better off alone than in bad company

As we entered the dim apartment block, my father stopped and smiled at me. 'Want to race up to Pilar's house?'

I nodded.

'You're both crazy,' my mother said. She was the sensible one and walked straight over to the lifts that rattled all the way up.

'OK. Ready . . . Set . . . *GO!*'

I skipped steps two at a time and pushed myself off the walls on the turns between floors. He was gaining on me, and in a few leaps, he disappeared around a corner. My mother was waiting by the door with my father at her side.

'Slowpoke, you may beat me some day, but it won't be soon . . .' my father said as he ruffled my hair.

We rang the doorbell and Pilar greeted us with a kiss on both cheeks. Pilar had a thin face, pointed nose and short dark hair. When we met her, she spoke softly and rarely smiled. She served coffee, hot chocolate and biscuits while she talked to my parents.

I sat quietly eating as many cookies as possible, looking around the room, trying not to drop any crumbs. The room appeared spotless, the lace on the coffee table gleamed bright white, and she had meticulously arranged the knick-knacks on the shelves that smelled of wood cleaner.

People from San Blas had *orgullo de barrio*, neighbourhood pride, and tried to keep the streets clean. Spanish housewives kept impeccable apartments. Their white laundry blew in the wind on the balconies. It was important to have an immaculate, dust-free home – cleanliness itself became an act of defiance against what the neighbourhood had become. There may have been a heroin-addicted son living at home, but a family's living room never betrayed the secret.

Pilar had photographs on the wall of her children during their first communions next to crucifixes with a bleeding Jesus. My parents said nothing about these. That might have been rude. To them, Catholics were obsessed with a suffering Jesus, frozen on the cross with a crown of thorns, while Protestants treasured the certainty that he rose from the dead and was no longer in pain.

While my mother and Pilar spoke, I eavesdropped, avoiding all eye contact. Their voices rose and fell, weaving around each other. At home Mom did not speak as often as Dad, uttering words only when they were better than silence. With her friends, though, the words unfurled themselves. I tried to follow the thread of their stories. They spoke of whose son was on drugs, whose daughter was walking the streets, who was in jail. When mothers spoke, they no longer felt alone; they tried to give context to each other's suffering, reminding each other that they belonged to a tribe that shared the burden of their struggles.

As I listened, it occurred to me that women were better talkers than men. They did not yak in clipped slang like the men on the streets, conveying their meanings by gestures and grunts. The colourful quilt of stories was something only women could make. I sat back, amazed by my mother, hoping that maybe one day I could talk to people like that too.

All the while, Dad stared off into space, probably thinking about J. R. R. Tolkien and C. S. Lewis, wondering what they debated at the gatherings of the Inklings in Oxford. Would they have invited him to join their circle?

Mom had a way of remembering everyone's name, how many children they had, and even what their birthdays were. She sent birthday cards to everyone and never sent the same one twice. I was more like my father, my mind prone to wander. But my mother had the kaleidoscope of faces, the calendars and family trees in her head. She would store away information from these conversations to retrieve later. Who needed to remember names or birthdays with her around?

Pilar said that at first San Blas was simply *el barrio*. Years before, the area had been dirt fields. It existed on the edge, standing forlorn between Madrid and the countryside towns.

'None of the older people are from San Blas. We moved in hope of something better.' She came like the hundreds of thousands of others from the provinces, leaving their dying villages in search of jobs. 'We lived like Gypsies then,' she said, 'and we had nothing.'

The first people to arrive in San Blas built crude shacks that sprouted overnight and then, like poppies, quickly disappeared. The better houses were made of bricks unevenly cobbled together, washed bone-white with lime.

General Franco's public works ministry developed large tracts of housing, and Pilar was among the lucky ones who moved into government-built housing.

'There were no drugs when Franco was alive. When he died, it all went to hell. San Blas devoured its young.'

I knew little about General Franco. His face was still on some coins, but he no longer existed, like some embarrassing, deranged uncle who was best forgotten. Dad said Franco was a dictator, but a friendly dictator, not like Hitler or Stalin.

When Franco died in 1975, Spain was free at last. Political parties were no longer banned, films no longer censored, and shops finally opened on Sunday. Not everything was for the better. Franco's regime shot drug dealers, keeping drugs scarce. Afterwards drugs were plentiful, and the *chavales* tried cannabis, amphetamines, cocaine and, above all, heroin.

Dad said Spain was finally catching up with the rest of the world, shuffling off the shackles of Franco's fascism. Spain had just joined NATO and was about to join the European market. But Pilar had her views, and we listened and nodded politely. We were there to win sheep, not correct them. I grinned, bobbed my head and drank my hot chocolate.

Four of Pilar's seven children became *yonkis*. The police killed her oldest son, José, in a shoot-out during a bank robbery. After his death, she was *muerta de disgusto*, dead from sadness. She recounted mundane stories in endless detail – José's *fútbol* games in the streets, walking him to school – details of little importance at the time, acquiring great resonance only after José's death.

Her daughter Begoña and a younger brother were junkies, and she feared they too would die like José. She pleaded with my parents for help.

I peeked at my Casio watch and pressed the button so the numbers would flash. Why did other people's stories take so long to tell? Would Pilar mind if I took another cookie while she finished?

As we said goodbye to Pilar, I felt really proud of the kindness we had showed her in listening to her troubles.

Some American families travel on vacation to Yosemite to learn how Sequoias can grow to three hundred feet or how geysers spew boiling water. Our vacations were visits to drug rehabs to learn if junkies would hurl when they went cold turkey.

Heroin sales were booming in Madrid, and the city did not have enough drug rehabs to cope with the wave of *yonkis* seeking help. When we travelled around Spain, we were not tracing the footsteps of pilgrims on the trail of Santiago de Compostela or gawping at Spanish cathedrals. We headed to Burgos, Vitoria and Santander, checking out drug rehabs. My parents were doing their research.

If my brothers and I could bring our *fútbol* and play in an open field near the rehab, we did not care about the ticking of time. But the worst of the trips was sitting in waiting rooms with uncomfortable, creaky chairs while my parents talked to administrators about detoxing. At least some rooms had televisions with *Superman* playing.

Our family piled into the fire-engine-red van my parents had bought to carry *yonkis* to distant centres up north. My mother packed sandwiches and Cokes, and my brothers and I sat in the back and talked to the addicts for hours as my father drove.

'How much does a gram of *caballo* cost?' I asked Cheli, the young woman accompanying us up north.

'Why do you care? You're too young to buy.'

'I'm not too young to know. How old were you when you started?'

'Sixteen. And I'm not telling you how much a gram costs.'

'Well ... Did you know that they've deciphered the hieroglyphs? Jean-François Champollion taught himself a dozen languages and figured out the hieroglyphs with the Rosetta Stone. I read it in my encyclopedia.'

'Talk to your brothers and leave me alone.' She took her coat and bunched it up against the window to sleep. 'Don't talk to me until we get there.'

'Did you know killer whales sleep with half their brain and only close one eye?'

'Did you know that you're annoying?'

Some people weren't as intrigued by *National Geographic* and that kind of stuff as I was.

I had already learned that others did not see the world the way I did. When I was six, I stayed home sick, while David and Peter caught the school bus. In that moment, I realised the world did not revolve around me. I spent the day reading through flash cards of animals and insects, memorising details of their lives and anatomy. One of the cards was of a fly with six thousand simple eyes that formed two large compound eyes. Who knew that little flies had so many eyes? I realised then that the world was like a giant apple, and we were all the little eyes, taking things in from a slightly different angle, trying to figure out the bigger picture. But I had difficulty seeing the world from the perspective of others.

I talked the whole way, while David calculated how many killer whales could fit between us and the car behind us, given the average length of a killer whale. He had invented the game to speed our rehab express trips along. The game was not much fun because he had memorised the length of all animals, just as he had memorised countless digits of pi.

Over the coming months, my father meticulously wrote the names of people we took to centres up north, but he stopped after sixty-three. Some addicts stayed but many hitchhiked back to San Blas faster than my father could drive. Dad said that if you put a *yonki* on the moon, he'd find a way back to earth without a spaceship. At least some heeded God's call, unlike the university students.

I had handed a pamphlet to Pilar's daughter Begoña on one of our Friday-night expeditions for *yonkis*. My parents took Begoña to a Christian centre up north. Begoña did not stay long and was back, walking the streets to pay for her habit. My father found her near Torre del Campo and offered to help, but she was uninterested: 'I'm pretty and can always get money,' she said. I thought she was beautiful and probably right.

My father sent one of her younger brothers to a centre on the northern coast. Every week he called home to reassure Pilar that he was doing better, and Begoña followed him. This time she stayed. She invited her friend Toñi to join her, and Toñi invited her husband José, who had just got out of jail for armed robbery, and he invited three of his friends. They all passed through our home – Hotel Tepper, as my mother called it, or Grand Central, as Lindsay called it – on their way to rehabs.

At last, my parents were finding their sheep, and I could scarcely believe the variety of the characters that came through our home. My parents, Lindsay and Myk were fighting heroin one addict at a time, and the church grew.

Our family living room could no longer fit everyone who came to us, so with tithes that my parents received from churches in the States they rented a small storefront in Lindsay's building. My father called the church Betel, which means 'House of God'.

In Madrid, Catholics outnumbered Protestants a thousand to one. We were an odd minority, but no one cared. One old lady who lived by the church asked if my father was a con man or a real minister because he did not wear a clerical collar and gave his sermons in a polo shirt.

We were there to help, and many mothers and family members of the addicts continued coming to our church meetings even after their sons and daughters returned to heroin. So many came that my mother and Myk organised a women's group that met every Tuesday. Pilar brought her friends, and they brought theirs, and the group grew.

If *yonkis* hustled and couldn't rest until they scored, my parents showed an equal obsession in their quest to save the lost sheep.

Sending addicts one by one to centres outside Madrid was like using a teacup to bail a sinking ship. San Blas needed a drug rehab close by that could take in lots of people.

After much prayer and discussion with Lindsay and Myk, my parents decided to found a centre of their own in Madrid. They put together a proposal for the mission to create a drug rehabilitation centre like the ones they had visited.

Despite the engulfing need, the mission my parents belonged to wanted nothing to do with the project. Converting people was much safer than helping them. My parents were free to go ahead, but they would not receive any support from the mission – unless, of course, the project was a wild success.

'How convenient,' my mother said. 'As the Spaniards say, *mejor solo que mal acompañado*. Better off alone than in bad company.'

Honestly, I think she was as distrustful of missionaries as drug addicts. Some missionaries once asked my mother if it was hard to work with addicts, and she said, 'Oh, it's much easier than working with normal people. At least addicts know they're broken and need help. They don't pretend.'

The mission deemed my parents reckless for starting a drug rehab when they had four young boys. Why not wait until we were older? Did they not know the danger they were putting me and my brothers in? It would wreck our lives. The addicts could rob or stab us handing out tracts.

'Excuses,' my father said. 'No one has hurt us so far. *Yonkis* want help to get off drugs.'

What did the mission know about San Blas? Sure, junkies had broken our car windows many times to steal the radio, but that was my father's fault, I told myself. You don't leave valuables out in San Blas. That was the rule.

Less excusable were the two kids on a motorbike who knocked my mother to the ground when they snatched her handbag. I mean, nobody was too badly hurt. Nasty bruises covered her arms, but she recovered.

As far as my brothers and me, we could take care of ourselves. Honestly, who would mess with a bunch of little blond kids anyway?

At least the mission wouldn't stand in the way. My parents had permission for the project. It was better than nothing. And nothing was all we had.

My parents and Lindsay refused to abandon the call, but they were flying solo. Starting a charity from scratch is a daunting task, and neither Lindsay nor my parents were trained to work with junkies. But they believed God would provide the addicts and the answers. There was no turning back.

While my parents argued with the mission, Raúl had left the centre my father had taken him to. He spent five months on the streets, robbing to support his habit. He said life was intolerable, and when drunk he often thought of killing himself.

But he kept coming back to our living room for lemonade and cookies, listening to my father's sermons. My father preached that every human life is infinitely valuable, as he quoted Romans 5:8, 'But God shows His love for us in that while we were sinners, Christ died for us.'

I knew the devotional messages by heart and drifted off into my memory of the order of American presidents and dates of wars as he spoke, but Raúl took it all in.

One day Raúl came to Lindsay for help. It was two weeks before he was required to appear in court over an armed robbery. He wanted to show up clean and sober, and therefore needed to check in to a drug rehab. But he didn't want to leave Madrid.

Without thinking, Lindsay offered to let him stay in his apartment to detox. Lindsay figured that most addicts never showed up for appointments; Raul would be no exception. But at nine o'clock the next morning Raúl showed up on Lindsay's doorstep, and we had our first addict in residence.

Raúl lived on Calle Porcelana near Torre del Campo. He came from a family of eight children. His father reeked of brandy, which he said made you warm and life more pleasant. I hated when Raúl's father pinched my cheeks, planted a wet kiss on them, and breathed on me when he hadn't brushed his teeth. The whiskers of his moustache scratched my face. When he stood at the entrance to the church, he smoked a cigarette with a drinking buddy who coughed and splattered speckles of bright red blood on the floor. David and I ran to the nearest bar to get sawdust so no one would track red footprints into church.

One Sunday after church, Raúl's mother invited us to her home and prepared Spanish *gazpacho* and *paella*. Her living room shelves were empty. Raúl had stolen the television and radio for a gram of *caballo*.

She called us *pequeños rubitos*, little blond boys, and ran her fingers through our fine hair, as if handling curious specimens. I found her equally strange. She giggled when we spoke English and gave me a twenty-five-*peseta* coin to buy sweets. Mothers giving us money infuriated my parents. Who knows how long they worked for it, my mother asked? But I mean, they offered, so I kept it anyway.

She told us stories of Raúl. He had quit school when he was thirteen to work as a plumber. When he was not working, he smoked weed. He quickly moved on to amphetamines and coke.

Raúl hoped the *mili*, a year of mandatory military service, might help him kick the habit. When he returned to the *barrio*, his friends had moved on from weed to shooting up. Raúl joined in. With heroin he had found his drug.

Injecting heroin gave him such a sense of peace that when he had the urge to vomit the first few times, even the queasiness provided a strange, soothing warmth inside. As he stumbled around, nothing mattered; vomiting, pissing, drinking – it was all the same, making him feel better than ever.

Like some addicts in San Blas, Raúl dealt to support his own habit, always chasing the white-powder bliss of the initial high. He spent all the money he made taking larger doses. Not much of a dealer, though, he soon held up supermarkets, his face covered by a mask, threatening the cashier with a gun. He robbed shops throughout Madrid by day, and at night terrorised people who were taking their evening *paseos* around the neighbourhood, as he held a knife to their necks.

One of Raúl's favourite methods for stealing was to pull a knife on a messenger of a *camello* to get the *papelinas*. Dealers wised up fast. After that, he pretended to be a dealer, and he took the customers to the toilets of Torre del Campo and pulled a knife. That didn't last long either. No one would buy heroin from him.

The thrill of the early high, though, was gone. 'It's not even about fun,' Raúl said, 'it's about surviving until the next fix.'

The first week Raúl lived with Lindsay in the apartment, his body functioned without heroin. Restlessness and insomnia troubled him, but Lindsay gave him chamomile tea and nothing stronger. For the first few days he said he had no feeling, no purpose, no desire to do anything. It was not painless, but Raúl did not hallucinate, his teeth did not gnash, and Lindsay did not need to tie him down. That stuff only happens in badly written movies by Hollywood types who have never used. In a week, Raúl was eating and sleeping well.

My father, Lindsay and Raúl became inseparable. Cooking, buying groceries, reading the Bible – they did everything together.

I visited Raúl with my father, and I sat quietly as they and Lindsay talked. He was getting the devotional treatment I got at home. I prayed God would give him patience.

One night, he sat alone in the living room in the dark and prayed, 'Whatever love and kindness you've given Lindsay, give that to me. Come into my heart, forgive me for my sins. Give me love for others.'

A warm sense of peace washed over him. He lay awake on the carpet, repeating 'God, God, God . . .'

When Raúl told me about it, I wondered: did his heart cocoon in his ribcage like a caterpillar before breaking out, transformed into a beautiful butterfly? Or did his spirit soar out like an eagle sweeping over San Blas?

I was a missionary kid, and I mean I was supposed to be saved and all that, but I had experienced nothing like it. Perhaps my heart was hard.

Raúl was a changed man, in the same way my father was when he said God had spoken to him after Harvard. All Raúl wanted to do was tell others about what had happened to him.

After four months of living with Lindsay, Raúl was eager to help his friends on the streets. He asked if he could bring in more *yonkis*. Lindsay agreed. Raúl rounded up Victor, Luis Mendoza, Paco Corrales, and others, and soon the small apartment heaved with eight men.

To me it sounded like an exciting sleepover of *yonkis*. I kept the faces of the early addicts in my head, like sculptures filling a mausoleum, each labelled with notes on their stories I had overheard, even if I couldn't remember all their names.

We were in business. At last, we had a drug centre, my father said. He'd bring back to the dinner table the stories of his time with Raúl and the men, and we lapped it up. Dad's stories were genuine and even better than reading encyclopedias.

Every *yonki*'s life told a story, and I could always remember the most colourful. Victor, known as *El Granos* because of his pock-marked face cut with deep grooves, had long hair and wore a raincoat in the summer. His brother died in a shoot-out with police, and ever since he had not cared about dying. In shops, he opened his coat, pointed to an enormous axe and waited for the cashier to obey. Often, he would trash the place even after he got his money, just so they'd remember him.

Even Manolo *Majara* wanted in. My father found him sleeping in the entrance to the church with his clothes in a black bag. He said he would not move until Raúl promised to let him move into the apartment. When he entered the centre, I avoided him unless Raúl was around.

Lindsay and Myk, my parents and the small band of men were like a first-century Christian community, sharing everything they had. As my father had read at church one Sunday morning from the book of Acts, the New Testament's account of the early church:

All the believers were one in heart and mind. No one claimed that any of their possessions was their own, but they shared everything they had . . .
For from time to time those who owned land or houses sold them, brought the money from the sales and put it at the apostles' feet, and it was distributed to anyone who had need.

This wasn't like socialism or some hippy commune where the dirty dishes piled up, my dad said. This was God's love poured out on a parched land.

To help pay for meals and expenses, my parents gave money from the tithes we lived on. Churches in America would send money to my parents, but much of it ended up funding the drug rehab. The mothers of the men came by, often to prepare lunch and dinner.

The centre had no method to its rehabilitation, no formal technique. My parents and Lindsay had no offices, no staff, no accreditation. Those things would come later. The start was just love. Just grace.

My parents' donations were touching, but they wouldn't feed all the men or house them. For that they needed a lot more money. Yet the government in Madrid hadn't even started spending money on drug prevention or rehabilitation.

Fundraising from America would take too long – letters took weeks to arrive – and it might not even raise much money anyway. Who wanted to give money to a bunch of addicts, much less in a foreign country? The men needed to eat.

My father had his MBA from Harvard, but he didn't write a business plan. People needed to eat, and working paid the bills. It was that simple. Betel was not the first charity to run a business, and it wouldn't be the last.

My father reminded us that Saint Benedict wrote in the sixth century, 'Idleness is the enemy of the soul.' Benedict ordered periods of manual labour followed by prayerful reading. *Ora et labora*, work and pray, and *lectio divina*, divinely inspired reading. Honestly, I wasn't sure you could call that a business plan.

Raúl had worked as a plumber before he became a *yonki*, and most of the men knew a trade as well. To keep busy and help pay for the rocketing costs of the community, the men took on odd jobs, but they weren't steady.

Eventually they saved enough to start a furniture shop. People donated furniture they no longer wanted, and Raúl and the men took it away for free. They repaired and restored the pieces and sold them cheaply. They loved taking something others thought was rubbish, cleaning it, caring for it and transforming it into something new with sandpaper, varnish and care.

Everyone in the centre worked. Once addicts made it through the first few weeks, Raúl gave them a job. No one sat around alone with their thoughts. Raúl was strict. Everyone had to attend morning devotionals and Sunday morning services.

The devotionals were like at our house. In Lindsay's living room, my father read from the Psalms or the Gospels or from Paul's letter to the Romans chapter 4:

> Blessed are they whose iniquities are forgiven, And whose sins are covered.
> Blessed is the man to whom the Lord will not count his sin against him.

My father had his go-to passages, but he always tried to find passages he thought would find an echo in the hearts of the men.

The only programme was work, discipline, love and grace. Grace was the oil that greased the centre's creaking wheels; it was the balm to forgive insults, to settle petty squabbles, to bear others with love. The men said that they had never seen anything like it on the street.

Raúl invited his old friends into the apartment. When they lived as *yonkis* on the street, they broke into cars together and shared needles together. Letting Raúl supervise the addicts might have been encouraging the wolf to lead the fox, but it worked.

When Raúl stayed up late to clean up their vomit, prepared cups of herbal tea for them, and gave up his own bed for the men, they knew he was no longer the man they had known on the streets.

Not all the addicts who came to church picked up the Christian ethos. The visiting *yonkis* frequently stripped old ladies' handbags of valuables during sermons and pickpocketed the older men as they hugged them after the services.

One Sunday, as my father opened the meeting, he invited the congregation to pray aloud. Hippy, a *yonki* with shoulder-length hair and a tie-dyed shirt, stood to pray. He careened forward but balanced himself on my brother David's shoulder.

'Thank you, Lord, that while we were stealing from the slot machines last night you didn't let the police catch us. Thank you, God, for looking after your sheep. Amen.'

'Amen,' said the addicts.

'We're going to have to go over the Ten Commandments again,' Raúl explained.

As more men entered the apartment, they slept on the beds, on the floors, and on the sofa in the living room. Lindsay became their older brother, mediating their fights, begging them to stay one more day.

The men always went out two by two as 'shadows' to buy bread, tools for plumbing jobs, or even go to the bathroom. They could never sneak away on their own to score a gram. Some hated it, but it worked, and many stayed.

The rules of the centre were clear:

Residents are to participate in the full schedule and activities of the community, keeping a structured day from 7 a.m. to 11 p.m.

Smoking or using any tobacco product is not permitted. Using drugs, alcohol or tobacco substitutes is not permitted.

All residents are to be accompanied by a 'shadow' during their first few months.

My father preferred to err on the side of grace, but Raúl said that rules were rules. People were making progress, or they were not. It was that simple. When they were not, Raúl encouraged them to leave.

Raúl often did not take men in the moment they needed help, forcing them to come to a few meetings first. The *yonkis* came to the Sunday services weeks in a row, even if they were high. And as Raúl promised, he took them in once they had proved they were serious. Although he made an exception for Juan Carlos *El Rubio*, the Blond, whose mother had given him a big chorizo for the centre. After all, Jesus had said that man should not live by bread alone.

Majara and *Veneno* entered the centre but did not stay long. But Carlos, a short man and skilful thief, was so shocked Lindsay would trust him that he swore he would not touch heroin again. He had been to jail for robbery and dealing heroin, but Raúl had given up his bed for him and slept on the floor. Carlos would repay that trust and he too would bring his friends into the centre. As my father said, people become noble because we love them and trust them, and they will do the same to others.

When I visited Lindsay's apartment, Carlos stood on the balcony with Raúl and me and pointed out his home. He lived about three hundred metres from our little apartment, close to the Gypsies' prefabricated houses. From Lindsay's balcony we could see the addicts on their way to score, and Carlos felt the hooks of temptation pulling him every day. But he stayed. He told me he did not belong to the street any more.

Over time, the patience of the older women in Lindsay's building wore thin. They complained about taking the lift with sweaty men marinated in beer whose arms were covered in menacing tattoos.

The protests mounted. Yet rather than fight them, my parents and Lindsay decided instead to search out a more suitable home for the men: a derelict farmhouse right outside the city near the airport. It had the benefit of being further away from the main points of drug sales in San Blas. At last, the men had their own place.

What began by accident, as a gesture of kindness to Raúl and his friends, was on its way to becoming a fully fledged drug centre. My parents and Lindsay formally founded *Asociación Betel*.

With the money the men earned and donations, the centre bought used vans. My father created a logo, and on the side of the vans they painted a blue dove flying over a broken heroin needle.

One by one, the *yonkis* were changing, and they in turn wanted to change San Blas.

No hay nada peligroso

There is nothing dangerous

'Out! Out! Go out and play soccer. This is the last time you horse around indoors,' my mother exclaimed. 'Don't come back until dinner time. Be here at eight thirty. And don't be late!'

She had become like the Spanish mothers in the neighbourhood.

My brothers and I knew nothing about baseball or American football. The only game that mattered was *fútbol*. In San Blas the sports newspapers *Marca* and *As* had a wider circulation than the national dailies such as *ABC* and *El País*. Few read books, but everyone read the sports newspapers.

Every kid in the neighbourhood played *fútbol* at all hours in those broiling summer days when school was a distant memory. We started early in the morning, played until lunch, had our siesta, and then returned to play some more. In the autumn, we felt deprived because we could only play on weekends.

David, Peter, Timothy and I joined in with the *chavales* and played *fútbol* in the courtyards between buildings. The lots were littered with dirty syringes and empty wine cartons, and the sour smell of urine lingered. We hated the stench, but the bare walls of the building were ideal for drawing goalposts with discarded chunks of plaster of Paris, and the small enclosures were perfect for a fast game on cement.

David, Peter and I bought *fútbol* cards and learned the name of every player in the Spanish league by heart, as if we were memorising Bible verses. On Fridays David filled out the *quiniela* for us all and furtively bet on the games. The money came from stealing the change my parents left on their dresser. David calculated the right percentage that would go unnoticed. Stealing and gambling were grave sins, but we figured that if we bet on Real Madrid and won, we could return it and donate money to Betel. We might even look like heroes.

Real Madrid was the greatest *fútbol* team ever, and it had all the best players. It was like supporting the Yankees. Raúl told us that *madrileños* carried football in their veins. He took us to the Santiago Bernabéu stadium, the high temple of soccer that could have filled a dozen cathedrals. As we left the Bernabéu on one of our early visits, Raúl told us, 'One day, you will be the first Americans to play for Real Madrid.'

When we played the game on the streets, David was the best. His body would move one way, the ball another, but they would reconnect further down the field, as if magically tethered to each other. After he scored goals, he would jump for joy while I did flips. Peter played midfield, passing balls up for him to score. I was goalie and Timothy was my trustworthy defender. He stood in the way of oncoming attacks without flinching before half a dozen players who were twice as big as him ran him over. Only the promise of an ice cream cone kept him from running home in tears.

As we played during the day, I saw the girls in the neighbourhood chatting and playing hopscotch. Rosa was the tall queen bee, and everyone buzzed around her. She was tanned, and even more striking towards the end of the summer. She felt no need to analyse the *fútbol* league and had no interest in me the few times I spoke to her. In her presence I had an unexpected tingling in my chest, my heart beating in my ears, my face burning red. I froze and could not say anything intelligent. Maybe one day when I was bigger, she'd notice me.

The only time the girls ever spoke to me first was to ask if I knew Tom Cruise. They lost interest when I didn't. Being American abroad in the 1980s was like being a hero and villain all at once. America was the land of Tom Cruise, Sylvester Stallone and Arnold Schwarzenegger, who always saved the world. Kids in the neighbourhood asked if I knew them, as if the US were a high school where we all grew up together and had each other's numbers. America was also the land of fat people, hicks who couldn't speak other languages, and too many guns.

At lunchtime we went home to eat and have a siesta, waiting out the bullying sun. The day was at its hottest and the sun pounded the earth. Before heading home, David, Peter, Timothy and I gathered our *pesetas* and shared flavoured popsicles, sucking on the blue ice until our tongues grew numb and the cold blood blasted the back of our brains.

After the *siesta*, we wandered out to play until the mothers called their children in for dinner.

Evening was the most beautiful time to play *fútbol*. Amber clouds of dust hung in the air as we played. The sun hung from the sky and dipped over the rooftops. In the distance we saw the street lamps lined up on Carretera de Vicálvaro, and when the tip of the sun had sunk behind the buildings in the half-light, the sky turned shades of lavender. Like fireflies the lamp-posts flickered and then swelled into a blue-green glow and burned a brilliant white. The lights lined the road like pearls on a long thread, and we played on until the sky grew black.

'David, we've got to go back!' I yelled.

'We've got a few more minutes,' he reassured us.

'I'm taking Timothy and heading home.'

'Wait, wait. We gotta go back together.'

We headed home sweaty, our legs cramped. After a few blocks, David, Peter, Timothy and I grew tired and marched with our arms locked around each other's shoulders, remembering the goals, commenting on the game, telling the stories repeatedly until they no longer resembled anything like the facts.

We rang the buzzer to our apartment since none of us ever carried keys. My mother's voice scolded us through the tinny speaker, 'You're late again.'

When we got upstairs, I wanted to wash my face in the sink and my feet in the bidet, but my father called us all into the living room. He was sombre. Perhaps we would not be let out for days.

We filed in and sat on the sofa side by side and glanced at each other. I was not looking forward to the punishment.

'We need to talk. Scientists discovered the virus for a terrible, terrible disease three years ago. Cases have cropped up in San Blas. It is called AIDS. It stands for Acquired Immune Deficiency Syndrome. People who are going to get AIDS test positive for the virus and ...'

'But Daddy, if AIDS is bad, why'd they say it's positive?' David asked.

'It isn't positive like when you say something's good. It means that the AIDS virus shows up in their lab tests.'

'So, Daddy? Why don't they change that? It's confusing and illogical.'

'That's the way it is.'

'Daddy, Daddy ...' I asked.

'Yeeees ...' I sensed he was growing weary with the questions, and his patience was not infinite.

'Daddy, how bad is it?'

'Yeah, is it worse than fever, like when I missed school this year?' Peter enquired.

'Please stop interrupting, children. As far as doctors know, it leads to death. The virus is a retrovirus, a really bad virus. Think of it sort of like ... like a spy. It enters the body and without warning attacks the human immune cells, called T cells. Those are the ones that protect us from colds. These retroviruses infect T cells, then replicate and quickly destroy the immune system.'

'But what happens to you?'

'Well, when the immune system has very few T cells, then the doctors say the patients officially have AIDS. And patients can get sick and die from almost anything. Even a common cold.'

The surgeon general's report, he said, put it bluntly, 'There is presently no cure for AIDS. There is presently no vaccine to prevent AIDS.'

AIDS was a death sentence.

We listened and did not know what to say.

'So far no one we know has it ... at least officially,' my mother reassured us. 'But we can't take anything for granted. Scientists invented the first AIDS test a little over a year ago. We don't even know who has it and who doesn't.'

My father continued. 'They say there are fewer than 20,000 cases in the entire world, but over a million could have it and not got tested. Scientists do not know much, but you can't get it by shaking people's hands at Parque El Paraíso. Addicts can get it by sharing needles shooting up. From now on, whatever you do, don't touch the dirty needles; you can get the virus from blood if you prick yourself.'

We had seen the needles everywhere in the street, and they were often splattered with fresh blood from the addicts who had shared them.

'Dad, we never pick needles up!' Peter said.

Why were my parents telling us not to handle syringes? It was common sense never to touch the bloodstained needles.

I thought AIDS was a gay disease that I knew little about. The first person to die from it in Spain was a gay man in Barcelona in 1981. The only time I had seen anything about AIDS was at the barbershop. The barber kept nudie magazines to entertain customers before their haircuts. *Interviú* had grainy black-and-white photos of men doing who knows what to each other with black squares covering their private parts and faces. And then there were photos of them covered in the horrible purple sores of Kaposi's sarcoma and stuff like that. I put the magazine down. No thanks. I liked girls, not boys. I grabbed another one to stare at Samantha Fox's big *tetas*. How were they so big?

'Jonathan, are you listening?'

I snapped back to the present.

My mother spoke up: 'Boys, there is nothing to be afraid of. AIDS is not easily contagious. You get it from blood and some bodily fluids. Make sure that when you spend time with the men on the farm you don't share toothbrushes with them because bloody gums are a problem . . .'

David jumped in, 'But we never do that! I've got my own toothbrush.'

Honestly, all the advice was pointless.

'I know. I know. I'm simply informing you. You're too young now, but when you get older, you will shave. You do not want to share razors with anyone in the drug centre. Razors often have blood from nicks and cuts.

'You don't have to worry. We can keep living exactly as we are, hugging everyone at church, shaking everyone's hand and giving them kisses on the cheek. There is nothing unsafe about our friends.'

She continued, 'We never need to mention the virus or AIDS, unless they bring it up. We have to love them even more and put them at ease.'

My father paused and looked at every one of us. 'We don't have to say anything more about it. Do we? All I ask is that you please be careful.'

'Can we go now?' David asked.

My father picked up the copy of *Time* magazine that sat on the coffee table. It said 'Keys to Life and Death. AIDS: New Research, New Danger.' It said the number of cases was doubling every ten months.

'Please read this article.'

'Can we go?' David asked.

'You can go.'

I thought we were lucky that no one we knew had AIDS so far.

As we slipped away, David stopped us in the hallway and whispered, 'That was close. At least Dad didn't punish us because we were late.'

Un hermano mayor y un ojo perdido

An older brother and a missing eyeball

THE CROWD WAS frozen in awe. Raúl was dressed as the devil and the men were his demons. They threw Lindsay on the ground and kicked him in the stomach and back as a throng of more than a hundred huddled nearby outside the Torre del Campo bar. I stood by with my brothers; we were transfixed. We knew it was a play, but it looked as real as any fight I had seen on the streets.

The skit was *Cadenas*, Chains, and it was wildly popular. Lindsay played a carefree youth who loved *fútbol*. He looked innocent, and the skit was believable. Raúl and the men dressed in ghoulish black tempted him with alcohol. Lindsay bit the forbidden fruit and drank. For this he got a small chain on his arm. The demons of drugs tempted him with cigarettes, and he liked them. He got another chain. Again, Raúl and the demons tempted him with hashish, and he enjoyed it, too. This time he got a larger chain on his leg. Like the *chavales* of San Blas, he slipped from one drug to the next; when the demons offered a syringe, he took it. This time, a chain choked his neck. Lindsay staggered around, shackled by heroin.

When Lindsay was on heroin, Raúl and the demons knocked him over and mercilessly kicked him in the ribs. Our men were unpredictable, and Lindsay thought perhaps they took too much pleasure in the realism and their roles.

Every time the men performed it, the crowds swelled. It spoke to the kids and the men in the neighbourhood because they had seen it and often lived it.

As the skit was ending, an old, short housewife arrived in time to see Lindsay shoot up. She had missed the first half of the skit and stood on her tiptoes trying to peer over the shoulders of the crowd.

'What's he doing? Is he shooting up?'

'Yeah, he's shooting up,' I told her.

Her face contorted. 'What's the neighbourhood coming to? Young people gathering around to watch other young people shoot up . . .' As she left, she muttered to herself, 'This place has gone to hell.'

After the play, David, Peter and I walked through the crowd to hand out our leaflets. This time, though, the scary skeleton was gone. We had Raúl's testimony of change.

While we did our work, Raúl stood out in front of the mass of people who had gathered and shared with them the story of how he had been a *yonki* and got off drugs. I would have been embarrassed with so many eyes watching, but Raúl said it was easy.

Raúl spoke to the crowd, 'The most beautiful story anyone can tell is the story of your own life. What do you want to tell with your life? Do you want to live a life of fear and shame, or get off drugs and come with us and live a life of love and hope?'

After he finished, he called out to people by name and invited them to follow him to Betel's Friday-night meeting. When he spoke, people followed.

Raúl was odd, but everyone followed him because he made you feel special to him. He had inside jokes with everyone. He had a high-pitched cackle that started and stopped abruptly. Whenever

I got into trouble, he asked, '¿Jonny, dónde están mis pistolas?' – Jonny, where are my guns?

I did not know where he got the phrase. My father said perhaps it was *Hidden Guns*, a Western starring John Carradine. Raúl himself could not remember. Often it was the oddity and obscurity of his jokes – so obscure that often even he had no idea where the punchlines came from or what they meant – that made them all the more ridiculous.

Raúl was solid, his hands meaty and strong, his fingernails curved and trimmed. His reddish cheeks had the scent of aftershave. His arms were thick as branches extending from his trunk, and when my brothers and I spotted him before church services, we tried to climb him. I held on to his arms and pulled myself up. Sometimes he would let me sit on his shoulders, but Timothy was his favourite to carry. Timothy delighted in looking down imperiously at David, Peter and me. He looked like a village boy who had tamed a wild elephant.

We elbowed and punched each other to be the closest to him. Raúl grinned and told us to punch him. At first, I refused to fall into a trap. Manolo *Majara* would fight with us and then tell my parents we were misbehaving.

'Come on, punch my arm. I promise I won't hit you back. Punch as hard as you can,' he said, rolling up the sleeve of his T-shirt.

I clenched my fist and threw a punch that landed on his shoulder.

'That was pathetic. Try again.'

I drew my arm back and held my breath and hit him as hard as I could.

'Jonny, you insult me.' No one but Raúl called me Jonny. 'Don't throw papers at me. I'm invincible, and you know it.'

No matter how hard I struck him, he laughed – and never had a bruise to show for any of my punches.

He smiled broadly, 'Let it be a lesson. Don't get into fights. There's always someone stronger than you.'

I felt relieved that Raúl was on our side.

My father showed no fear around the Gypsy camp or when people put guns or knives in his face. But one night he came home from Lindsay's apartment shaken. A deranged *yonki* named Lucio had threatened my father. The man ran for the kitchen and grabbed a knife, but Raúl put himself between the knife and my father. Raúl wrestled Lucio to the ground. He held Lucio by the neck with one arm and with the other squeezed his wrist so hard Lucio dropped the knife.

My father quoted from John 15:13: 'Greater love hath no man than this, that a man lay down his life for his friends.' The verse was nice, but the way I saw it, from that day we knew Raúl would take a knife for us. That was the greatest thing you could say about a friend in San Blas.

David, Peter, Timothy and I were like dogs: we could sniff out timidity. We bullied our Sunday-school teacher Ramón, who was too afraid to punish us. Ramón came from the Basque country and was about as out of place as we were. He had been a *yonki*, but he was so soft-spoken and his Spanish so proper, I wouldn't have guessed he did heroin by talking to him. We knew all the Bible stories already from our breakfast and dinner devotionals. David and Goliath were a given, but even Bildad the Shuhite and Zophar the Naamathite were too easy for us. Any half-intelligent child should know they were characters from the book of Job. Obviously. In that book God tests His servant Job and makes him lose everything. God could be a bit of a bully too sometimes.

But Raúl was different. When I got out of my seat during a lesson, he picked me up off the ground, holding my elbows, and put me back in my chair.

'*Cuidado o cobras*. Careful or you're gonna get it.'

That Friday, for the first time, my parents let us spend the weekend with Raúl and the men out at the farm in Barajas.

My mother had helped us pack for the weekend. After the Friday-night meeting, all of us boys were going except Timothy. He was only four, and that was too young for my parents to let him spend a weekend out at the farmhouse.

'I wanna go. Why can't I go?' Timothy cried. 'It's not fair. Why do I always have to stay home?'

My mother hugged him. 'When you're a few years older, you'll go. It will come sooner than you think.'

Raúl bent over, put his hands on Timmy's shoulders and looked him in the eye, 'When you're old enough, you can come out and stay with me.'

'Promise?'

'I promise.'

The men piled into their dilapidated vans. They were so beaten up we had to push them to get them moving. Raúl sat in the passenger seat by the driver. Peter, David and I fought, but I won and got to sit with Raúl. The old vans rattled with every vibration of the motor, and the air smelled of diesel fumes. The noise was so loud that talking was impossible. Raúl and I glanced over at each other and smiled at the din of the engine.

Two men had stayed at the farmhouse to cook dinner for everyone. Music spilled out from the kitchen as an old stereo player cranked out *'Para mi rey'*, a Christian Gypsy song in Spanish. *'No hay rey como tu, cambiaste mi lamento en baile.'* – There is no king like you, you changed my mourning into dancing. David, Peter and I offered to help to get closer to the food, but the cooks chased us away within seconds.

Once dinner was ready and the men had set the tables, Raúl gathered everyone into the dining room and waited for absolute silence.

'Lord, bless this food and the hands that prepared it. Please pour out your love over everyone in this house and touch everyone's hearts today. Make us more like you every day. In your blessed name, Amen.'

The moment he finished, the room erupted with the clanging of men serving food. Then they dipped their heads into the plates, almost inhaling the food. We ate a simple salad, and large plates of *tortilla española* and strips of chorizo. For dessert we ate *flanes* that Betel received as donations from supermarkets. Most of the food had passed its sell-by date, but no one cared. Good company could make even a simple meal a feast.

The dinner was noisy, the air filled with the men's yells for more food. Gluttony may have been one of the seven sins, but it was better than shooting up.

I asked Juan Carlos *El Rubio*, who was sitting next to me, why he entered Betel.

'I didn't even want to get off drugs. I was shooting up in an abandoned car with two friends by Carretera de Vicálvaro. They spent the night in the car, and when I came back the next morning, some kids had set fire to it. My friends were burned to death in their sleep. I don't want to die. That's why I'm here.'

I knew people shot up in the cars behind our apartment, but I had not imagined they were ovens that could cook people to death.

After dinner, Raúl gave us sheets and towels, and we followed him back to the large rooms filled with bunk beds. The floors smelled of bleach, but a ripe smell of men's bodies filled the air. I so often felt like a grown-up, smarter than everyone else, but I didn't even know what it was like to live among adults. I hoped I would not grow old and stink like that one day.

In our room, Raúl knelt and helped make our beds for us. After we had changed into our pyjamas, he said a brief prayer: 'Dear Lord, bless these children with a good night's sleep. Help them grow up to be kind, noble and wise. Protect them and guide them. In your name, Amen.'

He tucked each of us in before he turned the lights out.

I listened to the men hollering and laughing in the living room and dozed off. Throughout the night the loud, booming snores from the men startled me, but I fell asleep again when I overcame my fear.

When Raúl woke us, the stark light of day cast long shadows against the walls. He gave us towels and told us we should use the showers before the rush to use the bathroom began. By the time I got out, a line had formed for the showers.

At eight in the morning, the men gathered around in the dining hall for breakfast. I sat next to Luis Mendoza, who was short and had curly hair; when he smiled, he pursed his lips to hide his few unfortunate teeth. Luis dumped mountains of sugar into his *café con leche*. He dunked his cookies and ate them soggy. We talked about Real Madrid and their season; it was the failsafe opener for any conversation.

We wanted to be like the men, but Raúl would only let us have hot chocolate like the *yonkis* going cold turkey. He said we were rowdy enough without caffeine. As I drank my chocolate, I waited for Raúl to not pay attention to his glass so I could have a sip of coffee, but he swatted away my hand.

At the end of the table, Faris, an Iranian refugee who had ended up on drugs, stroked a glass of tea. He had prepared it himself with roots and leaves he had collected from the fields.

Raúl pointed and spoke loud enough for Faris to hear him, 'He thinks it'll make him trip out, but he doesn't need the tea for that. He's already nuts.' Faris laughed as he caressed his tea.

After breakfast, the men moved all the chairs and tables out of the way. Everyone sat in a circle waiting for the devotional. Some of the newer men draped themselves in blankets, even though it was summer, and held mop buckets between their legs. They lurched forward as if they were going to vomit, but nothing came out. Raúl sang boldly, but off key, and the men joined in.

When Raúl gave the devotional message, he spoke *simple y llanamente*, simply and candidly, in a way the men would understand. His speech was eloquent because it was heartfelt, vigorous and direct. Only two years earlier I had seen him in my living room with track marks on his arms and the sharp stench of gin. As he spoke, you knew why his friends from the streets of San Blas followed him into Betel.

'I'm going to keep this short. Open your Bibles to First Corinthians chapter one. Let's read the passage together.'

The men did not know the order of the books in the Bible, and my brothers and I helped them find First Corinthians. At last we put our home devotionals to good use.

'Some of you think we're a bit nuts or perhaps a strange sect. I get it. For years, I thought God was a bully only here to beat us when we disobey. But that isn't God's love.' Raúl began reading:

> *God hath chosen the foolish things of the world to confound the wise; and God hath chosen the weak things of the world to confound the things which are mighty.*

He offered his thoughts on the text. 'Do you know what is wise in the world? It's being the toughest. But it doesn't matter to God. What matters is becoming the kindest, the most loving. That takes guts.'

'I want you to know that it doesn't matter who you are or what you've done. You might be sick or weak. You're important. You might be the least educated junkie in the world, but God loves you. You might be a criminal, but you can put it behind you.'

The men nodded as he spoke. His message was simple and unadorned, and they listened.

'We do not measure our love by what we do for those who are stronger than us. Jesus came to heal the weak and the suffering. He said, "Truly I say unto you, As you have done it unto one of the least of these my brethren, you have done it unto me."'

When Raúl had finished speaking and closed the devotion with a prayer, the men divided up the jobs for the day. David, Peter and I helped them sweep and mop the house and pull the weeds in the garden. We worked around the house all morning until lunchtime. The men knew how to eat. The cooks had prepared a giant *paella* with a simple message written in thin red pepper slices in the centre: *DIOS ES AMOR* – God is love.

Before the meal, Raúl thanked God for His many blessings. Almost every head bowed, but as I peeked around the room, I saw the new men exchanging glances and snickering while he prayed. Not everyone shared our religion.

Growing up in a religious home was like being a goldfish; the invisible walls of my family and beliefs had been my world. In the bowl you think the water is all there is, and everything outside is blurry. Some drink and join, but to others the fishbowl of religion will always be small and alien.

Was it the fear of dying alone that made the men put up with too many *aleluyas* for breakfast and Christian messages in their *paella*? Was it death that made people believe?

All the men on the farm were young. I had met old alcoholics, but never old heroin addicts. Some died quickly overdosing; others died slowly from things like hepatitis C. *Yonkis* who mixed alcohol with heroin were more likely to throw up, sometimes choking on their vomit in their sleep. I had seen others overdosed in the ditches by the Gypsy camp, and I told myself that they were frozen in a deep dream.

After lunch we had a *siesta* because a workday was never complete without one. Then came our favourite part of the day: *fútbol*.

The men headed over to an empty field, and David, Peter and I ran ahead, kicking the ball as we yelled to Raúl to hurry. Raúl had taught us dribbling tricks and how to hit a header from a corner shot.

'¡Joder, me cago en la hostia!' I had kicked the ball too far into a ditch.

'What'd you say, Jonny?'

'*Joder, me cago en la hostia.*'

'You know what it means?'

'Of course I do,' I said, running after the ball.

'Come back here! Right now!'

I grabbed the ball, put it under my arm and ran back.

He glared at me. 'Well, if you say you do, what does it mean then?'

'I . . . I . . .'

'I can't hear you. Speak up!'

'I dunno.'

'Jonny,' he said, grabbing my shoulders and lifting me off the ground. He stared at me, 'It means "fuck", which is a curse word, "I shit in the host", and that's the body of Christ in the communion. You're not a parrot. You can't go around repeating everything you hear on the streets. *Colleja!* Bend your neck. Assume the position.'

He gave *collejas* to the men in the centre every time they cursed. If there was one thing I hated, it was *collejas*.

He put me back down, and I tilted my head, exposing the back of my neck. With his thick hand he slapped hard. I felt its sting and tried not to cry like a weak kid.

'That'll teach you. Don't you ever say that again. Now, let's play some *fútbol*.'

The *colleja* taught me an important lesson: I needed to learn my curse words better.

I knew many curse words, but my parents knew almost none, as the men and women did not use foul language around ministers.

One visiting missionary preached that God wanted our spirits to be free like a butterfly. My father was translating and used the word *marica*, queer, instead of *mariposa*, butterfly. And the preacher pranced around the stage. The congregation roared with laughter. The preacher felt he was connecting, so he repeated it again and again, which only led to cackles and hoots. I was mortified, but couldn't contain my laughter. God wants us to float like fairies, he repeated. No one had the heart to correct my father, and the preacher sashayed around the stage until some *yonkis* were laughing so hard they had to leave the service.

Those were the perils of being a missionary and learning another language.

With thirty men in the programme, we had enough to put together two fútbol teams. Not everyone could play flat out. Some men could barely get themselves out of bed, and one guy named Miguel Jambrina was so thin that the men joked he would break if they ran into him. But no one kept him off the field; the game had to be played.

The men split into teams, and David joined in as well. Peter and I stood at the sidelines, watching the action, begging to be let on the field, but Raúl had ruled we were too young.

Midway through the game, an addict held his hand to his eye.

'Stop! Stop running!' Raúl yelled, 'Manuel *El Vasco*'s eyeball has fallen out. Be still and help look.'

'Not again! Can't he go a day without losing his eyeball?'

Manuel had come from the Basque country, and he had been knifed in the eye on the streets years earlier. His glass eye never stayed in its place, falling out at the most inopportune moments. When he travelled on the subway, dishevelled and tired, he would fall asleep, but only one eyelid closed fully, and the glass eye continued to stare at his fellow passengers.

'Help search for it. The sooner we find it, the sooner we play.'

Raúl held the ball and leaned over, scouring the ground, sifting through the pebbles for the missing eyeball. After a few minutes of searching, we found an eyeball that looked like it had come from a costume shop. Manuel *El Vasco* thanked us and went back to the bathroom to wash it off.

After the game everyone was sweaty and covered with dust, and we changed into our bathing suits to join Raúl and the men in the pool. It was small, only reaching Raúl's shoulders, but it was deep enough for baptisms and for us to dive in.

Lolo, a young addict, kept a pet ferret he took with him into the pool. The creature was a splendid swimmer. It tucked its front paws under its chin, poked its nose out of the water, and paddled with its hind legs, using its tail as a rudder, gliding through the water until it struggled, and Lolo pulled it out.

After breakfast on Sunday morning, David, Peter and I got into the vans to head to the Betel church service where we would see Timothy again. Perhaps my parents would let us bring him along next time.

Jambri and Manuel *El Vasco* stayed behind at Barajas. They had come down with a fever overnight. I did not know how they could be sick when they'd looked fine on Saturday night.

As we drove back to San Blas, the steering wheel vibrated from the clattering of the engine's pistons. Gusts roared in through the windows. I closed my eyes, felt the wind on my face and hoped the summer would never end.

A few months later, my father drove his fire-engine-red van and stopped by the *fútbol* field as we played. The Betel leaders had piled in, and they were all heading to the hospital. My father said Luis Mendoza was sick with pneumonia. Beyond his poor teeth, he was thin, and did not look too good even on the farm.

'Can I come along?'

'Hospitals are not for children. I'll see you at dinner,' my father said.

Hospitals remained a mystery to me. My father had taught us that if you ate well, exercised and looked after yourself, sickness and death would be a distant danger that should cause us no fear. My brothers and I had never been seriously ill, nor had we broken a single bone. We were lucky. I hadn't set foot in a hospital since my birth.

I wasn't sure why they were not a place for kids. Were nurses always in a hurry and did doctors run around barking orders like they did on TV? Did the patients' rooms look like the ones in Betel, with bunk beds, or were they spacious like hotel rooms with a television and room service? I'd have to ask Dad when he returned.

That night at dinner my father was subdued, and it wasn't just that he was lost in thought, thinking of St Augustine or C. S. Lewis, as usual.

'What's wrong, Dad?'

My father recounted his visit to the hospital ward. It was overflowing with AIDS patients, all suffering from the dry pneumonia Luis had, tuberculosis, and a variety of opportunistic diseases I had never even heard of.

When my father reached Luis's floor, family members stood out in the hallway, afraid to enter the rooms, fearful the patients might transmit the virus. Their horror was partly watching their son suffer, and another measure was the embarrassment of having a son with AIDS.

People were deathly afraid of AIDS in Spain and even in the US. In 1984, two years earlier, Ryan White had been barred from attending school in Kokomo, Indiana after contracting the disease from a blood transfusion due to his haemophilia. Ryan and his family were shunned by the community. It took over a year and court fights for him to be able to attend school. It didn't matter what doctors or experts said. The disease afflicted homosexuals, Haitians, haemophiliacs and heroin addicts. Having the virus was like being a leper.

My father gave Luis a hug when they saw him, because it was the simple acts of love that matter, not any grand heroics, he said.

Luis was dressed in his hospital pyjamas; his pained breathing fogged his mask while the oxygen canister gurgled and whirred. He coughed and struggled to breathe.

My father said Luis was approaching eternity and the arms of God. But even the certainty of heaven did not quiet my father's worry.

'If there is one case in Betel, there are many more,' my father said. 'They've all shared needles.'

For AIDS, the average incubation period was over five years. All the junkies could appear perfectly happy with no symptoms and be HIV+. Everyone could have the virus.

Luis died a few weeks later. I did not get to go to the funeral. Funerals were like hospitals; they were not for kids. And I hated being a kid. Why was the world a conspiracy to keep me as an innocent child for ever? They wanted to keep me an ignorant child because they didn't like the world of adults. But I had read books and encyclopedias and knew how the world worked.

I felt sorry for Luis with no more tomorrows to look forward to. The idea of his death struck a strange chord with me, as he was the first person I knew who had died. I did not know him well, but he probably left a hole in someone's life. He was someone's son and brother. He had played *fútbol* in the fields by my street and shot up by my house. He was gone. And he was going to miss next season's Real Madrid games, too.

El Mercedes del ministro

The minister's Mercedes

I took my little yellow bike and pedalled furiously under the blazing summer sun. Dodging cars, I raced through the streets of the neighbourhood. I was relieved to be out of school, with no teachers telling me what to do, and I wanted to see how Betel's *rastro* worked.

When I arrived, drops of sweat were rolling into my eyes. I wiped them away with my forearm. I parked the bike and went to the sweet shop next door to buy an ice lolly to cool myself off from the dry Madrid heat.

The used furniture shop on Calle Esfinge had a white façade with a large sign in deep blue letters, and it had bars on the windows. Jambri was standing in the small office where he coordinated the collection and delivery of furniture. The *rastro* sold beds, wardrobes, dressers, dining tables, bookshelves filled with books and anything else people donated. In the back of the shop the recovering addicts ran a small workshop where they repaired the furniture and reupholstered chairs and sofas.

'Hey!' Jambri yelled out to the men, 'It's one of the Dalton Brothers! Make sure this gangster doesn't shoplift!' He bounded to the front of the shop and welcomed me into the *rastro*.

The men in the centre had nicknamed us the Dalton Brothers, after the notorious gang of bank and train robbers of the American West. We took it as a compliment.

Jambri's name was Miguel Jambrina, although everyone called him by his nickname. He was twenty-four and even though I was just a kid, he treated me as a friend. Jambri was softly spoken, with an almost imperceptible lisp. He was tall with a thin, angular face. His forehead was slanted, as was his nose; when he played *fútbol* without a shirt, his ribs protruded. Many of the *yonkis* entered the centre emaciated. I could not remember what Jambri looked like when he came to us, but I couldn't imagine him any thinner.

The *rastro* buzzed with activity. Raúl showed up with a team of men between plumbing or brick-masonry jobs to see that everything was going smoothly.

Jambri did not need to be checked on. He never stopped working. He took calls from people who wanted to throw away old furniture. He organised the men and vans to put together collection schedules. He supervised the workshops where the men in the programme disassembled and restored the pieces. And he was the sales manager, haggling with the customers over the price for a dresser or a wardrobe. As I followed him around, I sensed the pride he had in his job.

At first, I watched, but I wanted to work.

'Can I help? I can help them over there.' I pointed at the men unloading furniture from one of the Betel vans.

'Jonathan, don't be stupid. This is a man's job. I don't want your parents telling me you got hurt helping here. The furniture weighs more than you.' He laughed. 'Let's see. How old are you?'

He held my hand and pulled me away from the men moving big pieces of furniture through the shop.

'I'm already ten.'

'Ooof! Definitely too young...'

'Come on! Please. Please.' I was embarrassed and knew that throwing a fit would not help my case.

I hated the way adults infantilised children, even if I was a child. I hated singing Sunday-school songs in front of church, wearing costumes for Christmas plays, and being told I couldn't do adult things. What did adults know?

'You get in the way around here. But stick with me. Maybe I'll figure something out.'

Jambri relented and let me answer the phones. I was sure that was a job I could handle. The receiver hung on the end, and the cable snaked around the desk. I waited with pen in hand for the ring, like a mongoose ready to pounce, ready to take notes on where to pick up furniture. I was a kid, but at least I sounded completely Spanish now. As long as they couldn't see my blond hair and blue eyes, they had no idea I was American.

It finally rang. The first few calls were easy. I checked the schedule for deliveries, booked appointments in the empty slots and wrote the addresses and contact information of the donors. I felt grown-up, no longer pretending to work. Even though I was coming in at noon, following Jambri around and answering a few phone calls, I believed I was no longer a little kid playing *fútbol* or bottle caps in the neighbourhood.

After an hour of answering the phone, my bike beckoned. What were the other kids in the neighbourhood doing? Were they out scoring goals? What colour ice lollies would I buy with the coins?

'Can I help tomorrow? Honestly, I think I'm done for the day.'

He chuckled. 'Tired from work already? You can leave. Go ahead. Take a book.'

He went back to the shelves and gave me *The Poem of El Cid*, which I'd tried to read at home, but the Old Spanish was difficult. I came back and got a copy of *Don Quixote*, which was much longer but easier to read. Reading page after page was like eating cherries – you could never have enough. Each had one brilliant line after another. Cervantes had thought of everything, 'He who loses wealth, loses much; he who loses a friend loses more, but he that loses courage, loses all.'

Jambri let me come back every day and work with the men. Some days he was sick with awful colds and fevers, which I could not understand. I never stayed if he was not at the *rastro*. But when he was there, he and the men shared their chorizo *bocadillos* with me and gave me cold Coke cans that he would roll against his cheek to cool himself down when his fevers came on.

The men had all been *yonkis*, but many were pickpockets, thieves and some had even gone to jail for murder. Their bodies told their stories through their tattoos, scars and often broken noses and bones.

They shared their lunches with me and taught me the feral slang of buying heroin. Every trade has its jargon, and everything in San Blas had a precise taxonomy. Drug dealers were *camellos*, camels. Errand boys carrying drugs were *mulas*, mules. Quitting heroin was *pasando el mono*, passing the monkey. Heroin was *caballo*, horse. As Jambri said, you rode the animal at first, but in the end, it always rode you.

'Have you seen the latest VEN?' Jambri gave me the pamphlet we handed out at parks.

When VEN started, it had the skeleton representing drugs, but now every issue told the testimony of a recovered addict like Raúl. The latest had Jambri on the front cover.

I took the VEN back to my desk to read. It turned out that I barely knew anything about his life. And what a story! It beat anything made up by Lewis or Tolkien.

He grew up in one of the four-storey red-brick buildings, one street down from Raúl on Calle Porcelana. Raúl was four years older, and they were part of different gangs.

Everyone worked. The street near his apartment bore faded blue plaques with names like Brick-Masons' Street, Sculptors' Street and Chisellers' Street. Jambri's father was a tradesman, and his mother made her living cleaning the *portales* of the buildings in the neighbourhood. The skin on her knees was thick and hardened from scrubbing floors. They raised his four sisters and older brother, but they almost all dropped out of school.

As a teenager Jambri became an apprentice spray-painting cars. He earned good money, but it didn't last long. He started drinking and smoking weed with his friends, and soon he was shooting up. He quit painting and got involved in a gang that robbed banks. He never wore a mask or pointed a gun at anyone – he drove the getaway car. The gang was slick and pulled off a few heists but no matter how big the robbery, they blew the cash on drugs within days.

When he robbed banks, he never used the same car twice. He did not want the police to catch him and trace a bank robbery to him, so he stole cars downtown to use as getaway cars. One day he found a powerful Mercedes Benz. The next day he and his friends went to a small town outside of Madrid and held up a bank. They made their escape easily.

Jambri was flushed with pride, and he and his friends were going to rob another one the same day. Within the next hour they had found another bank, and his friends entered the bank with their guns. He waited at the wheel for them to come out. Everything was taking far too long. By the time his friends had made it out of the bank, the Spanish Civil Guard had already set up roadblocks at the exits to the town.

Jambri knew that if he was caught with weapons and money he was going to go to jail for a long time. And he was only seventeen. 'Let's ditch the car on a side street and make a run for it,' he told his accomplice.

'I can't run.' His accomplice had a limp. He pulled out his revolver and put it to Jambri's head, 'I've been in *el talego*. No way am I going back.'

Jambri shifted gears and the Mercedes rocketed to 140 miles an hour and rammed the police barricade. In that moment, the Civil Guards unloaded dozens of rounds into the car with their machine guns. The car made it through, and Jambri kept his foot on the pedal until he reached an empty field. He and his friends stepped out of the car unharmed, set it on fire and escaped.

The following day Jambri bought a newspaper. A photograph of the Mercedes appeared below the headline: 'MINISTER'S CAR STOLEN, USED IN BANK ROBBERY'. The article explained that the car was the official bulletproof vehicle of a politician.

The story was so incredible, I didn't know if it was true or not. But who cared? It was so crazy it *had* to be true.

The police caught up with Jambri when he was eighteen. A judge sentenced him to five years in Carabanchel, the largest prison in Madrid. He passed his hours looking at the sky through the bars in his window, reading *Papillon* by Henri Charrière and fantasising about escaping.

In jail heroin was more plentiful than on the outside. In the entire cell block, there were only two syringes, which were shared between more than two hundred prisoners. They knew it spread hepatitis and other sicknesses, but they didn't care.

After Jambri got out of jail, however, his problems with the law did not end. The prosecutors indicted Jambri along with three other members of his gang for another bank robbery. The prosecutor asked for a sentence of eleven years. He went into the courtroom afraid and lonely, but the prosecutor told him a fire in the offices had destroyed much of the paperwork. They had no choice but to drop the charges.

Jambri thought that God, fate, *someone* was looking after him. He was going to turn his life around. He stopped the bank robberies but not the drugs.

When my father and Lindsay went around the neighbourhood to talk to the addicts, they attracted attention – Raúl was with them. When he spoke to them, they knew he looked different. He was not there to buy a gram of heroin. Some addicts were intrigued by what my father had to say about how only God's love could fill the hole they had in their heart. Others threw empty beer bottles and stones as greetings. They called him priest and *facha*, and no one liked fascists. Jambri even shouted, 'Go back to your own country!'

The addicts usually left after a while to buy heroin somewhere else, undisturbed by the street preaching. But Jambri stayed and listened to what my father had to say. He was tired of going in and out of jail, being homeless, and seeing friends die of overdoses. Jambri came to a Friday-night meeting at Betel and finally asked to enter the centre.

Jambri gave up heroin and drinking, but he had been a smoker since he was thirteen. When no one was around in the field behind the farmhouse, he made cigarettes with pages from a Bible. The thin paper was ideal for rolling and he crushed dried leaves to use instead of tobacco. The cigarette burned his insides and gave him no high. Sitting alone and feeling miserable, he tried to remember the prayers my father had said.

'God, I'm sorry for all my sins. Accept me as your son. Come into my heart. Give me love and peace. Guide me. In your name, Amen. Dear God, I hope that was right.'

Jambri worked diligently in Betel's second-hand shops, volunteering for work around the farm and helping Raúl run the house, encouraging the new addicts when they were going through withdrawal. On weekends, he volunteered to visit Carabanchel prison and invite his old friends to come to Betel when they got out. Raúl gave him the responsibility for running the *rastro* on Calle Esfinge. In less than a year he had gone from robbing banks and shooting up to managing a legitimate business.

When I finished reading the VEN, I couldn't believe it.

'Jambri, you're a lot more interesting than you seem.'

'Is that an insult or a compliment?'

'No . . . Not an insult. I mean, you've lived a lot and don't talk much.'

'I don't dwell on the past. I'm ashamed of it, and all I want now is to transmit love. Hate destroys you, but love transforms us and the world around us.'

He was sounding more like my dad and Raúl every day. Soon he was going to be preaching at me.

'Do you mind if I take it?' I stuffed the VEN in my pocket.

Besides running the *rastro*, Jambri was a leader in the men's residence. It is risky having *yonkis* who have been off heroin for one year supervise recovering addicts who have been off heroin for a few weeks. For all my father and Lindsay knew, the men could have all been drinking and smoking, and covering up for each other. That, though, was how Betel worked. Faith, my father preached, is taking a risk and stepping out into the unknown.

Betel supported itself almost entirely with the businesses it operated. Like Raúl and Jambri, the former addicts had left school when they were kids. None of them had Harvard MBAs or knew anything about accounting, but they intuitively understood cash: the centre's businesses needed to have more cash in the evening than they had in the morning. They were good at that.

Jambri was never happier than when he restored furniture. When the used or abandoned furniture entered through the doorway, the pieces came in with scrapes and dents, disfigured by years of neglect and abuse. The former owners had been unkind to the dressers, wardrobes and desks. The handles were missing, the mirrors cracked and shattered, and often layers of faded paint covered what had once been solid oak.

No one wanted the battered and worn pieces, and the donors were more than happy for Betel to take them off their hands. Seeing the furniture come from the vans into the repair shop, I couldn't imagine what they might have looked like if they had been treated with love and care.

Jambri and the men in the *rastro* took the furniture apart piece by piece, revealing stains and scratches in the wood, and peeling off all the old coats of paint. Then they doused the pieces with harsh, acrid chemicals that ate away at the ugly exterior. The men sanded for hours, smoothing the uneven surfaces, exposing the grain of the wood until they saw the beautiful hidden patterns.

When the original piece had been laid bare, the guys applied coat after coat of varnish until the wardrobes or dressers shone again as they had when they were first made. A box full of bright, polished brass handles sat in the back of the repair shop, and the men found the most appropriate ones to screw onto the drawers. They took out shards of glass, measured the size of the mirrors and replaced them. At last, they saw their own reflection, undisturbed by cracks.

Jambri had been patient with me that summer, giving me many books, and I wanted to give him a gift. Some American missionaries had given me a green T-shirt that read in English: 'If you meet me and forget me you have missed nothing, but if you meet Jesus and forget him you have lost everything.' It was not much of a gift, but at least I didn't have to spend any money on it. I folded the T-shirt, put it in a plastic bag and rode my bike to the *rastro* to say goodbye before the new school year started.

I gave him the shirt and translated the writing, impressed by my ability to read in two languages. I could think in Spanish as easily as English and switched between the two with ease.

He read the English with his Spanish accent, '*If you forget me . . .*' He coughed and then stared at me.

'I can't forget you, Jonathan. I can't even get rid of you. You just keep coming back.'

Nuestro propio pequeño universo

Our own little universe

'CHILDREN, BE SILENT,' my father ordered. 'At the table, children should be seen and not heard.'

Christianity was our religion, but in our house reading had its own rituals.

Every morning before school we had a long devotional that, beyond providing spiritual edification, gave us patience and taught endurance, which we suspected was one of the desired results.

My father insisted on silence and attention when he read. Often, though, he'd pause and hand his book across the table. 'Mary, why don't you read this? You have a beautiful voice.'

David, Peter, Timothy and I sat around the table, buttering our toast and drinking our orange juice trying to avoid the clinking of knives on plates or clanking of glasses on the tabletop. We dared not disturb the readings, out of fear of spankings.

My father paused for interludes, commenting upon the passages, adding marginalia to the text. This practice was his 'pontification', as he liked to call it. He enlightened us as to the difference between Koine and classical Attic Greek, and he elucidated the meaning in the Apostle Paul's writings. The New Testament was written in a common Greek, not a literary one. God spoke to everyone, the learned and junkies alike.

No one in San Blas spoke Greek. I couldn't understand why it mattered, and my mind drifted off like a kite. But Peter cared about what words meant in Greek and Hebrew with their squiggly lines that my father wrote on napkins and studied them like an ancient code. His enthusiasm only cheered my father on, and Peter ignored me even when I kicked him under the table.

Devotionals bled into dinner and continued late. My father kept few clocks in the house to avoid being rushed for anything, which made it hard to prove the pontifications were too long.

'Everything will happen at the right time, and not before,' he would say. That was why our church services never started on time. Schedules were the tyranny of small minds.

We listened while my parents shared light readings from texts such as the *Inferno* from Dante's *Divine Comedy*, Thomas à Kempis's *The Imitation of Christ*, John Bunyan's *Pilgrim's Progress* and Saint Augustine's *Confessions* and *City of God*.

Saint Augustine had lived a life of sin and then randomly opened the Bible when he heard the voice, 'Take up and read.' And he sold all he had, gave it to the poor, and followed the call. The story loomed over our dinners.

Everything was a jumping-off point for asides. Who knew that the graffiti down the hill by the Gypsy camp, 'Abandon all hope, you who enter,' came from the *Divine Comedy*? My father read the lines that followed, as the poet Virgil leads Dante into hell:

And he said to me: 'This miserable way
Belongs to the sad souls of those
Who lived without infamy and without praise.
They are mixed with that craven crew
Of Angels who were neither rebellious
Nor were loyal to God, but were for themselves.'

One of the greatest sins is simply living for oneself, not looking after those who are hurting. We would end up in hell like the tortured souls in Dante's underworld if we did not love others and care for them.

'Boys, who can tell me what were the cities Augustine wrote about?'

Theology was not as interesting as my history books, so I let Peter answer that one.

'Anyone? Was anyone listening? Do you not care about the readings?'

He looked at my mother and shook his head. There were no grades in the pontifications, but he treated us like students in a tutorial, and we were failing him.

'The earthly city and the heavenly city,' Peter replied.

'And those who follow the earthly path, where do they go?'

'Hell.'

'That's right. Hell is just a metaphor in *The City of God*, but in Dante's *Inferno* it's a real, physical place. And I can tell you it *is* real. God gave me a vision of heaven and hell at Harvard.'

David and I stared at each other over the empty plates. I had never seen heaven or hell, and my father's vision still sounded strange to me.

Still, the readings were a gateway to a different world. Our parents read history books and biographies of William Wilberforce, George Müller, C. S. Lewis, and C. T. Studd, as they exhorted us to be great men.

Reading to touch the past is a constant in human history, as my father pointed out when he read from Tablet I of *The Epic of Gilgamesh*, the world's oldest story: 'Take and read out from the lapis lazuli tablet, How Gilgamesh went through every hardship.' I imagined that stone, wondered who'd carved the first story, and if Gilgamesh's parents made him sit still at the dinner table too.

We had no icons in our Protestant house – just books. It was God's word, not icons, that saved. My father said the Catholics left Jesus hanging from the cross, and often forgot the Resurrection. Hope cannot die. Death has no sting.

When my parents found something worth sharing, they read it aloud. They'd skip from page to page, picking snippets, as if picking apples from tree to tree. Sometimes they brought a pile of books and placed them next to the pots. My parents laid the books on the table, fitting them tightly together with no other mortar than curiosity, laying a bridge to places we had never even dreamed of visiting.

'Because we read,' Dad said, 'we're different from other families in San Blas.'

Although we did not have money, we could travel wherever reading transported us. Books could open doors to another world. My father read C. S. Lewis's *An Experiment in Criticism*, in which he wrote, 'In reading great literature I become a thousand men and yet remain myself.'

Lewis was the guiding light for my father, proving to us all that you could believe in God and not be an illiterate fool. Lewis taught at Oxford and Cambridge, and wrote fairy tales but also scholarly works on medieval English literature.

Reading set us apart, but with humility we could mix with princes and paupers and still be ourselves.

'*Logos*,' Dad explained, 'means 'word' in Greek. But it also means light. Reason. Even God Himself.' Creation, he reminded us, began with speech: *Let there be light*.

And we learned that words have awesome power as we poked at the last specks of our refried beans and rice.

As a boy, my father never had his Bar Mitzvah because he spent all his time wrestling, and he regretted it. He had great nostalgia for the synagogue. My father said you could not be a man in Judaism until the Rabbi called you up to read the Torah. Reading made you a man. Jesus himself didn't become a man until he read and argued with rabbis in the temple. My father said we should aspire to *Torah lishmah*, the highest form of learning. Not for vanity or prizes. Learning for learning's sake.

And this was about all I knew about my father's life as a Jew before he converted. Jews liked the Old Testament, and Christians preferred the New. Everyone must have a different taste in books, I thought.

When the gatherings were too long – even by the standard of your average pontification – we pretended to doze off to cut them short. Our heads drooped slowly, our hair grazing the remains of dinner.

'Jonathan, you're getting food on your hair,' my father said, interrupting his reading. 'Don't you want to hear what Saint Augustine has to say to us tonight?'

'Sorry . . . sorry, Dad. I'm tired.'

'Are you pulling a stunt? Do you want a spanking? I don't believe in "Spare the rod, spoil the child." You will not grow up to be a brat.'

My father never joked about the rod. He had Bible verses written on the paddle he used on us for years. The verses only worsened the sting. We gave up rebelling and he stopped spanking us, but we let our minds wander and play hooky while our bodies were still present.

I knew how to survive and keep my place. If I had been in World War II, I wouldn't have taken up a gun against the Germans but might have put sugar in their gas tanks or cut some cables along the railways, as long as I wasn't caught.

'Now, Elliott, it's enough for this evening . . . I think it's everyone's bedtime.' My mother rarely spoke at the dinner table, preferring to conserve her words as a marksman manages his ammunition for the perfect shot. 'Even I'm falling asleep . . .'

'As Joseph's brothers said in Genesis before they tore his coloured coat and sold him into slavery, "Behold, the dreamer cometh." One day, you will thank me for this reading. You'll thank me for the pontifications when you go to university and become great men.'

'Yes, one day. For now, they're children, Elliott. This is not a classroom. They need to go to bed. And if you're going to quote Genesis, let's do Genesis 21:12, when God ordered Abraham, "Whatever Sarah has said to you, listen to her voice."'

Two could play the game, and we were grateful for a mother who with the least effort curbed his devotional excesses.

Her interruptions only made him love her more. He got up from his chair and told us, 'Look away, boys, look away,' before he kissed her. And we scurried to our rooms.

Dad could be a stern disciplinarian, but his love of learning was infectious, and he transmitted it to us. It did not matter if it was pulling encyclopedias from the shelf to explain how cryptography worked or how Latin turned into Spanish and Italian. No subject was so complicated that my father could not explain it with a fountain pen and a few drawings. But he said we did not even need him for explanations. If we had books, we could teach ourselves anything. The world was ours if we could read.

My parents quoted Thomas Macaulay often: 'I would rather be a poor man in a garret with plenty of books than a king who did not love reading.' I didn't know if they quoted it in praise of reading or to excuse our poverty as missionaries.

At dinner, my father told us that if we ever saw Cambridge's colleges, the beauty of the Gothic spires and the grass courtyards that gardeners had gently trimmed for centuries would overwhelm us. He kept his memories like framed prints, often returning to them as if to dust them off and admire them. My father finished any mention of the great university with, 'One day you will go to Cambridge.' He said it as if he were passing on his dream as a gift to us. It had the lightness of hope and the weight of responsibility.

When the dinner ended, my father retreated to the kitchen to scrub the pots and pans. I quickly found the BBC by spinning the dials. We sat around waiting for the news coming in on his short-wave radio over the crackle of the ionosphere.

Then a voice with a strange enunciation began, 'This is the BBC broadcasting from Bush House, London ...'

In our little kitchen in San Blas my father taught us to follow events around the world. Gorbachev and Reagan were having a summit in Iceland. Maybe Americans and Russians, the evil empire, would at last be friends. If junkies could change, maybe countries could too. In my mind I kept a well-stocked pantheon of foreign leaders, and it filled me with pride that I knew what was happening in distant countries.

While theological treatises bored me, we loved an engrossing story, the kind you couldn't put down at night. We read *Robinson Crusoe*, *The Prince and the Pauper*, *The Odyssey*, *The Iliad* and countless more. Every night we were eager to take our baths, brush our teeth and hear what might happen to Odysseus and his poor crew or Robinson and Friday.

Books were not dead. Reading breathed life into them. Reading was powerful and stirred such intense feelings. A great book had the power to change us and shake us to our core.

It was the power of words that exhilarated and transfixed us when my parents read to us before going to bed. J. R. R. Tolkien, C. S. Lewis and Jules Verne conjured new worlds of Middle Earth, Narnia and eerie voyages for us to explore. Words sizzled and popped off the page, and our minds soared in pursuit. Words were light itself, more real than everyday life, and far more exotic.

Books have immense power, my father told us, and we must be careful about what we read. We choose our books, and they shape us.

Not all books were created equal; we read *The Lion, the Witch and the Wardrobe* until the sharp corners of the pages became rounded and fuzzy. When Lucy entered Narnia, we felt the thrill of pressing through the warm fur coats and emerging in soft, cold snow on the other side of the wardrobe, a doorway into another world.

We cried when my parents read from *The Song of Roland* about evil Ganelon's betrayal of Roland and Oliver. I knew Roland as a friend and dreamed we had been in battle together before he died. In my mind, I pictured the Saracens killing him down the street, by the entrance to the Gypsy camp. If I had been at his side, I would have protected him.

My father read the scene to us:

The count Roland, when dead he saw his peers,
And Oliver, he held so very dear,
Grew tender, and began to shed a tear;
Out of his face the colour disappeared;
No longer could he stand, for so much grief,
Will he or nil, he swooned upon the field.

The author wrote, 'He has learned much who knows the pain of struggle.' Even though I had never known anyone close to me who had died, and sadness existed only in books, the story put a strange softness in my chest. That night I went to bed with a feeling of heaviness that I had never felt before.

Peter teared up and asked, 'Dad, why did Roland have to die? Can't he come back like Aslan?'

In *The Lion, The Witch and the Wardrobe*, Aslan returns from death like Christ after three days. In literature, death is the great antagonist, always conquered in Act Three. But my father told us that in life – here in the physical world – death is final. We do not come back. But there is hope. What is Christianity if not the Resurrection story and the triumph of life over death? We can meet on the other side in heaven when we too have died. That is when we will be reunited with those who have come before us as we gather at the walls of Zion.

When the very last readings were done, my father turned off the lights and transformed our room into a planetarium with a small light bulb and a toilet roll peppered with holes. He gave us our own little universe with Perseus, Orion and a zodiac swirling above.

'Dream dreams of Zion,' my father exhorted.

'Now, Elliott...' my mother said, 'let them sleep.'

He tucked us in, prayed and recited Psalm 23: 'The Lord is my shepherd; I shall not want. He maketh me to lie down in green pastures; He leadeth me beside the still waters. He restoreth my soul...' We went to sleep with our feet in San Blas and heads among the stars.

Casas en ruinas

Houses in ruins

M Y FATHER LOVED ruins. Landlords always offered a lower rent for a derelict property than for a new one, and few landlords wanted to rent a refurbished place to a bunch of *yonkis*. Betel did not have a large budget, but it had lots of manual labour. If anything needed fixing or rebuilding, the men could do it. Derelict properties were easier and cheaper to rent, but my father loved them because he saw in them what others could not.

Betel's first church and office were in a shopfront on Carretera de Vicálvaro, and the main room could hold a hundred people at most for a service. Sunday mornings it was standing room only and people spilled into the hallway and out of the front door. The office was so small it only had space for one desk. When Ramón or Raúl taught us Sunday-school lessons, they had to teach us in the kitchen, but that was inciting misbehaviour. Peter and I raided the refrigerators for ham and cheese when we were bored. We knew all the Bible stories and verses anyway.

Raúl and my father scoured the neighbourhood for properties. They looked at abandoned nightclubs, warehouses, factories – anything with a lot of room. Finally, they found an old dance hall on Calle Raza, right off Calle Alcalá, one of the busiest streets on the north side of the neighbourhood. No one had rented the place in over twenty years. Half of the ceiling had caved in, the paint on the walls had peeled off, revealing layers of green and blue, and water leaks had damaged the bricks and plaster. Weeds sprouted through the tiles and overran the courtyard.

Yet my father knew it was Betel's next headquarters, and called the landlord until he secured it. The building was much bigger than the old church, but the rent was ten times as much.

Raúl doubted that Betel had the money, but he did not argue. As we left the building, he turned to me, '*Este hombre es demasiado. Pero aprendo cantidad.*' – This man is too much. But I'm learning a ton.

I had never seen my father so excited. He paced about, measuring rooms and making mental notes. 'The offices will be here. We'll put up walls of plaster and hang new ceilings. And over there,' he said as he pointed, 'we'll have a reception area with sofas. We'll fix the walls, treat them for water damage and instal pine sideboards.'

He looked up, his eyes darting left and right as he pictured in his own mind how the ceilings and walls would look one day.

'Dad, it's a mess,' I said. 'We can't have a church here. It would take an army of men to fix it.'

'"Oh ye of little faith!" Trust me. We will have a big, beautiful church,' he said; it was like he was letting us in on the grand opening before anyone else.

As soon as my father signed the contract and got keys to enter the building, Betel's vans pulled up to rebuild the place and everyone went to work. The men poured out of the back doors armed with paint buckets, rollers, ladders, hammers, saws, picks and shovels. Raúl, Jambri and Juan Carlos tore up the place. If you put your fingers to the bricks, they turned to dust. The men smashed the bricks and plaster, and Raúl and the plumbers put in new pipes and sealed all the leaks. Peter and I followed behind, collecting the discarded rubble.

Out on the street, men mounted ladders and prepared the façade. They were going to put up Betel's trademark blue dove and broken needle, but my father intervened; the needle had to go. 'Let's not scare the neighbours.'

The rebuilding took a month, but on the last day of work, after we had swept and mopped the building, it looked exactly as my father had said it would. The roof was fixed. The courtyards were clear of weeds, and the men had put potted plants around the steps. The entranceway had sofas we took from Jambri's *rastro*. The church hall shone as distinct rays of sunshine streamed through the windows near the ceiling. And my father beamed as happily as he had when the vision appeared in his mind's eye for the first time.

I wondered whether my father was addicted to the buzz of the challenge – the worse the mess, the bigger the challenge. The landlord of Betel's farmhouse liked the way we had fixed it up, and he gave us a month to leave before he sold it. A *chico* in the centre said he knew of an abandoned house and farm in the town of Mejorada del Campo that he had used as a shooting gallery. The place he took us to was a ten-minute drive from San Blas. It had been a warehouse in the Spanish Civil War and had lain unused for decades. To reach the house you had to drive through winding, uneven dirt roads. Our car lurched from side to side as it hugged the ruts.

The house sat at the bottom of a hill, right by a small creek. There must have been a factory upstream because the banks bubbled with white soap suds. The main building had three twenty-five-foot-high walls and no roof. Next to it were living quarters with five rooms. They had no windows, and the doors hung askew. Stray dogs had left their marks. I took shallow breaths, trying not to fill my lungs.

'This is ideal,' my father said.

'You can't make the guys stay there,' I protested. I did not like visiting, and I could not imagine it would be any better to live there.

'It'll be grand.'

'Not even the dogs stay,' I said as I glanced over at my brothers, who were equally astonished.

'As the prophet Zechariah said, "Do not despise the day of small beginnings, for the Lord rejoices to see the work begin." We'll rebuild the house, and the church will grow. Trust me.'

When we first went to the church at Calle Raza, if I strained my imagination, it was possible to see what he saw. But at the Mejorada farmhouse I only saw decay no matter how hard I tried.

His dreams and visions were strange, but the men and even our family followed. We protested, but who else saw things that weren't there and made them come to life? He was Odysseus, and we were the tired sailors rowing away, hoping we'd make it home to Ithaca in one piece. He was a dreamer, but also a doer, and we were in awe of him and trusted him even when our heads said we shouldn't.

My father thought empty dreams were useless, but the ones you held onto in the sunlight could change the world. As T. E. Lawrence wrote,

All men dream, but not equally. Those who dream by night in the dusty recesses of their minds, wake in the day to find that it was vanity: but the dreamers of the day are dangerous men, for they may act on their dreams with open eyes, to make them possible.

Raúl, Jambri and the thirty-five other men moved all their things from the old farmhouse in Barajas to the ruin in Mejorada. They worked from early in the morning until late at night fixing and cleaning the place. Without a kitchen, the men prepared simple food in the open air. For dinner we ate *pan tomaca*, bread smothered in olive oil and crushed tomatoes, and strips of chorizo roasted over an open fire. Food never tasted so good as after work.

A young missionary couple had joined Betel, and their first visit was to Mejorada. They seemed in shock – culture shock perhaps, but much more likely they didn't expect to see cows and pigs living on the ground floor near the men. Peter was exuberant as he showed them around, jumping out of the cow stalls, slapping the pigs and sending them away squealing. They didn't follow a word of what my father told them on his tour, they just followed Peter's comic relief, his boyish silliness and his pride, which wouldn't have been out of place on a tour of the royal palace downtown.

Dad said the centres needed to be in the middle of nowhere. Drug addicts who had the virus were the twentieth century's lepers. Nobody wanted drug addicts in their neighbourhood, and not in their same building. That's why we needed ruins. We needed to be out of sight. I was too focused on getting in line for the food and joking with the men to ask who might be HIV+.

My father and the brick-masons built the fourth wall, and they slept beneath the stars that beat like hearts. A few days later, he helped them put a roof on the house. David, Peter, Timothy and I stood below, watching my father dangling from the scaffolding. Day after day we returned. With small hammers we tried to crack the large boulders. We could only chip off small pieces, but Dad and Raúl descended and broke them effortlessly with sledgehammers. My brothers and I carted the chunks of stone away. We were not much use, but we were helping my father do what he loved most – fix damaged things.

The day the men moved into the farmhouse, my father led the devotional. He always had the right verse for everything. The Bible was useful that way. He read from Isaiah chapter 58:

And if thou draw out thy soul to the hungry,
And satisfy the afflicted soul; . . .
Thou shalt raise up the foundations of many generations;
And thou shalt be called The repairer of the breach,
The restorer of paths to dwell in.

The story of love was mending the split, repairing the rifts.

The house was remote and Raúl led the men in an ascetic existence. During the day they may have worked in Betel's rag-tag businesses, but at night they communed with nature. Overhead the pylons looked like giant iron men with outstretched arms, and they crackled with electricity. Yet below, the house was not connected to the grid. In the evenings the generators whirred loudly and the light bulbs flickered, attracting swarms of mosquitoes that buzzed in sympathy. When I visited with my father for a morning devotional, it felt to me like a monastery built for *yonkis*. The fifty men sang, raising their voices in unison, and the hills echoed in response.

On the slope of the hill, the men gathered large stones and painted them cobalt blue and white in Betel's colours. They lined them up so planes on the flight path overhead could read: *DIOS ES AMOR*. God is love.

The only visitors who came to the isolated community were the police. They drove up in many cars with *ordenes de busca y captura* – search and arrest warrants – and with their hands on their holsters, ready to take one of our men into custody. Almost everyone had been in so many armed robberies they had lost track of their crimes. Sometimes my father convinced the judge to allow the men to serve their sentences in Betel, but other times the centre could do nothing for them.

Manolo *Majara*, who had re-entered Betel, was the first they came for. They locked him up for two years for a heist he'd done on an electronics warehouse, but the judge let him to come to Betel on weekends.

If my father wanted to turn convicted felons into ordained ministers, he had his work cut out. For many years the men's minds had been in disrepair. Most of the men could not read or write well because they had dropped out of school in their early teenage years. The only thing most addicts read on the streets was the sports paper *Marca* for the weekly scores. My father and a Canadian missionary created a small Bible school to train the men to read and write and teach them theology. In the evenings Raúl, Jambri and the men studied patristics, apologetics, hermeneutics and many other subjects I did not understand.

None of the men found studying easy. Jambri told me he doubted he could learn anything, but the moment the classes began, he couldn't stop reading. He was driven by the verse, Romans 12:2: 'Be ye transformed by the renewing of your mind'. After two years of study, the mission ordained Raúl, Jambri and three other leaders in Betel. My father was immensely proud to see them as ministers in the church they had rebuilt with their own hands. I was too when I saw how happy Jambri was.

Not everyone was as pleased with Betel's workers.

As a newly ordained pastor, Raúl went with my father to meetings of the Protestant pastors in Spain to represent Betel. In one meeting, a pastor asked why a drug rehab centre was ordaining ministers and starting churches. He pointed to Raúl, 'Why don't you do what you do best? You do rehabilitation work. We run churches. We'll send you our guys to get off drugs, and when they're on the straight and narrow, you send them back for pastoral care.'

Raúl stood up and faced all the pastors.

'*Your* guys? *Your* guys? Let me get this straight. You want us to do all the dirty work, so you can have them back all cleaned up, sitting politely in your church? No. It doesn't work that way. You can call them *your* guys when you've cleaned their sores, sat up all night through their withdrawal, dealt with them when they're threatening, and then slowly watched them change. Only then can you call them *your* guys.'

The episode gained Betel few friends, but when my father recounted the story at the dinner table, I sensed in his smile the same satisfaction he had when my brothers and I did something well.

Raúl led the men in the Mejorada house, as he had in Barajas. He gave them *collejas* whenever they cursed, made them wash the dinner dishes for a month if he caught them smoking, and forced them to leave if they were not making progress. Many feared him when they entered the centre, but he was fiercely protective of the *chicos*, and they respected him for it.

One Saturday evening the men were in their underwear, stretched out on folding chairs, cooling off after a long summer day of work. A missionary couple stopped by unannounced. They wanted to see the *yonkis* and strolled around the house and garden. The men called over to Raúl to talk to them. The conversation did not get far, and he swiftly sent the missionaries away.

'There's nothing for you to see here. We are not apes in a zoo on display for you. This is our house!'

Just as Raúl moved into Lindsay's apartment with no grand design, almost every step in Betel's growth followed a similar pattern. The farmhouses kept filling with men, and whenever a house was full and the men were running the *rastros* responsibly, Betel opened another house and another shop. The *yonkis* needed help, and they kept coming.

My brothers and I had a front seat at the growth of Betel. Every week my parents updated us on the news, as if projecting flickering newsreels transmitting news of distant, momentous events.

At first the new residences were all in Madrid, but soon Betel opened centres in other cities. Myk and Lindsay got married, which came as a surprise to no one but themselves. The two of them went to Valencia, a city on the east coast of Spain, and started a centre with some men from Madrid.

Jambri had been a selfless leader in his house in Loeches and had run the *rastro* well, so my father, Lindsay and Raúl gave him the job of opening a centre in Cuenca, a city about an hour and a half east of Madrid. Cuenca is a town of medieval architectural curiosities and stone homes perched on the edge of the cliffs. Jambri took Juan Carlos *El Rubio*, the Blond, Pedro *El Puñe*, the Fist, and Manolito to help him.

My father and Jambri found a ruin that was cheap to rent. The ancient house had thick stone walls and massive oak beams. Jambri, his men, a van loaded with used furniture and bags of tools, cement and plaster of Paris – that was all he needed to start a new centre. It did not take them long to fix the whole place up and return it to its former splendour.

I visited Jambri and got to know Manolito, who was a puppy dog of a man. He was loyal, small, with a jaunty energy, and he loved to joke around. We traded letters, keeping each other updated on goings on in Madrid and Cuenca. He didn't last long, though. He had fallen in love with a young woman in Madrid, but she broke up with him by letter. They said he stopped eating and died of heartbreak, but it didn't make much sense to me. I reckoned AIDS killed him, and I felt sorry for him.

Jambri got sick easily and was so skinny he always looked like someone who had just checked into Betel, even though he was the leader of the house. The townspeople rarely believed him when he insisted he was the director of Betel in Cuenca. Even some of the new men teased him. One evening a man who had entered the centre refused to do a simple chore to help clean up the *rastro*. Jambri asked him politely to follow the rules like everyone else.

'Why should I listen to you? You look worse than me,' the new guy taunted him.

Jambri picked up a crowbar that was among some tools nearby and raised it to strike the guy. For an instant, he hesitated and put it back down.

'I knew you were a coward,' the new guy gloated.

Jambri slapped him with all his force. The guy left the centre without saying a word.

Jambri glanced around the room. Everyone stared at him in disbelief. For months he had worked diligently at the men's house, been conscientious with his men, and tried to live humbly, turning the other cheek. Jambri packed his bags, unable to speak.

No Betel leader could behave in such an un-Christian way. Jambri came back to Madrid.

When I saw Jambri, we said nothing about it. I knew what had happened, and he knew that I knew. Dad and Raúl punished him, but it did not matter. When we worked together, he never raised his voice at any of the men in the *rastro*. Whoever he hit deserved it. He was my friend, and that was all I needed to know.

One day Raúl burst in through our front door, his chest exploding with pride. He was smiling more broadly than I had ever seen him smile. When he was ecstatic, his eyes would squint and his cheeks would turn red, as if we had caught him having too much fun. He brought some ice cream and gathered us all in the living room. My parents stood near the doorway and beamed.

Raúl was going to marry Jenny, a young missionary from New Zealand. They had known each other for over a year. She had briefly shared an apartment with Myk. I often saw her when she went out to the parks with us to talk to the addicts. And I had seen her talking to Raúl after some of the Betel *fútbol* games. When he met Jenny earlier that morning, the first thing he asked was if she wanted to go for a walk. They walked without saying a word. Nervously, he stopped and, affecting great casualness, held her hand. He said he had practised that all week.

'You know I'm a rough man, and I know you don't speak Spanish well yet, so you don't have to say much.' Raúl never liked to waste time. 'Just say yes or no. Will you marry me?'

She said yes. Raúl took her downtown and showed her his favourite spots in Madrid. He paid for a large meal in Plaza Mayor but was so nervous he did not eat a bite.

Jenny grew up as a devout Anglican Sunday-school girl in New Zealand, but once she left home, she lost interest in the Church. With her new friends she tried heroin, but it only made her vomit. Cocaine and hashish, though, were drugs she had briefly enjoyed.

When Raúl told us his plans, David, Peter, Timothy and I looked at each other in astonishment. We immediately focused on the most important issue at hand: did this mean he was going to spend less time with us? Would the marriage threaten our regular *fútbol* games? Raúl had brought the ice cream to share in his happiness, but I was sure he had also done it to bribe us and soften the blow.

Raúl assured us, 'Don't worry. You're not losing me. I'm becoming *medio guiri*, half foreign, like one of you.'

My father married Raúl and Jenny four months later. The October day was so unusually warm and bright they held the wedding on the church's patio. Never had the church been so striking, and Raúl's men even found doves to release after the ceremony. David, Peter, Timothy and I enthusiastically pelted Raúl and Jenny with rice.

Almost a year later, Raúl and Jenny took four men and a van full of furniture to open a *rastro* and drug rehab centre in Barcelona. Thay had had a little girl shortly before arriving. Raúl said only Betel could make him move to Barcelona, where they did not support Real Madrid. Jesus loved tax collectors, prostitutes and Roman soldiers, so loving people from Barcelona couldn't be that hard.

Raúl and Jenny shared an apartment with the men until they found a suitably dilapidated wreck to rebuild. The men wanted Raúl to have some privacy, so they divided the apartment with a large blanket and a rope. After a few months of living in the apartment, Raúl found an abandoned house. My family came to visit, and the same excitement flickered in Raúl's eyes that I had seen in my father's at Mejorada.

Jambri was not far behind Raúl. At the Betel meetings, he met a nineteen-year-old girl named Mari Carmen. After Jambri got married, the Betel leaders and my parents sent him back to Cuenca with Mari Carmen to run the centre. Mari Carmen did not care that Jambri had been a *yonki* or a bank robber. Her older brother and sister had been on drugs too. They had both died of AIDS.

The virus was spreading in Madrid, baring its fangs and biting at the heels of friends. Yet I thought little of it.

I missed Raúl and Jambri but was happy for them – at last they had got their own ruins.

I did not get to become friends with Raúl's replacement as leader at the Mejorada farm. Ramonet did not have Raúl's charisma, but he had the optimistic, quiet ability to get things done and encourage others, no matter how badly he felt. Although he was physically weak, he was the first to volunteer and push the Betel vans when they needed to be jump-started.

Yet one morning, as he gave a devotional amid hacking coughs, he could not continue. His ghastly rattle was so dreadful that my father ordered Ramonet to go to the hospital immediately. As soon as he had been admitted, the doctors prohibited him from leaving. He was tubercular, and the doctors were horrified he had not sought medical help sooner.

For the first time, my father took me with him to the hospital in Alcala. As we approached in the fire-engine-red van, I was bouncing with excitement. At last I'd get to see what doctors did and find out if hospitals looked anything like the ones on TV.

We went to pay Ramonet a visit and wish him a speedy recovery. He looked fatigued, and strained to speak between his gasps for breath between coughs. He was soaked from a fever and chills, yet he smiled and promised he'd be back at work soon, helping out at the Mejorada farm. Perhaps a giddy optimism in the power of faith or the magic of medicine comforted him. I knew little about medicine, but I didn't see how he was going to be pushing vans anytime soon. In fact, he looked deathly ill, and if death had a smell, he had it.

Ramonet died the next day. Dying from tuberculosis so quickly was not normal. The doctors said AIDS had killed him.

The virus incubated for much longer than anyone knew and killed far quicker than we feared. Some of the men said Ramonet's eagerness to serve killed him. He should have got help earlier, but that may have only given him a few more weeks or months. AIDS was deadly, and there was no beating it – borrowing time was the most anyone could hope for.

At church, the men got up to speak about Ramonet, tell stories about him and remember him. He never hogged attention. He shone by helping others. He was the sort of person who bettered the world by finding and celebrating the small things that made others unique. Many of the recovering *yonkis* didn't have any stories, but they remembered how Ramonet made them feel loved, and that was why they decided to stick it out when they were going cold turkey.

In the months that followed the news came slowly and unevenly, like the first drops of a distant downpour. Victor *El Granos*, who used to rob shops with an axe he hid under his trench coat, died of pneumonia. Lolo, the young man who kept the ferret on the farm, also died in the infectious diseases ward. I assumed it was pneumonia as well. Cheli, the young woman I had regaled with stories of Champollion deciphering the hieroglyphs, had died too. And many more.

By the time I started paying attention to the disease, it was too late. Many addicts were HIV+. No one knew who got it first, or who gave it to who. It was like an invisible, deadly chain letter people received and passed on to many others without knowing it.

Sardinas y lentejas

Sardines and lentils

We lived well on little and never wanted for anything because in the early 1980s the almighty dollar went a long way in Spain. But it was too good to last.

My parents received no fixed salary as missionaries. They lived day to day from offerings they received from churches in the United States. Any large donations they received, they gave to Betel instead of saving.

My father explained the dollar was too strong, and after the Plaza Accords in 1985, it had fallen precipitously against the *peseta*. Like a Babylonian god who withheld rain from the crops one year and made the rivers flood over the next, the foreign exchange markets gave and took away. Currency markets were more terrifying than anything I had read about in books. From one year to the next my grandparents' birthday cheques bought fewer Big Macs. Not even my father's dry economic diagrams on the back of a napkin explaining Purchasing Power Parity and references to *The Economist* could soften the blow.

Not only were the dollars not going as far as they used to, but churches were sending fewer of them. The offerings slowed to a trickle. Perhaps my parents' faith was inadequate.

My parents called David, Peter, Timothy and me into the living room. My parents did not have enough money to send us all to the missionary school. Only David would go because he was the oldest and needed to prepare for university. But we would stay at home to learn. What were Peter, Timothy and I going to do all by ourselves?

Our lives changed in the mundane details. We were eating less beef and more sardines and lentils, my parents stopped buying ice cream, and my brothers and I received our one-hundred-*peseta* allowances infrequently and then not at all. As the winter set in, my parents set the thermostat lower and lower. We covered ourselves in blankets as my father ploughed ahead in his pontifications. And I learned to hate the cold.

The founder of Worldwide Evangelization for Christ, C. T. Studd, was the son of a wealthy tea planter. Studd became captain of the Eton and Cambridge cricket teams. He could have lived a life of comfort in London. Instead, he gave up his inheritance and died penniless, aged seventy-one, in Africa. It was the way of a true missionary.

Before Studd died, he wrote, 'If Jesus Christ be God and died for me, then no sacrifice can be too great for me to make for Him.' My parents had it hanging on the wall at home. It sat next to a Bible verse warning against pride that said: 'What does it profit a man if he gains the whole world and loses his soul?' The verse was pointless; there was no danger of us gaining anything.

When I grew up, I would not be a missionary. I'd get a job, something where you got paid well and *regularly*. I covered myself with blankets and rubbed my feet together to fight the cold. How foolish I was to want the life of Eric Liddell in China!

I felt angry, and was surprised by the depth of feeling. Reading others was difficult, and reading myself was even harder. As preacher's kids, we were always supposed to be thinking of others, not ourselves. I sat back, coolly detached, observing the world spin around me and struggling to make sense of it.

Being the son of a minister was like being the child of a sitcom dad. He is your father, but once a week he appears as the father in another family, in everyone's home. Everyone feels they know him and have a piece of him. And your family secrets end up as a punchline in a sermon.

Being a preacher's kid meant being the first to church and last to leave as my parents hugged and spoke to everybody. It meant sleeping on sofas at a Betel farm while my father finished a sermon. Everyone wanted to be near my parents, and we know they weren't really ours – they were collective property. We could jealously guard our parents, but they belonged to the world. Our life revolved around theirs and people knew us as the preacher's kids. '*Los hijos de Elías y María*. Elliott and Mary's kids.'

I sometimes thought my brothers and I took second place to the hundreds of other sons and daughters my father spent so much time with. He missed birthdays, *fútbol* games, and was away too often visiting distant drug rehabs. Rarely did we get a compliment for good behaviour; it was what was expected.

Our house was Hotel Tepper, and the misfits often were not the addicts but the visiting ministers. Catholics may have been too hierarchical, but in the world of Protestants, anyone could declare themselves an 'international minister'. My father had a high tolerance for the visitors who prophesied in highfalutin King James English and anointed him with olive oil from the kitchen.

I hated being a Christian with all the crackpot ambassadors for Christ. I refused to speak to them before or after the services and did not want to acknowledge that we might be part of the same tribe, even if it was a tribe I had not chosen.

The worst preached sermons that wandered so far astray my father cut the service short and contradicted their message. No. God would not multiply their tithes seven-fold. Our calling was to serve and love others. That was its own reward.

My parents accepted anyone who came by and had little time for doctrinal debates with Catholics, Baptists or Anglicans; they would cut off most theological conversations with, 'It will all be sorted out in heaven.'

Dad reminded us of C. S. Lewis, who wrote in *The Screwtape Letters* that is easier to love the idea of church than the people in the next pew where 'neighbours sing out of tune, or have boots that squeak, or double chins, or odd clothes'. It is always easier to love the idea of something than the thing itself.

'Why do you put up with the crackpots?' I asked my father.

My father replied, 'The Apostle Paul wrote that we are "treasures in earthen vessels". God sometimes chooses flawed people to bring His message.'

We may all be earthen vessels, I thought, but some of us are more cracked than others.

The life of a missionary was not for me. I did not understand why Timothy wanted to be a medical missionary to Africa. He was only five but dreamed of being like David Livingstone, the Scottish missionary who fought the slave trade. My mother sometimes called him 'my little missionary'.

Timothy didn't know enough. He'd learn.

One night, I eavesdropped on my parents in the kitchen, counting *pesetas*, debating whether to ask for expired food from the drug centre or withdraw from our tiny bank accounts. David had worked out the mathematical beauty of compounding and had enough for a few shopping trips. Over his objections, they took his Banesto bank booklet and emptied his account. The sums were insignificant, but it had come to that.

How had we become as penniless as the people we came to help? Why had my father not gone into business after Harvard? If he had, we would not be eating lentils and refried beans that made you fart all day, and my mother would not have to teach us at home.

Why had my parents chosen to be missionaries? I hadn't. How could my father live with himself? Just because he had done LSD at Harvard, we were stuck on a permanent acid trip. We weren't poor because of some great social wrong conspiring against us. No. We were poor by choice. Our reward might be in heaven, but that was a long way away.

My father's friends from Harvard Business School lived in Park Avenue penthouses and were running banks on Wall Street. We lived in San Blas and pretended we weren't hungry.

My father's vision now embarrassed me. Every time he mentioned it, I thought, 'Oh no, not again.' Was it medically possible to die of shame? He had scars on his shoulders from going through the glass storefront. I hoped other kids wouldn't notice them when we went to the pool. I thought God was strange. He had called on Abraham to sacrifice his son, Isaac, then provided a ram instead. As a child, I may not have had the wisdom to run the universe, but I'd create stories that made more sense if I ran things. And I wouldn't ask anyone to sacrifice his son. Come to think of it, I mean really, that's the central story of Christianity: a father sacrificing his son.

That year, Gordon Gekko preached in *Wall Street* that 'greed, for lack of a better word, is good'; my parents were busy giving their money away. Gekko was the villain, but as I saw it, he had a point. We could have done with a little more greed and less idealism.

At breakfast a few days later, my mother gave the devotional. We read from the Apostle Paul's letters to the Philippians verses 4:11–13, 'I have learned to be content whatever the circumstances . . . whether well fed or hungry, whether living in plenty or in want.'

My mother commented, 'Our happiness always comes from within. Never let circumstances rob you of your joy.'

My father reminded us of a quote from John Bunyan's *Pilgrim's Progress*: 'A man there was, though some did count him mad, the more he cast away the more he had.' So too, my father said, we were casting aside earthly things for even greater heavenly ones.

My parents had the Apostle Paul and Bunyan on their side, but it provided no comfort to me.

We ended with a hymn, even though we rarely sang together – my father's favourite and the one he sang the most often, 'Be Thou My Vision'. My mother held the faded Baptist hymnal she had grown up with and sang:

Be Thou my Vision, O Lord of my heart;
Naught be all else to me, save that Thou art
Thou my best Thought, by day or by night,
Waking or sleeping, Thy presence my light.

Riches I heed not, nor man's empty praise,
Thou mine Inheritance, now and always:
Thou and Thou only, first in my heart,
High King of Heaven, my Treasure Thou art.

As my mother sang the words of the hymn, tears rolled down my father's cheeks.

Maybe we were becoming more Christ-like by suffering, but even Jesus felt pangs of hunger as the devil tempted him in the desert.

'Everyone, please come into the living room,' my father said. Those were my least favourite words. I was afraid he wanted to talk about AIDS again, or maybe God had spoken and told us to go to some new, distant place.

It was even worse: we were leaving our little apartment. I stormed out of the family meeting and ran to my room. My father followed me and sat on the edge of my bed. 'I know what it is like to leave one's friends and home,' he said. 'When my parents divorced, I had to move. Our landlord wants the apartment. We don't have a choice.'

We were going to move from a small apartment on our street, Calle Butrón, to a small house on Calle Caspe in Canillejas at the other end of the neighbourhood. The area was once a quiet town, but San Blas ate it up as it grew. Our new house looked a world away from the apartment on Calle Butrón. The garden was bigger than my father had described it, and it had a mulberry tree. I had never seen so much greenery in San Blas. Yet I would have traded all our mulberries to be close to the dump, the Gypsies and the vast rows of apartment blocks. They were the only world I knew.

Our garden had a small shed with a caved-in roof, and my father said it would be our classroom. He and a few of the men from Betel repaired the beams and whitewashed the walls. I could not believe that my parents were going through with their idea. Only in books had I read about one-room schoolhouses on the American prairie. How was I going to learn without classmates and lessons? What would I use for schoolbooks?

My parents said that Pearl Buck had been a Presbyterian missionary kid in China, and she had been home-schooled. She won a Pulitzer and a Nobel Prize. We had no excuses for not learning or achieving great things.

The small, sparse room barely fitted a desk for my mother, two tiny desks for Peter and me and an even smaller one for Timothy. We sat in a circle, crowding around an electric heater whose coils glowed orange and filled the air with a burning tang.

At nine-thirty in the morning, we put our hands on our hearts, stared at a small Stars and Stripes on my mother's desk and recited our oath of loyalty to a country we barely remembered.

The Pledge of Allegiance felt alien to me. In the neighbourhood we never saw the red and yellow Spanish flag or heard the national anthem. It still had the whiff of fascism. When General Franco died almost all the street names changed. The only time I heard his name was when children in the streets sang dirty limericks about him.

We reverently learned about the Boston Tea Party, the Gettysburg Address and D-Day. Even though we were in Madrid, we might as well have been in small-town America.

My mother sipped cups of hot tea, corrected our work and answered our questions. She wasn't a teacher like the ones at school. She believed children were born with curiosity and the irrepressible desire to learn. Adults could push it down like a beach ball under water, but it would just come shooting up in the end.

'My job is not to teach you,' she said. 'My job is to get you to love learning so you can teach yourselves.'

Learning was the freedom to become whoever we wanted to be.

The only formal texts that served as instruction were thin packets with correspondence coursework, which we raced through every morning, propelled in a competition against each other.

With ink on my fingers, I scribbled furiously, attempting to finish everything by recess. But Peter always retained the advantage. I switched to pencil and eraser, retracing my steps, trying to find my error. I squeezed the desk, hoping the answers would appear miraculously. Peter glanced over his notebook, never resorting to an eraser. The one year, two months and one day that divided us in age shrank as he grew older and smarter.

But the true education did not start until she dismissed us from our coursework and gave us complete freedom to go into the study to climb and pull books off the shelves.

At first, the only thing that guided our tastes were the covers of books and their photographs. But with time we moved on to even thicker, more serious books. Our appetites were omnivorous, driven by the magic of learning. Peter and I fought over

Roget's Thesaurus and the *American Heritage Dictionary* as we read definitions from adze to zygote.

But my favourite books were the medical ones. *The American Medical Association Complete Encyclopedia* had anatomical diagrams of sexual organs and disappointingly dry discussions of intercourse and insemination. The best chapters, though, were the ones on first aid. As I read them, I imagined myself a hero. Yes, some day fate would call on me in a great accident to staunch a severed artery, and the world would marvel at my knowledge.

Then Peter and I moved on to the faded *National Geographic* magazines. They always had enthralling articles about sharks and orang-utans, but we loved the ones with Pygmies and Masai warriors. We read, giggling, and showed pictures of bare-breasted women with large, saggy nipples to Timothy.

The more tired my mother was, the less of a threat television became to our intelligence, and we could watch it if we kept silent. She introduced us to movies she'd seen as a young girl and in college, like *West Side Story*, *The Sound of Music* and *High Noon*. Gary Cooper and Julie Andrews were as familiar to us as our friends from the streets. She told stories from her childhood of a country far more exotic than Spain. My mother confessed she had a crush on Rock Hudson too. Hudson died of AIDS in 1985, and after that, everyone in the world knew about the virus.

Before she became a missionary, she had started training to be a stewardess so she could travel widely. That came to a swift end when she broke her ankles sliding too quickly down the emergency exit of a plane. She would have to find a less dangerous way to see the world.

My father travelled to distant new Betel centres, God's calling creating a permanent restlessness. Through his absences, it was my father who became an even larger figure than Mom, who was with us, pouring herself into us every day.

Most days I was relieved not to be at school. My body was not as I remembered it. Why was my voice changing, and why was I growing hair in odd places? Would I have hair on my back and legs like my father? I hated the minefield of puberty and the daily tripwires I discovered. My private moments revolved around the bathroom mirror and I sniffed my armpits, mortified at what was becoming of me. I pleaded for the changes to stop, but the mirror pitilessly revealed my flaws.

Throughout the day, Peter scoured the house, collecting samples of liquids and powders. He had a restless self-confidence; the world was his and with enough curiosity he would figure out how it all worked. An alchemist, he and Timothy would make potions from the liquids they pilfered from the kitchen and my mother's dresser. They hoped to copy Alexander Fleming's discovery of penicillin. With Timothy's help, they wrote meticulous labels for the benefit of future generations.

In the early afternoon, once we had finished all our coursework and read until we felt our brains were full, I hurried with Peter and Timothy to Betel's offices to watch the new men enter the centre.

Seeing the men check in never ceased to excite me. The office took no photographs of people when they entered the centre, but if I glimpsed their haggard appearance, whenever I met them again, the first image would return to me, as clearly as if I had retrieved the faded card of a *fútbol* player from my desk drawer.

One day, a blond boy who was smaller than me slouched on a sofa in the entranceway. The boy was skinny, his eyes blackened, his lower eyelids drooped. He waited with his father who was no better. The boy looked at me with an empty, haunted stare and then turned away. I glimpsed the abscesses on his arms.

Never had I seen such a young heroin addict. Raúl, Jambri and all the men had started in their early teens to drink *litronas*, smoke weed and chocolate; then they moved on to *tripis* and coca, and even when they shot up they did not enter the centre until they had been hooked for years. There were many stops along the way, and heroin was always the end of the line.

I asked a secretary about the kid. His name was Jorge, and he had been shooting up for about a year before he entered Betel. He was ten and I could not believe he was three years younger than me. I often fantasised: what if there was another me in the same city, living a life perpendicular to mine? At that moment, the lines had crossed.

How did he ever start shooting up? Was it fun at first? Was he a Real Madrid fan like me? I hoped he would not leave the centre and would answer all my questions.

Little Jorge did not leave, and during Betel's church services I watched him from across the room. After the meetings, I loitered nearby, trying to come closer, hoping that he might introduce himself. But he never said much and always sat next to his father.

One day I sat next to him at a lunch at the men's house. His father was sitting far away. At last. I had no fear of asking Jambri about shooting up, but I was strangely afraid to talk to Jorge.

'Did you . . . You used to . . .'

'What?'

'You used to shoot up, didn't you? I saw the track marks.'

He started to speak and then caught himself. He looked around the room. His father was far away.

'Yeah. I did. But not at first . . .'

When Jorge was nine years old, he started working as a *correo*, delivering heroin to his father's regular customers. Jorge took the *papelinas* of tin foil to the right person and always brought back the exact amount of change. He was an efficient, obedient foot soldier, and the police never stopped him.

One day, out of curiosity Jorge opened a packet and snorted the heroin, as he had seen his father do to test the powder. What began as an occasional indulgence, like eating sweets when he wasn't supposed to, became a habit. Jorge hid it from his father, but once he found out, he did what only a disturbed drug-dealing father would do. He set his son straight and showed him how to shoot up instead of sniffing.

Jorge left Betel a few weeks after we talked. I never saw him again.

What kind of father involved his son in his own work like that, putting him in the way of heroin and needles? And why did his mother not stop it?

The kids were always dragged along by the riptide of their parents' lives.

El ojo de la tormenta

The eye of the storm

THE PHONE IN the entrance rang like an irritated child, spoiling our dinner.

'*¡Buenos dias! ¿Dígame?*'

My mother's voice carried into the dining room. It became even brighter when she answered the phone. And then silence. Her voice dimmed.

David and I glanced at each other.

'Elliott ... Elliott, it's for you. Jambri and Mari Carmen ... You'd better come to the phone.'

That evening, as Jambri and Mari Carmen were returning to Cuenca from Madrid, a drunken truck driver crossed into their lane on a sharp turn. In an explosion of glass and steel, their car hurtled off the road. They were trapped in the twisted wreck, and they drifted out of consciousness while they waited for an ambulance. The mechanical Jaws of Life arrived and cut them loose, but by the time they reached the hospital, they had lost a lot of blood and their situation was grave.

Jambri was at the hospital, and I wanted to see him. I hoped the doctors were looking after him.

As we took the large hospital lift, my mother and father said nothing. I overheard the anguished conversations of families all arriving at once during visiting hours. A mother wiped her tears away in the lift as she composed herself and forced a smile. We got out on Jambri and Mari Carmen's floor and searched for their rooms. My parents had told me about the accident, but even knowing the catalogue of injuries was not enough to prepare me. Mari Carmen's eyebrow was slashed, her right eye had come out of its socket, her ribs were broken and her spleen had ruptured. She could barely see or speak.

I stood at the back of her room, already hoping we would not stay in the hospital too long.

When I went to Jambri's room, he was lying immobilised, bound by bandages and pulleys. Pins and screws went straight into holes in his arms, and his exposed skin was a wounded purple. The accident had shattered his wrists and broken his arms, legs and ribs in many different places. Just looking at his body made my stomach queasy. I wanted to look away and leave the room.

'Does it scare you to see me like this?' he asked.

'Of course not.' I steadied myself at the edge of his bed and squeezed his iron bedposts. 'How are you?'

'I'm lucky to be alive.'

I tried not to say much and let my parents do all the talking.

After the accident, the doctors and nurses had worked for hours and saved Jambri and Mari Carmen's lives. But some of them did not want to touch Jambri. He was HIV+. The hospital staff feared needle pricks and scalpel cuts. In the operating room, they wore surgical goggles, waterproof gowns and double latex gloves. The chances of infection were not high, but even the smallest possibility was too great a risk.

My father said the doctors were professionals and did their jobs by rote and reflex, but once the operation was over, Jambri felt the coldness of the interns as they did their rounds and the nurses whispered in the hallway before they entered his room.

It was months before Jambri and Mari Carmen left hospital and got back to Cuenca. When I saw him again, we shook hands, but he held mine at an angle and could not squeeze. The bones had set badly. Was that normal or was that what happened when nurses were scared to touch a patient?

Why were people afraid of Jambri? Jambri was hurt, not sick; surely he would be fine. When I worked with Jambri at the *rastro*, I had shaken his hand, hugged him, and nothing had happened to me. I was living proof.

My parents had told us not to worry about befriending people who were HIV+, and we didn't. We had already lived with ex-*yonkis* for the past few years. It was a little late for worrying about HIV.

Raúl, meanwhile, had caught a fever, but thought all he needed was a little rest. His condition did not improve, and staying in bed, taking vitamins and drinking water did not help. His fever got worse and he started losing weight. Jenny took him to the hospital near their home. Surely, he would be back in a few days as soon as the doctors figured out what his problem was. Each day she went to visit him, and his fevers persisted, and he lost more weight.

When Jenny became pregnant, the doctor told her and Raúl to take some routine blood tests. Raúl was HIV+ but Jenny and their daughter were not.

The day the doctor told him he was HIV+, he called my parents. The words fought to come out between the sobs. Raúl understood he had a virus that had no cure. He had a disease that was claiming the lives of his friends one by one. With no cure in sight, the diagnosis sounded like a judge handing down a death sentence.

My parents did not tell us the news about Raúl and his diagnosis. If he wanted to tell us, he would, they figured. It was only when he was in the hospital, losing weight, that we found out.

What? How come no one told us before? How could he be sick? It made no sense to me. Bad things happen to *other* people. We are not other people. It couldn't be happening to Raúl.

The doctors in the hospital in Barcelona told Jenny that persistent, unexplained fevers were common. Night sweats were a grim ritual for people with AIDS; you had to get used to them, they said. She would have to be patient.

The vague reassurances and platitudes of the doctors became meaningless as the days led to weeks and the weeks turned into a month. There had to be a specific reason Raúl's health did not improve, a hook to hang their hypotheses on.

The number of doctors that came by his bed increased week by week. Older doctors came by with younger residents, and they looked at his medical records and talked to him. For some of them Raúl was a strange AIDS case, and they could not come by often enough. He did not yet show the classic low T cell counts and signs of many opportunistic diseases, yet his weight kept falling. It was an intriguing mystery. But despite the doctors' medical interest, Raúl continued to lose weight and grow weaker. He stayed in hospital awaiting a breakthrough that appeared ever more unlikely.

September passed and then October. Jenny came to the hospital every day to visit him. Sometimes she brought their baby daughter, Séfora, along. Her second birthday was in November, and on her birthday the family shared a cake and blew out the candles in Raúl's hospital bedroom. Jenny was almost seven months pregnant with their second daughter, and she feared the baby would be born before Raúl got out of hospital.

Raúl had been in the hospital almost three months and the doctors still did not know what he had. He had lost almost half his weight and was in agony. The doctors kept coming by to look at his charts, but they were incapable of anything but empty expressions of curiosity.

One day, during their regular visits, Jenny pleaded with the head doctor, 'If you don't do something, he could die!'

The thought had not occurred to her before, and she wanted to take the words back as soon as she had said them.

'Yes, he could.'

The doctor was surprised she didn't understand the awfulness of the virus.

One day, after dozens of tests, the doctors found the source of his sickness. He had contracted tuberculosis of the stomach and intestines, rare in Europe but not uncommon in Africa. It had punctured the stomach wall and spread. The doctors began a new treatment, and though Raúl's condition improved, the damage was done.

Raúl was too frail to return to run the Barcelona centre again. When he left hospital, my father recommended he and Jenny come back to Madrid. They took a flight so he would not have to face the seven-hour drive; the men in Betel Barcelona loaded up a van with their things and followed them to Madrid.

I accompanied my parents to see Raúl and Jenny. They had moved into an apartment on Calle Butrón, our old street in San Blas. Raúl was sitting on the sofa, wearing pyjamas and wrapped in a blanket. He gave me a hug, put his arm on my shoulder and said 'How are you, Jonny?'

His arm was so skinny. He was *El Tocho*: he was not supposed to look like that. Would I ever punch his arm again, and would he only ever be strong in old photographs?

'I've often preached from Job,' he said. 'Man that is born of a woman is of few days and full of trouble.' But now, I finally understand the book. Some people say they're going through a wilderness – at times I think that I am never going to come out of one.' Raúl struggled for words. 'I want ... I *need* to work again.'

Raúl and Jenny agreed to stay in Madrid and help my parents pastor the church. It would be less physically demanding than running one of Betel's businesses or overseeing the men's residences.

The first time Raúl came to church, Timothy ran up to him to hug him.

'I don't want you to die.'

I looked away in embarrassment. You can't censor children.

'We will all die. Every one of us. Some of us sooner than others. Some of us know it, and others don't,' Raúl said.

Timothy started crying. Raúl dried his tears with his thumb.

'I'll be here as long as I can. Who else is going to give you *collejas*?'

Timothy let go of Raúl, smiling amid the tears.

Just as Raúl had not known that he was HIV+ when he entered Betel, many of the other leaders did not know either. After Luis Mendoza died, my parents, Lindsay and Myk encouraged all the directors and staff in Betel to have their blood tested. The centre also asked all new addicts to get blood tests as soon as they entered the programme. With each set of lab results, the Betel central office updated the medical files, adding pieces to the puzzle.

After everyone took their tests, perhaps when they felt we were old enough to know, my parents told us the news. Jambri, *Majara* and *Veneno* had contracted the virus. Almost every addict I had grown up with was HIV+. Unless scientists made a breakthrough with medicines, everyone would die soon.

It did not even seem real. How could all my friends be HIV+? It couldn't be true.

Spain was unique when it came to AIDS. In the US it started out as a gay disease. Before it was AIDS it was even called

Gay-Related Immune Deficiency (GRID). But it wasn't only a gay disease. In Africa, AIDS was a heterosexual disease. In Spain it was a disease of the *yonkis*. And San Blas was the epicentre of the earthquake.

AIDS hit Spain a few years after it had exploded in San Francisco and New York, and it was just as deadly. Spain had the distinction of having the most AIDS cases in all of Europe. It was the only country in the world where most came through intravenous infection. The Spanish government estimated that two thirds of all AIDS cases involved heroin addicts. An estimated 40 per cent of all heroin addicts were infected. In jails hundreds of addicts must have shared a few needles. How else did it spread so quickly?

It wasn't just the addicts who spread the virus. Mothers were passing it on to their kids as well. Shortly after Raúl and Jenny came back from Barcelona, their second daughter Raquel was born. The first blood tests showed that mother and daughter were both HIV+. Jenny had become HIV+ too. The doctors did not know if Raquel became infected during pregnancy or delivery.

Why did Jenny and little Raquel have to suffer when they didn't even shoot up? How many wives and daughters in San Blas were HIV+? No one knew how far the virus had spread.

So many leaders in the centre were infected that my parents and Raúl organised a conference. Between coffee breaks and meals, we packed into the church to hear doctors and ask questions. Many addicts knew so little about AIDS that it appeared as random and capricious as a biblical plague.

All the leaders of the centre came from around Spain to the conference, and my brothers and I sat at the back of the room and listened. Like nestlings with open beaks, we awaited the answers that came our way. We all learned how the disease developed, how the virus spread and how researchers were struggling to find a cure.

Should they take their Retrovir and other drugs if they were getting headaches and nausea? How should they behave in Betel's residences if more than half of the men and women were HIV+? Should they marry and have family if they could give the virus to their kids? Could they build a life for themselves amid the bombs and trenches? Would they *ever* live a normal life?

Everyone was struggling under the weight of the questions. For many this was the first chance they ever had to ask.

Some addicts were too ashamed to tell their fathers and mothers or even their own children. Many in the neighbourhood died without their families knowing why they were ill. They lived and died behind a wall of silence. To them, a physical death was less frightening than rejection and a social death.

The diagnosis of being HIV+ was the dark line of demarcation splitting their lives in half. Before and after. Before was a more innocent, even naive time. After was the certainty of death. After was the shame of being infected. And there was the shame of feeling ashamed.

Raúl led a round-table discussion on living with AIDS. He had regained most of his weight, although the tuberculosis had run down his defences over time. His T cell count was extremely low, like fallen soldiers leaving his immune system undefended. Jambri, Juan Carlos *El Rubio* and others spoke, and then Raúl.

'AIDS has been positive,' he declared.

The audience gasped while people exchanged glances.

'Every time someone has died, it has produced more seriousness, more compassion and more love. We have cried tears for them and are sad that they are gone, but we are aware more than ever that we must make each day count. With our limited days, we have to live a life of quality instead of quantity.'

'What God has done, and I don't think He could have done it another way, is that He has broken something inside me. Having AIDS gives me more love and empathy for others. We are all on the same level.'

'AIDS makes us realise there is no time to waste.'

Faced with the disease, Raúl was going to continue working in Betel and showing God's love to his last breath. Others spoke openly, many for the first time, about carrying the disease and knowing they were going to die; their words were all variations on Raúl's theme.

I did not have the virus, but knowing that almost all of my friends had it made me despair. They were HIV+ and had to live with it, yet it did not make them withdraw from life. The virus forced people to choose how they wanted to live.

Some addicts I talked to in the neighbourhood knew they had the virus ticking inside them, ready to explode, and it made them more reckless. They said nothing was worse than getting AIDS.

Stories circulated in the neighbourhood about addicts who robbed passengers on the subway, not with knives or guns but with needles with infected blood. If *yonkis* were going to die, they were going to take others with them. The story did not ring true to me, but others believed it.

After the conference, my parents cleared a shelf in the study and little by little the trove of information grew. I devoured the books and scientific journals, in my attempt to understand. Our 1976 *World Book Encyclopedia* had nothing on the disease. But I read *Time*, *Scientific American* and *The Economist*, collecting articles about it. Some were harrowing; they projected up to a billion people would become infected. Others were dry scientific texts that depressed me. Even if doctors produced the medicine to suppress the virus, it would mutate and become resistant to drugs. Nothing could stop AIDS.

What was the point of reading? More information did not give me any more control over the virus. Did I think that information was a switchblade to defend me, as if the disease were a knife fight in San Blas? AIDS is impersonal and you could not fight it – not on your own terms.

In America, Reverend Jerry Falwell made the grand pronouncement that 'AIDS is the wrath of God upon homosexuals'. This was sheer insanity to me, given a global epidemic was attacking everyone: gays, heterosexuals, haemophiliacs, children, rich and poor. Falwell loathed 'faggots'. My parents thought Falwell was an embarrassment to Christianity, even worse than the American televangelists they so despised. Those who preach and rail most loudly about the immorality of others often secretly live in breach of it themselves. No, that's not Jesus, my parents said. Some Christians were the worst possible advertisements for Christianity. If God is love, the Christian response to those who are hurting should always be more love.

Everyone lives with some great fault in their lives. But what does society do to people who've smoked too much, eaten too much, drunk too much, shot up too often or had unsafe sex? A good society cares for them and does not put them out to pasture to die alone. We can never lose our humanity.

Why was it that some Christians took parts of the Bible so literally – the seven-day creation, the flood and the endless genealogies – yet viewed the Sermon on the Mount with its call to meekness, kindness and love, and the Ten Commandments, as mere suggestions?

I was proud of my parents' response. As my father wrote to churches in America, 'AIDS breaks your heart. It makes you compassionate and softens you.'

I had gay friends in Betel, and I loved them. All my gay friends were HIV+, and it was impossible to know if they had got the virus from sex or from shooting up. Most were hairdressers, and they gave me haircuts when I spent weekends out in Betel's residences. And I loved hearing their stories of working downtown, cutting and styling the hair of Pedro Almodóvar and other celebrities.

I read Randy Shilts's *And The Band Played On*. The newspapers had photographs of ACT UP protesters chaining themselves to federal office buildings, fighting the police, demanding more funding for AIDS research and carrying banners that read 'SILENCE = DEATH'. From where I was in Madrid, none of it made sense to me. It wasn't the National Institute of Health or even the political establishment that was killing my friends in San Blas. It was the virus. ACT UP's struggle was thousands of miles from mine.

Yonkis were pariahs, outcasts with no political power. They had no Rock Hudson of their own, no poets or playwrights putting on off-Broadway shows. No one even cared enough about them to protest in Madrid. In Spain, AIDS was *their* disease.

I didn't care about protests or die-ins. I didn't want Raúl or Jambri to die – that was the only thing I cared about.

Soon the press became interested in Betel's experience with AIDS. A Dutch television station came to make a documentary on the centre and the church. My father, Peter and I took them to the men's residences, the used furniture shops, the Simancas Metro stop and the Gypsy camp to interview *yonkis*. By the camp, the paramedics resuscitated a man who had overdosed, while my father prayed at their side. At the Metro stop, the reporters met young prostitutes who had been in the centre. They had a complete picture of Betel and San Blas.

When the package with the video arrived, my father opened it eagerly. He read the title: 'Half the Church Has AIDS'. From the outside, all people saw of Betel was the disease – a modern scarlet letter. It robbed them of any other identity besides the virus.

When they interviewed Jambri, he told them that everyone with AIDS would die, but so would everyone *without* AIDS. As a teenager he had shared needles with his friends and become infected. Nothing could change that, but he was going to spend the rest of his life in Betel trying to rescue others.

Jambri was not the only one who thought that way. When AIDS exploded in Spain, Betel grew exponentially. In a little over two years Betel grew from around two hundred addicts to more than six hundred. Death has a way of focusing the mind, my father said.

The new men in the centre were becoming leaders much faster than usual and opened houses in new cities. My parents hoped they would not rob the centre's money, mismanage the shops or shoot up in the programme. Betel trusted the men and women, and they repaid the trust.

My father and Lindsay ordained the ex-*yonkis* as ministers more quickly than the mission's guidelines allowed. As my father wrote in his quarterly newsletter to churches back in the United States:

> *We are moving quickly because of the urgency of the task: a lost and dying world; and because of the fragile nature of the vessels God has given us to build His house. Half our church and more than half of our leaders are HIV+. We have no time to waste and cannot wait on or follow the traditional methodologies of preparation. We are cast upon the Lord, trusting in his supernatural enablement, and in His mercy to heal or extend the lives of His servants until all that has been committed into our hands has been done. Perhaps God is doing something new. Perhaps we are only in the eye of the storm. Either way we will finish the course.*

It made little sense to send the men and women in Betel away to seminary for three years to study theology when they could die at any moment.

When Protestant pastors and missionaries in Madrid complained about what they viewed as Betel's lax standards in ordination, Raúl cut them off.

'You may be right, but we don't have time for your methods. Read the Bible more carefully. It was Jesus who once told the Pharisees, "I tell you the truth, the tax collectors and the prostitutes are entering the kingdom of God ahead of you."'

Un amor supremo

A love supreme

It was 1990, and my father and I were glued to the television every morning. The Berlin Wall had fallen and millions of people were suddenly free. Thousands of East Germans stormed the Stasi headquarters in Berlin to view their own files. F. W. De Klerk released Nelson Mandela from prison, and Apartheid crumbled. Ian Charleson, who had played our great hero Eric Liddell in *Chariots of Fire*, died of AIDS. We did not know that he was gay or that he was even sick. The news was as shocking as finding out that Milli Vanilli didn't sing their own songs.

News dominated our mornings. As soon as I woke, I got dressed, brushed my teeth and combed my hair in front of the mirror with a parting on the left side, the way my father did. My father and I were always up first and had a cup of hot tea and watched the American news together to follow global events. He hated most of the news and corrected the fallacies that reporters peddled.

'Jonathan, they're doing it again . . .' he would bristle as the news shows stoked his irritation.

With the stainless-steel fountain pen he always carried, he drew graphs showing me the relationship between inflation and unemployment and how to calculate GNP, correcting what journalists had said about exchange rates or trade. He taught me about the Phillips curve, Gini coefficients and Pareto distributions. I was only fourteen but prided myself in the belief that I knew as much as adults. It was a mystery to me how they could make such a mess of the world. My father taught me to love the morning news the same way we had enjoyed hearing the BBC over the short-wave radio years earlier. And I inherited his opinions and political prejudices, much like the family moles and birthmarks we shared.

No morning could be complete without his pontifications. After Dad and I had watched the news together, my family still all sat at the breakfast table while my parents held devotionals and read from whatever book they had brought. This was our morning routine, and when we were not travelling to distant drug rehab centres, it never varied.

Missionaries live at the whim of exchange rates and the irregular generosity of Christians. Churches in America had been generous once again, and I almost wished they had not. After almost two years of home-schooling, my parents once again had money to send all of us to the missionary school Evangelical Christian Academy.

As soon as the devotion was finished, I made sure Timothy was in his elementary school uniform of light grey trousers, white shirt and blue jumper. David, Peter and Timothy fought for their slots to use the bathroom, and Timothy was always the last one to get it all to himself. When he finally had his turn, I helped him comb his hair exactly the same way my father had taught me. He brushed his teeth, scrubbing his two large front ones more than the rest.

Timothy was four years younger than Peter, five years younger than me and seven years younger than David. My mother wanted one of us to walk him to school. Peter was the closest to Timothy in age, but they fought and teased each other endlessly. Sending them together would be like asking Real Madrid and Barcelona fans to get along. David was the oldest and there were few things worse than being seen with young, immature brothers. Walking Timothy to school fell on me because I was fourteen and vaguely responsible. We already shared a bunk bed and did not fight.

David's world was already floating away from ours, and he spent more time with the men and women in the centre, helping in Betel's office, chatting with the endless visitors who came through Hotel Tepper and dreaming of going to university. The world of children was too limiting for him.

We had the same parents, grew up in the same house, went to the same school, and played *fútbol* on the same streets. We even looked alike in so many small ways. How could we be so different?

We walked from our house on Calle Caspe, winding through apartment buildings and made our way to Calle Alcalá. Timothy had an ebullience that was infectious. He would sing the Beach Boys' 'Barbara Ann' loudly and off-key in the street. David and Peter paced ahead even more quickly to avoid association with us.

'Shut up! You're annoying me. And everyone thinks you're nuts.'

'I can't hear you ...'

'Someone is going to beat the shit out of you if you don't stop.'

'Ah! You said the S-H-I-T word. You're in so much trouble with Daddy. No allowances for a while. I'm telling unless you sing ...'

And once I had started singing, I couldn't stop either.

An hour after my father taught me lessons, I relayed them to Timothy. He was my little experiment, his brain a laboratory for my prodding and probing. I marvelled at how lucky he was to have me as his teacher. We covered America's growing trade deficit with Japan, our high fiscal budget deficit, and the decline of

America's manufacturing base. He learned of Newton's laws of motion and the basics of thermodynamics – stuff every child should know. Every day he absorbed new words, which he casually inserted into his conversations with his teachers: 'Miss Clark, Andrew is uttering platitudes.' I couldn't afford an ice cream, but I gave him five *pesetas* for each word he used at school. I thought I was teaching him, but I was teaching myself.

At breaktime Timothy played games with his classmates and teased them. He was often blissfully unaware of how different our lives were from theirs. One day I overheard him telling some little girls that they had AIDS.

I pulled him over by the shirt collar. 'What are you doing? You can't go around saying stuff like that.'

'They told me I had cooties, and I don't have cooties!'

'They are just winding you up.'

'But I don't have cooties!'

'They're imaginary, Timothy! AIDS is real and people are scared of it. You don't want them repeating it to a teacher, do you? No one is going to understand. Do you want us to get kicked out of school?'

'Are you deaf or something? I said I don't have cooties!'

'Fine! You don't have cooties. But don't you ever say that again about AIDS. If you do, I'll give you a *colleja*.'

Timothy was only nine, but we never let that foil our plans. We expected him to keep up with our conversations. He was the vessel we poured information and lessons into. David taught him mathematics, even forcing him to take the maths section of the SAT to see just how smart he was. Timothy cried and begged to go out and play, but when the test was all over, he was proud when he got a respectable score even for a high-schooler. David insisted on explaining all the problems he had missed. Maths was elegant, and if only Timothy saw its beauty, he'd solve any problem perfectly.

One summer we went to a town on the Costa Brava, on the north-east coast of Spain. During the day we went diving in the crystalline waters near the rocky beaches, and my father read books by C. S. Lewis and the poems of T. S. Eliot to us at night.

Near the coves, a rock jutted out like a railroad spike from the sea. My father would swim out to the rock, climb up and dive in. One morning, my father and Peter had jumped, but the rocks were high and even David feared smacking the water from such a height. I stood with Timothy at the peak. He held tight to the rocks.

'I'll buy you an ice cream if you jump.'

He kept looking below at the water, weighing the decision. As the minutes passed, the water dried on our skin, leaving a sticky, salty feeling. Perhaps he was calculating the variables, trying to judge the distance, how hard he would hit the water, whether or not it would hurt.

He looked over at me and asked, 'What kind of ice cream?'

'Any kind you want.'

'It's going to be chocolate.'

He grinned at David and me and jumped into the sea. The turquoise water parted into bubbles, and when he surfaced, he jubilantly waved at us to join him.

Spanish television played American black-and-white movies early on Saturday mornings, and I watched them and caught glimpses of American culture. The Kirk Douglas film *Young Man with a Horn*, based on the life of the great jazz cornetist Bix Beiderbecke, was unforgettable. Beiderbecke was one of the greatest players of all time, and Louis Armstrong once said that if Beiderbecke had lived, he would have been the greatest. But he was an alcoholic and died in 1931. He was only twenty-eight. From that moment, I wanted to play the trumpet.

My father did not share my love of jazz. In his mind jazz was associated with the drug culture in New York in the 1950s. 'I've been to jazz clubs with my father in the Village,' he said. 'They were no place for kids.'

'You mean bars like Torre del Campo in San Blas?' I asked. 'Sounds pretty bad.'

My father was lost for words. 'It . . . It doesn't even sound beautiful.'

'What are you talking about? Have you even heard Mingus's "Better Get It In Your Soul"?'

'I haven't, but that's not the point.'

Timothy and I had played the track a hundred times. The song was a raucous, joyous piece that pounded like feet stomping in a revival camp meeting.

'Who said you get to decide what's beautiful and what's not? Or that you're the final judge of everything? *We* like it.'

'Well . . . keep it down. Do not play it around me.'

Arguing with parents is never fair. They're not just the opposing team; they play the referee and linesman too. And they always keep the score.

If Timothy and I wanted to play it, we had to play our tapes hidden away, like a 1920s speakeasy, as we broke laws that made no sense. And what could be more jazzy than a speakeasy?

In a moment of clarity, my parents' disdain for television, which was so high-minded before, struck me as disguised prudishness. Their taste in music and books was no longer gospel. I had reached the age where I knew more than my parents, and I winced at their ignorance.

As brothers, we shifted our exploration away from our parents. Timothy watched *The A-Team* at a friend's house because my parents thought we should not be exposed to violence. David had to watch *Porky's* and *Weird Science* at friends' homes too. We already knew of violence and even sex. We were kids from San

Blas, for goodness' sakes. David could never stay out as late as his friends because bad things happened at night, even though if you wanted to find drugs every junkie knew where to find them during daylight hours.

We never worked out why New York in the 1950s was worse than San Blas in the 1980s or why heroin in a jam session was any worse than in a Madrid dump. Not everything had to be Dylan and Baez either. Who made Dad the judge of truth and all things right?

We knew my father loved us, but he was the autocrat of the breakfast table, the inspiration for learning, the oracle of good taste and the arbiter of ideas. The solar system of the house revolved around his gravitational pull. As little children, we tilted towards him like flowers to the sun, but those days were over. Sometimes we simply wanted to be like comets and fly away free into our own orbits in the distant universe.

Dad said a big problem in San Blas was lack of discipline and strong father figures. Fathers were absent or drank too much while children ran wild and free. My brothers and I often cringed at him and sometimes wished we had a little more space and less of a father figure.

Dad was *somewhat* right, even if I hated to admit it. Jazz and heroin had a long history, and it is impossible to talk honestly about jazz without talking about heroin. As Miles Davis said, 'Jazz is like blues with a shot of heroin.'

Heroin was a problem for Stan Getz, Miles Davis, Chet Baker, John Coltrane and Charlie 'Bird' Parker. Bird died of an overdose at thirty-four. Chet Baker spent most of his life on heroin. Getz struggled with his addiction and died an alcoholic, like Beiderbecke. Davis kicked the habit cold turkey. Coltrane quit his habit after Davis fired him from his band, spending many days alone in his room, fasting in a profound religious experience. Coltrane later dedicated his album *A Love Supreme* to God. 'My goal,' he said, 'is to live the truly religious life, and express it through my music.'

Sure, there was lots of heroin in jazz. But boy could Miles Davis play, and his notes were effortless, like pebbles bouncing across the water. I liked to think that jazz musicians with their many addictions would have been at home with Raúl and Jambri in Betel.

Timothy and I planned to be famous musicians and play in clubs like Minton's Playhouse in Harlem or the Village Vanguard. We were going to be like Dizzy Gillespie and Bird. They had an explosive relationship, but despite their differences they were *the* duo of jazz history. Dizzy once described Parker as 'the other half of my heartbeat'.

We idolised Wynton Marsalis who played trumpet, and his brother Branford who played the sax. We'd be like them with rhythm and pizzazz, even if we were white.

Timothy was as stubborn as Bird but wanted to play the trumpet. But it could not be. Dizzy and Bird played the trumpet and saxophone, not two trumpets. Dizzy was older; *I* was older and *I* was Dizzy. End of story.

Whenever Timothy tired of my pontifications on jazz, he hid one of my music books and told me I could not get it back until I taught him to play my trumpet. I searched for the books, but he always found a secure hiding place. Defeated by his ingenuity, I relented and imparted the secrets of my horn. As soon as we were playing scales and arpeggios, I forgot about my book and was glad he had outwitted me. A few days later, he returned the book unharmed but would not reveal where he'd hidden it.

We hatched intricate, elaborate plans. We were going to play the trumpet and sax together and we would attend Harvard to get a decent education. My father's stories of Cambridge and Harvard resounded in our ears. Our age gap meant I would have graduated before Timothy was a freshman, but we'd figured that one out too. I'd find a job in Boston and Timothy could share an apartment with me to save some money.

We even knew what we were going to do after Harvard. Timothy and I planned that I would be president for two terms, and Timothy would be my vice president. After that, assuming the country had not tired of us, we'd just reverse roles. It was not clear how we'd combine the presidency with playing at the Village Vanguard, which was not even in Washington, but if Reagan was an actor and president, then it wasn't too far-fetched to think we could be musicians and presidents.

Our plotting was obsessive, bordering on the maniacal. One day I had detention and told Timothy to go home with David. I didn't want Mom to worry about him.

When I got out of detention, I found him playing basketball with Salva, the school caretaker who had been a *yonki*. They were giggling as Salva cracked jokes.

'What are you doing here? I told you to go home.'

'I wanted to walk home with you. We've got a lot of planning to do.'

Salsa y poemas

Salsa and poems

THE UNITED STATES was a strangely familiar place. I looked to our rare trips back with a mixture of anticipation and nervousness. It was the promised land, but everything was so foreign to me. It was supposed to be 'home'. I had an American passport and had lived there in first grade, but now I only recognised it from all the movies on television on Saturday mornings in San Blas. Nevertheless, I derived comfort from the familiarity.

As missionaries, we had to go on a furlough back to the United States every four years to visit churches that supported us. The town where my mother grew up, Wilmington, North Carolina, was our base while my parents travelled.

Furloughs are something every missionary family loves and hates. Like salmon in our migratory pattern, we returned to where we were born. Going back to the United States is a holiday from the mission field and a chance to see family again. The furlough would have days at the beach and barbecues, but it was also as gruelling as the political rubber chicken circuit, with endless lunches and dinners of cold drumsticks with potato salad, the canned speeches given over and over again, and nodding even when you felt like keeling over in a pew. But the donations from the churches paid my parents' salary and helped make Betel possible.

David at least looked forward to visiting Penn, Yale and Princeton, which he had set his sights on. He'd soon leave us and high school behind for the world of adults. Peter could look after himself, and I'd spend my time entertaining Timothy.

The Presbyterian church my parents were members of found a place in downtown Wilmington for us to have during the summer. The elegant pre-Civil War house was surrounded by tall oaks draped with Spanish moss amid azaleas and oleanders. Not far from the house was the old red-brick Cotton Exchange. I missed the busy streets of San Blas and thought of Louis Armstrong's song 'When It's Sleepy Time Down South'.

We loved downtown, and most of all we enjoyed the public library. David, Peter, Timothy and I had never seen such a palace built for books. We strode through the front door and were awestruck. The staircases ascended and cascaded floor after floor. Like vast waterfalls, each row of books tumbled upon the other, multiplying our horizons and imaginations. In a classroom, teachers told you what to read; in libraries, we could roam wherever we wanted. And education was free if you read books fast enough and avoided late charges.

We were overcome with anticipation and figured out that between the four of us we could check out as many books as we liked. David checked out books on mathematical puzzles and IQ tests to learn new equations and matrices. Peter checked out as many science and engineering books as he could find.

In Madrid I walked Timothy to school and in Wilmington we fell into our comfortable routine once again with trips to the library. I loved feeding him ideas and information. He had read books on instruments and musicology. He had memorised as much as any nine-year-old could about the history of the saxophone.

That summer our grandparents took him to buy a saxophone. The salesman asked Timothy, 'How much do you know about saxophones?'

Without hesitating, Timothy replied, 'Adolphe Sax invented the saxophone in 1841 to merge brass and reed instruments. There are fourteen saxophones, but the four main ones are the soprano, alto, tenor and baritone saxophones. And Charlie Parker played the alto. That's the one I want.'

He smiled and looked pleased with himself, but he could not have been half as pleased as I was.

Timothy and I spent our days in the music section, and we could not believe our luck. The local radio had gospel in the air, but jazz was our drug of choice. The library shelves stocked biographies of John Coltrane, Miles Davis, Bix Beiderbecke, Charlie Parker and Charles Mingus. Best of all, the library had recordings of every major jazz album.

The records were old and hissed and popped as the needle slid through the vinyl grooves, but we were hearing jazz history. Timothy smiled and tapped his feet to the syncopated, animated dialogue between Miles's horn and Coltrane's sax on *Milestones*: *Ta, ta, Ta, ta. Ta, ta, Ta, ta, Taaa* . . .

We played the tracks at home and then played them again so as not to miss a note.

'Isn't this the happiest song ever?' Timothy asked.

'It is.'

'You can't listen to it and not be happy to be alive,' he said smiling. 'Play it again.'

While my brothers and I were content mining the recesses of the library for books, my father was incapable of staying still. God may have been perfect, but if a flaw remained in His well-ordered world, there were not enough hours in the day to set it right.

Dad was always hungrily searching for new things to read or see. In Wilmington he missed Spain and visiting the Betel centres, so he kept himself busy that summer between his preaching trips by taking us to the gym to play squash and to the beach to swim.

One weekend in July my mother had gone to a women's conference with some women from our church. My father announced we'd have a men's retreat of our own.

'We're going to Kitty Hawk. Pack your bags. You'll see where Orville and Wilbur Wright flew the first plane.'

The night before my father took us to the library and checked out *Zorba the Greek* to watch. He told us stories of travelling around the Greek islands during his 'reading days' at Cambridge and how he ate sardines roasted over an open fire and drank ouzo on the beach with local fishermen.

Timothy's stomach was queasy, and he left halfway through the movie to go to bed. I followed him, found him already asleep, and took his shoes off and tucked him in.

The next morning, Timothy and I would have preferred to go to the library or to the Cotton Exchange for an ice cream.

'Can't we stay in Wilmington and read?'

'Life is an adventure. There are no rewards for staying home.' For Dad, life belonged to those who do things, not to those who watch.

'Dad, please. Timothy really doesn't want to go. I'll watch him.'

'You'll be glad you went. That's it.' He had decided, and he was the boss. As always, that was it.

I went upstairs to help Timothy pack.

'Can Daddy let me stay here with you?' he asked. 'I don't want to go.'

'I tried. I don't either. He says we're all going.' I wished I were stronger or more forceful, but nothing stopped my father when he wanted something.

I packed some books on jazz and put our clothes in a small bag. We would travel light. At least we'd be back in a day.

In a few weeks David would turn seventeen, and he was anxious to drive. He drove while my father enjoyed the trip. Peter had made sandwiches that morning. My father gave us Cokes and snacks of salsa and Doritos, then read to us from the Bible as he always did. Timothy sat in the front and slept.

He began with Psalm 120 and read through to Psalm 127:

Children are a heritage of the Lord;
The fruit of the womb is a reward.
As arrows in the hand of a mighty man,
So are the children of one's youth.
Happy is the man that hath his quiver full of them;
They shall not be put to shame,
When they speak with their enemies in the gate.

He prayed, and he told us how much he loved us, how proud he was to have us as his children, and he said that one day we would be great men.

Why did he always have to be so preachy and address us like we were a congregation? Couldn't he give it a break?

The drive up to Kitty Hawk on the day of 19 July 1991 was ordinary and unremarkable up until 10.45 a.m.

I looked up from the book I was reading seconds before it happened. I glimpsed a white stripe delineating the edge of the winding country road and the grass beyond. A few inches from the side, the ground slumped into a ditch. One wheel strayed over the line, and then the minivan lost its balance and rolled over.

The accident probably lasted only a few seconds. Timothy was in the front seat asleep. My father was sitting in the middle seat, and Peter and I were reading books in the back. The car rolled over with a deafening roar as grass and gravel scraped the side of the car.

Then my father yelled, 'Hold on, boys!'

The minivan rolled and rolled, bellowing with the crunching of steel. We were thrown around against the van's sides, the roof and the floor. My father kept yelling, and I tried to hold on as he said, but couldn't. Books flew everywhere, and all my father's notes for his poems and sermons rained down like a ticker-tape parade. I fell on top of Peter. My head and my shoulders slammed against the roof and the floor of the van.

Suddenly, everything was quiet.

I was on the floor of the car and my body was coursing with adrenaline. I looked around and grabbed the seat with my hand and then squeezed my arm; it was all there and real. Peter was lying next to me, looking as frightened as I felt. Dad reached up front to see if David and Timothy were fine.

'Is everyone all right?'

'I don't know.' I pulled myself back up.

'Daddy, what happened?' Peter asked.

We looked to the front.

David screamed, 'Timothy! Where's Timothy?'

Timothy was not in his seat. The side doors were jammed. We all climbed out through the windshield. I leaned over the dashboard and pushed myself out, taking care not to cut myself on the glass. Timothy lay unconscious next to the minivan, blood gushing from his mouth and ears. I had read the American Medical Association encyclopedia on Mom's bookshelf. Instantly, I knew he was going to die.

I yelled harder than I had ever yelled. 'No! No! No! God, why did you do this to Timothy? Why?'

I howled with rage.

My throat constricted and my lungs ached. I fell to my knees by the car and pounded the freshly cut green grass that was covered in Timothy's blood until my fists hurt.

And in the back of my mind, the verse came to me from Matthew when Jesus cries out from the cross: 'My God, my God, why have you forsaken me?'

Why does the mind work in such strange ways?

The sight of Timothy was overwhelming. I needed to get away from the wreck.

Our car had landed on someone's property, and I ran to the nearby house with Peter to use their phone. Someone had already called an ambulance, so I tried to call my mother at the women's conference. I called the church to ask someone to pick us up at the hospital where the ambulance would take us. I asked them to find my mother. I called my grandparents in Wilmington but could not reach them. I tried to bring order to the situation. But the truth is I avoided standing at my brother's side.

When I returned to the car, I found my father kneeling and holding Timothy in his arms as he prayed. My father asked God to show mercy on little Timmy, to heal him, if possible, and to take him gently if not.

My father prayed while the paramedics struggled.

They could do nothing; they pronounced him dead.

After they put Timothy on a stretcher, my father stood by the minivan crying silently. I noticed that part of his face was covered with blood. I raised my hand to clean his cheek, but it was the red salsa from the snacks we'd brought. I tried to rub it off with my hand. I did not want the paramedics to see him like that.

I was struck by how absurd death is. It does not announce itself. It does not dress itself in melodrama. Timothy was unconscious before he died, and there were no parting words imbued with meaning. Before the journey my father had only just read us the Psalms and told us he loved us, but that was what he always did; he did not know they were the last words he would read to us as the band of four brothers. No, death sucker-punches you when you're going about your day.

As for my mother, I had left a message that we had had an accident, but I did not tell her yet that Timothy had died. I did not want her to hear the news alone. I could not even begin to think how my mother would react.

The ambulance took Timothy, David and my father to the hospital. Before they put Timothy in the ambulance, I looked at him and saw his two large front teeth. They were the front teeth he brushed every morning before we went to school. They were the same large teeth I had at his age. We looked so much alike. Why had I survived? Timothy looked at peace, as he was the night before when he was sleeping, but now all was not well with the world. Nothing could ever be well again.

A painter stopped by the roadside to see if he could be of any help, and he drove Peter and me to the hospital in his van. I lay in the back of the van between the brushes, the canvases and the cans of paint and wept until I felt my body had run out of tears.

At the hospital my father, Peter and I sat in the waiting room while the doctors treated cuts to David's shoulder. My father answered questions for a hospital administrator. Was David insured? What was Timothy's full name for the death certificate? His birthday and age? And social security number? My father struggled to remember the numbers. Couldn't he answer them later?

As I sat by my father, I thought of all the people in Betel and all the people that Timothy wanted to help in Africa as a medical missionary. I held my father's arm with both hands, 'Daddy, death is real ... I could have died today ... Timothy wanted to be a missionary in Africa. That's what he wanted. I need to take his place. I need to help as many people as possible before I die.'

He looked at me with tears in his eyes. His voice cracked as he said, 'Jonathan, you don't need to make any decisions now ... From now on, you have to live life one day at a time.'

My head drummed with headache.

My brother, my brother! Why? Why had it all happened?

I asked for an aspirin. A nurse took me back to a room. Did I hurt anywhere? My head and maybe my shoulder a little. Did I have any cuts? I didn't know. I hadn't stopped to check. I needed to sit. A chair. Where was a chair? Please. She examined me, and I had some cuts. I needed a tetanus shot. And a painkiller. I think that's what she said. The nurse gave me the shot and told me I needed to be X-rayed. She put me in a wheelchair and took me to a dark room and left me while they prepared the machine. I sat in the wheelchair by myself in this room without windows or lights and cried once again. It may have only been a few minutes, but it felt as if I had been left alone for hours. Where was David? My father and Peter? And then from the back of my mind: *You will never see Timothy again.* I gasped for breath. My arms wouldn't move when I told them to. Where was I?

The room. I needed to get out of the room.

I sat in the wheelchair, shrieking, calling out for a nurse to come back and take me to my father. The nurse returned and apologised for leaving me alone. She said it was normal to panic; we had had a bad day.

News of the accident reached my mother at the women's conference. She was having lunch in the dining hall when one of her friends led her to a hallway. Half a dozen women surrounded her. They asked her to sit and gave her the news. There had been an accident, but they did not know who had been hurt.

One woman said she would drive my mother to the hospital in North Carolina – a six-hour drive. My mother was in a total state of shock. When she arrived, we were already back in Wilmington.

A nurse said, 'Somebody's gotta tell her.'

My mother called my grandparents' house in Wilmington. Before she could even ask, my father told her.

She cried out, 'Oh, Timothy, my little Timothy, my little missionary!'

When she returned to Wilmington, we met my mother at her parents' house. David, Peter and I stood at a distance as my parents slowly approached each other.

'I'm sorry, Mary. I'm so sorry . . .' my father said. 'It's my fault. I shouldn't have let David drive.'

'Timothy . . .' she sobbed as she hugged my father, 'My little Timmy.'

My mother turned towards David, Peter and me and we walked over to her and embraced her; then we stood in a broken circle.

None of us could speak that night. We could not sleep and heard each other weeping in the dark.

As soon as Lindsay and Myk and the leaders of Betel found out Timothy had died, they bought Raúl a ticket to the United States. He would represent Betel at the funeral. Raúl boarded a plane from Spain to New York and from New York to Raleigh, North Carolina, and from Raleigh on a small plane with two propellers to Wilmington. He was exhausted and suffering from a fever when he arrived. Nonetheless, he came.

I was the first one to see him at the small airport. He looked weary and sick, but he dropped his bags in the middle of the ramp and ran towards me with his arms outstretched, embraced me, and cried.

'Os quiero, os quiero, os quiero.' – I love you all, I love you all, I love you all.

The day of the funeral, the funeral home sent a car to my grandparents' house to pick us up and take us to the church. Raúl rode with my family, and at the service he sat in the front row, next to my mother and father. My father introduced Raúl as his son, and Raúl delivered a solemn, moving eulogy in Spanish, which my father translated. He spoke of the great love that everyone in Betel had for our family and he said that Timothy, David, Peter and I were his brothers.

My father recounted how we went back to the wreck after the accident to pick up our books. The clock on the dashboard was frozen to the time of the accident. He found his notes and a crumpled, dirty sheet of paper amid the shards of glass and debris. It was the poem 'To an Athlete Dying Young' by A. E. Housman. My father had read the poem to us many times before:

The time you won your town the race
We chaired you through the market-place;
Man and boy stood cheering by,
And home we brought you shoulder-high.

Today, the road all runners come,
Shoulder-high we bring you home,
And set you at your threshold down,
Townsman of a stiller town.

Smart lad, to slip betimes away
From fields where glory does not stay,
And early though the laurel grows
It withers quicker than the rose.

Eyes the shady night has shut
Cannot see the record cut,
And silence sounds no worse than cheers
After earth has stopped the ears.

Now you will not swell the rout
Of lads that wore their honours out,
Runners whom renown outran
And the name died before the man.

So set, before its echoes fade,
The fleet foot on the sill of shade,
And hold to the low lintel up
The still-defended challenge-cup.

And round that early-laurelled head
Will flock to gaze the strengthless dead,
And find unwithered on its curls
The garland briefer than a girl's.

We had seen many young men's lives cut short in San Blas. We had the experience but not the meaning.

My father said he had consoled many parents in San Blas who had lost sons to overdoses or AIDS. He had counselled them and read verses of the Bible to comfort them. Suffering until now had always been something that happened to others. We were now other people.

Dozens of cars drove slowly from the church, and at the cemetery, rows of plaques dotted the ground. I did the maths in my head. On every gravestone, the dates were of births and deaths of people who had died in their old age. We were at the cemetery because of the accident. They were there because – just as accidentally – they had survived so long.

By the graveside, David saw the family friend who had loaned us the minivan for the summer. David apologised about wrecking the car.

'The car doesn't matter. Nothing is more valuable than a life.'

The burning, blinding sun pounded my head. I looked to the sky and then closed my eyes. The sun's negative seared on my retina. The wind whistled in the trees, and engines throbbed on a distant road. When my eyes opened, everything was blurred. Standing by the coffin was a young boy no older than five. He had the same blue eyes and fine blond hair Timothy had. He smiled at me, and I smiled back. For a moment, Timothy's presence was with me.

After the service, family friends came to the house where we were staying. It was oppressively hot and humid, and I went upstairs to change my clothes. A knock came from the door. The little boy appeared.

'Are you sad?'

His question did not deserve an answer.

He entered and wandered around the room. 'Whose are these?' he asked as he picked up Timothy's toys.

'They're Timothy's.'

'Can I have 'em?'

'No.'

'He isn't gonna need 'em any more...'

'Please leave.' I wanted to push him out the door and slam it in his face, but he was just a little kid. 'Don't come back.'

He left without arguing. I sat at the end of my bed and looked at Timothy's things. We would have to do something with them, and it had not occurred to me before.

In the days that followed the funeral, friends and aunts and uncles and second and third cousins I didn't even know prepared dinners for the many guests that came to the house to offer their condolences, and they washed dishes and cleaned the house.

My parents knew them, but we had strangers in our home. They were making Southern meals I had not tasted before – collard greens, okra and sausage, gravy and biscuits. The only thing I remember about them is they had no taste, and I left the food almost uneaten most meals.

'You must be Jonathan,' an elderly woman said. 'You're the second oldest, right?'

I nodded and did not even have the energy to ask who she was.

'When I lost my husband, I feared I'd never be happy again, but time heals. You'll be better in a few years,' she said.

Well, that *makes me feel much better*, I thought.

Be kind. Be Christian. That is what my parents wanted.

'Thank you. I appreciate it,' was all I could muster.

Raúl stayed with my family in Wilmington for a week. David, Peter and I tried to escape the well-wishers, taking him to the waterfront and to the old Cotton Exchange. Raúl was tired, and he stayed in my room to rest. We carefully took apart the bunk bed that I shared with Timothy and made two beds. Timothy was small and slept on the top bunk, but Raúl feared he would come crashing down on me in the middle of the night. It was comforting to share the room with him. And it postponed accepting Timothy's bunk bed would be empty.

I gathered Timothy's notebooks and toys and put them in his backpack. I was not going to give anyone Timothy's toys. But I did not know what to do.

All I could think of were the words of my father: 'From now on, you have to live life one day at a time.'

Una litera vacía

An empty bunk

THE PLANE TOUCHED down in Madrid, and it was the same city, but everything had changed.

We made it through passport control and picked up our bags, moving through the day as if on autopilot, but we dreaded the thought of returning to our empty house. The sliding terminal doors opened to reveal crowds awaiting their friends and relatives. It looked like half of Betel was there. My father held my mother's hand and guided her through the crowd as she looked down, almost catatonic. She did not want to return to Madrid and leave her home and family in Wilmington, but she came.

We could barely speak to each other after Timothy died; how would we be able to speak to the people in Betel?

We embraced the blur of people amid a haze of tears. People grabbed our bags and ushered us to a Betel van. I slid the van door closed and tears streamed down my face. Why wasn't Timothy coming home with us? I didn't want to go without him.

The door slid open again and a hand reached over and pinched my cheeks.

'Why are you crying? You should be happy. You're home back in Madrid.' It was Maribel, the wife of a leader in Betel.

I ignored her.

She pinched my cheeks again.

'Come on. Smile. We love you. We're all here for you.'
'My brother died. Leave me alone.'
I pushed her away and slid the van door shut.

There is nothing so savage as a graceless act of kindness in grief.

When we made it home, Timothy was gone, but his presence lingered everywhere. His bunk was empty, and he would never sleep in it again. I counted the number of plates before dinner, and we would never again set out six plates. He would never wear the neatly folded clothes in his drawers.

Even the smallest detail at home in Madrid exposed the hole in our lives. I found Peter and Timothy's rock collection in his side of the closet. When I cleared out his drawers, I found some of my trumpet books beneath his underwear and shirts. He had hidden them to force me to go out to play basketball. I smiled as I cried. He had the last laugh.

As I cleaned out the drawers of the desk we shared, I found a diary in a small ringed notebook I did not even know he kept. In his childish scrawl, I read entry after entry:

9 October 1990
I don't like the cold wether but I like it when it snows. But I walk to school every day and its very cold. I freeze even when I have a coat on.

24 October 1990
People know Im a Christian because we help them and we treat them nice. We have devotions.

14 November 1990
When I feel sad, I go and punch my pillow. Then I go to my friends house. Then I come back and I punch my pillow again. Then I sing the beach boys song and then I'm not sad.

14 January 1991
I know that Martin Luther King had a dream that whites and blacks should be equal. He boycotted everything.

1 February 1991
My family is a missionary family and it helps toxicomanos get cured.

He even wrote about David, Peter and me: 'They take care of me and I like them.' We dragged him around the neighbourhood when he was little and bullied him into becoming our co-conspirator. What a relief he knew we loved him!

Timothy wrote about his toys, slime monsters and giant pizzas, but he also wrote comments on the Gulf War and the US debt. He penned short thoughts about what he would do if he were president, how he would have more robots to make American automobile factories productive and how he would deal with the trade deficit with Japan. It was astonishing stuff for a nine-year-old kid. He had paid far more attention on our walks to school than I ever imagined.

Reading his diary, I realised we do not know the smallest sliver of the thoughts and character of those we love. And I had so many questions.

My parents, David, Peter and I all scoured the house for pictures of him to frame and keep. We looked for traces of him and talked about him at the dinner table.

Who knew that he hid a piggy bank full of *pesetas* beneath the clothes in his drawer? Or that he had saved videos of his friends' birthday parties? We caught him in the corner of the frame clowning around. The small things about him became big, and for a moment, I felt he was with us again.

But Timothy was gone. Had he been sick, perhaps I could have readied myself for the loss, but nothing could prepare me for seeing my brother die so suddenly and violently. How could life as I knew it change in an instant?

Never again would I sing Beach Boys songs with him on the way to school. Nor watch him jump triumphantly off the cliff into the sea.

How could he be dead? Only a few weeks earlier he was here. He couldn't be gone.

Many mornings I woke up thinking that it was all a bad dream, that somehow Timothy would be sharing my room with me once again, that I would walk him to school. Then the empty feeling came as the morning light seeped in, accompanied by the hollow noise of day. I was in my bed, and he was not in his.

Timothy died five days before his tenth birthday. We buried him in Wilmington at a cemetery that is less than half a mile from the hospital where he was born. It was so unnatural, a father and mother burying their son like that. Old people die, I told myself – not nine-year-olds.

After Timothy died, my mother had gone to see his body in the mortuary, and she said he looked at peace. I did not want to see him; it would have been too final, admitting the inadmissible. I struggled to accept that he was gone. I kept all his things, just in case he returned and needed them.

I operated in a magical twilight, writing letters to Timothy and burning them, hoping the rising ashes would carry my thoughts to him. This practice continued until my mother asked, 'Is there a reason you keep taking the kitchen matches and why are there ashes on the patio?'

I confessed, but she did not scold me.

As we settled back at home, the flowers sent as condolences stopped arriving, and those we kept wilted and withered. Life for those around us returned to 'normal', and we did our best to play the part and go along.

Sadness had touched my life before, but grief was altogether different. Timothy's death was an exposed wound that would not heal. Soon the sharp pain gave way to a dull, unshakeable sadness. I lost my appetite. I couldn't sleep. At dinners, in class and even playing *fútbol*, I excused myself from everyone to cry. I glanced around to make sure no one was watching, even though I told myself I didn't care if people knew.

For months after Timothy's death, even the shortest car journey induced panic and sheer terror if the car hit the slightest bump. When I travelled with friends, I clenched my seatbelt with white knuckles and did my best to hide it, but when I was with my family, my mother sat next to me and held me tight in her arms, 'Breathe, Jonathan, breathe . . .' The van went over the side of the road. It would happen again; I was sure of it. I stared out the window and looked at the white line delineating the side of the road as tears rolled down my cheeks.

Why had my father let David drive? What an unbearable burden for my father – and even worse for David. I pushed the thought away and would not even acknowledge it. Enough. I would never speak of it. There are some things we must leave in the cupboard of the mind and never touch again if we are to function and survive.

The worst part of losing Timothy was losing even my memory of him. How could I forget someone I loved so much? I shared a room with him, yet I found it hard to remember his face. The image flickered in my brain, disappearing if I concentrated on any detail.

We are nothing more than the sum of our memories, and what did forgetting say about me?

We told faint memories we recounted again and again, hoping they would grow stronger with each retelling. We held on to them like pieces of a puzzle, feeling their uneven outlines, fitting them together, gluing them in our memory, waiting for the scattered fragments to form an image and become clearer in our minds. But the more you hold on to a memory, the more elusive it becomes.

If at the age of only fifteen I struggled to remember the outline of his smile and the sound of his mischievous laugh, what would I remember when I was old? Time moves slowly when we look ahead and disappears when we look behind. One day I might go to college, find a job, get married, have children, work and retire. My youth would be a distant memory, and the person I would be then would certainly be different from the teenager I was. Timothy, though, would be forever young, a nine-year-old boy with a frozen smile on my mantelpiece. And what I'd remember would be the static picture and not the messy, boisterous, complicated, curious boy he was. The memories would disappear, and the photographs would become the memories.

The plans Timothy and I had painted together on the vast canvas of our future were gone. There would be no tomorrows with great concerts or recordings of the next Dizzy and Bird. We would not share a room in Boston when he would follow me to Harvard. I read his diary many times looking for clues to his thoughts and found an entry dated 14 February 1991: 'I like my brother Jonathan because he shows me how to play the trumpet.' We project our goals and dreams onto others. He did not want to play the sax; he wanted to be like me and play the trumpet.

For all my grief, life did not come to a standstill. The school year resumed in September in its pitiless march, and I had to start tenth grade, even though I didn't want to.

The routines that had given me so much comfort before Timothy died now tormented me. Walking to school alone was unbearable – tracing the steps where I had taught him Newton's laws of motion or the right way to use difficult words without sounding too pretentious – so I went with Peter and David. In

Betel we still had Friday night and Sunday morning meetings to go to. There again I felt alone. Timothy used to sit in the front row, and if he was tired during a sermon, he would rest his head on my shoulder and fall asleep. I started sitting at the back of the church.

David sat at the back of the church, helping the young mothers in Betel look after their children, many of whom were HIV+. He often held Raúl's young daughter in his lap throughout the sermon. For so long, he had distanced himself from children and even from us as teenagers. We were too childish and immature for his liking, yet now he cradled fleeting life in his hands.

Grief appeared in waves: like a surge it came crashing in and receded slowly. In the lulls I forgot the pain of Timothy's death for brief instants. The little daily chores of life took over. One morning, as I tied my shoelaces before going to school it occurred to me I had not remembered Timothy yet that day.

Brief moments of peace and contentment appeared unannounced. But then the remorse over forgetting my brother was even worse. The small mercies of friendship or simple pleasures of life became an affront to his memory and the agony of losing him. In that moment, my grief lapsed into guilt. My tears were no longer about the anguish of losing him, but the self-pity of losing my own sadness. Timothy would not have wanted me to be as disconsolate as I was, but a sense of shame haunted me if I was *not* in mourning.

His death was so senseless. Friends and strangers offered answers for why he had died. None of them were satisfactory.

Some Christian friends of my parents said that God was trying to test my father's character like He had Job's. Was God a callous force experimenting on a man who loved Him? If He was, I wanted nothing to do with the divine bully. If that was the kind of God my family had so faithfully followed to Spain, God had a lot to answer for.

Others said that we took loved ones for granted and we could only realise how much we cared for them when they were gone, so God had to take them. If that were true, I could not imagine a punishment so out of all proportion to the crime.

None of the answers made any sense. We groped blindly for some greater meaning, for some method in the madness of grief. We were like children peering through a foggy window, trying to understand a hazy, senseless world.

One missionary friend reminded my mother it is the grit in the oyster that makes pearls, the heat that makes the diamonds. The dark threads give colour to our lives, not the strands of endless white. None of this can be appreciated at the time. It is only looking back that we can see the pattern of our lives.

Maybe one day we'd see she was right, but how is it that encouragement in a time of grief feels so much like a poke in the eye?

My parents turned to books, but they offered nothing to me. My father read C. S. Lewis's *A Grief Observed*, originally published in 1961 under the pseudonym N. W. Clerk, at the dinner table. Lewis taught English literature at Oxford. Late in life he met Helen Joy Davidman, an American writer, and they married. She died of cancer a few years later. In journals, he wrote his private thoughts:

> *There are moments, most unexpectedly, when something inside me tries to assure me that I don't really mind so much, not so very much, after all. Love is not the whole of a man's life . . . People get over these things . . . Then comes a sudden jab of red-hot memory and all this 'commonsense' vanishes like an ant in the mouth of a furnace.*

Lewis, the great man of faith and letters whom Dad always looked to for guidance at devotionals, struggled with death and grief, but he had no better answers than I did.

My father rarely said that Timothy had died. Perhaps he couldn't accept it. He talked about Timothy's 'homecoming to God', his 'graduation' to a better life, how he was 'called on by God' – anything but saying Timothy was dead. He trafficked in euphemism.

It was odd to me not to say it.

Timothy died. He was dead. And he was never coming back.

When I asked my father why he watered down the truth, as ever, he had more answers than I expected or wanted.

Throughout history everyone has called death by another name. Henry Longfellow wrote of 'a covered bridge leading from light to light, through a brief darkness'. The Apostle Paul wrote, 'Brothers, we do not want you to be ignorant about those who fall asleep, or to grieve like the rest of men, who have no hope.' Shakespeare wrote in *Hamlet* about 'this sleep of death', and in *King Lear* that 'Men must endure, their going hence, even as their coming hither; Ripeness is all.' Life was short, and all you could do was taste and savour the few days you had.

My father had Shakespeare and the Apostle Paul on his side, but it didn't bring Timothy any closer.

'Timothy was noble and has gone before us,' my father said. 'He's now in the great cloud of witnesses, and one day we will join him and not be ashamed.'

My father's faith was firm before the accident, and afterwards it appeared unshaken. To him Timothy's death was an agonising reminder that we live on the edge of eternity, balanced precariously on a tightrope between birth and death. We are always a step away from the abyss.

My father found a sliver of meaning in Timothy's death. Even the verse he chose for Timothy's gravestone was drenched in optimism. The inscription came from John 12:24: 'Except a corn of wheat fall into the ground and die, it abides alone: but if it die, it brings forth much fruit.'

But what greater cosmic gain could come from ending the life of such a young boy? What great harvest could come from such bitter seeds? Perhaps it could produce long-suffering and patience in our family and give us compassion for others. God, the stern schoolmaster, would use a death in our family like a birch switch, its sting would teach us the pain of all the families in San Blas. If that was God's plan, I would return my ticket to get my money back at the door. I wanted no part of it.

It was ridiculous. My parents were not self-absorbed people. Nor did we do good deeds self-righteously. My parents loved helping others, and if God had some grand plan, how did taking Timothy away fit in with it all?

There were days when I wanted to go to sleep and never wake up. If death was a path to heaven, and Timothy was already there, wouldn't it make sense to kill myself? Surely after dying I would not suffer pain or grief; I'd be with Timothy. Death would be the ultimate relief.

Thoughts of suicide seduced me. Various plots and plans competed in my mind. Stepping in front of a bus on the walk to school was probably effective, but I might not die immediately. I was too much of a coward for that kind of pain. I'd hang myself with my leather jump rope, but if it went wrong, how would I explain it? I wanted to be dead, not almost braindead. Sleeping pills were the best option, but what pharmacist would sell them to me? Nothing was right.

Every few days the dreams of killing myself returned, but I spoke to no one about them. I lacked the courage to follow through. But the real and only reason I never killed myself was that I did not want my parents to lose another son.

When David, Peter, Timothy and I were younger, we were inseparable and wandered around the neighbourhood together. We had shared everything: ice cream, toys, chicken pox, lice. If we stuck together, nothing could go wrong. At first, we retold stories trying to enlarge them, hoping to bring Timothy back to life. Then we spoke less and less. All the joking and mischief disappeared. We walked to school together in the morning and rarely spoke a word.

If anyone ever asked how many brothers we were, it was always four. Timothy was gone, but we'd always be a band of four brothers. Yet the Dalton Brothers gang could never be complete again. The loss of Timothy was like a missing limb; we felt his absence every day.

The spring before the accident, the students at our missionary school had elected David student body president and president of the National Honour Society, and Peter, Timothy and I were proud of him. David had always led the band of brothers when we went out to roam the streets. He was the brains and always knew what to do.

David's intelligence burned brightly, and he could crack anything with ease. He taught himself calculus and trigonometry on his own from books when he was twelve. He picked up the clarinet and saxophone in weeks. I asked him how he did it, and he looked at me like I was an idiot. 'It's simple maths. Notes are numbers and measures keep time, and scales are just patterns of steps. There's nothing to it.' Ah, so simple, yet why was playing the trumpet so hard for me? Why is it that those who have a gift are most likely to take it for granted?

After the accident, though, he went from being a tall, athletic, extroverted teenager to an introspective young man. He had entered his senior year in high school, and he wanted to go to Princeton to study mathematics. Did he know why he poured himself into his studies the way he did? Books were the wonderful carapace we had always withdrawn into as kids to create our own world at home. I was not looking forward to seeing him go to college. He would be so far away from our family, Betel and the neighbourhood.

David had been driving the car when the accident happened, and he held himself personally responsible for Timothy's death. My father had let David drive, even though he had only got his licence a month earlier. But it was a freak accident, and Timothy would probably still be alive if his seatbelt hadn't failed. After all, David was in the front and only had a few cuts to show for the wreck.

As we slept at night, David's voice whispered, 'Why? Why'd it happen? I should have died instead of him.'

Peter would get up from bed and hug David.

'It's not your fault. I love you.'

We tried to reassure him, but nothing we said lifted the load he had placed on himself.

One morning on the way to school, Peter said, 'I guess I'm the youngest now. Before Timothy was. He was the joker.' He had been giving this much thought. 'I need to be the clown now ... but I don't know if I can. I can't laugh any more ...'

Peter choked up.

'No one's going to take anyone's place, you hear me? You've just got to be yourself,' I said.

And who could match Timothy's impishness and irrepressible sense of humour? With an earnest look he would ask my parents the most ridiculous questions: 'If we need to save the environment by recycling paper, why don't we recycle toilet paper?'

In our lives there was only before and after. Timothy's death was the equinox, and when he was gone every day became a little dimmer. The grey haze of depression grew thicker, blocking out anything that might have raised our sights from the ground before us. Sometimes we struggled to see even the next step ahead. David, Peter and I walked together to school, but we strained to speak and couldn't make sense of things.

I didn't know why Timothy was gone or why I had survived. These questions were unanswerable. Life was random, like some cosmic lottery we had never asked to play.

El corazón de una madre

The heart of a mother

THE HOUSE WAS still, the rooms dark, and my brothers had gone out with my father to visit the Mejorada farm. From my mother's room, I saw the soft glow from her reading lamp and heard her crying quietly. I peered around her doorway. She sat at the end of her bed, surrounded by photos. The pictures formed a collage of memories: Timothy dressed as a pilgrim for Thanksgiving; standing with her on a mountain on vacation in Austria; holding his little dog, Fuzzy, when we brought him home for the first time; being baptised at church. Timothy had a knack for being in the centre of any group photo. Every frame told a story, and Timothy looked so alive. He was her 'little missionary', her favourite.

We were all collecting photos like children building castles on the beach, tracing with our finger in the sand, hoping the tides of time wouldn't wash away our memories and pretty pictures.

The quiver of her lip and the tears streaming down her cheeks cut deep, and it hurt to watch her cry. All I could do was kneel at her side and hold her hand as we wept.

'He had such a kind heart,' my mother said.

'He did, but he was tough too. Remember when you punished him for using his karate at church?'

How could my mother forget? My parents let us take karate classes to get our energy and aggression out in a healthy way.

One Sunday morning outside church an addict pinched Timothy's shoulder so hard Timothy started crying. Timothy kicked him in the balls and punched him in the face. The man was writhing on the floor at the church door while people entering the Sunday service couldn't stop laughing that a kid had done that to a grown man. After that, we never went to any more karate classes. We had not behaved in a Christ-like way.

'We punished him, but I was so proud of him for standing up for himself,' she said. 'I couldn't tell your father that, of course.'

My mother and I laughed so hard remembering the incident; we snorted and coughed as we wiped away our tears.

We had teased Timothy and called him 'Mommy's boy'. He was much tougher than boys his age but like all jokes and insults, there was a cutting truth to the jab. Timothy was the youngest, and my mother spent more time with him than with any of us. She loved all of us, but I think she loved Timothy in a way that mothers can love only their youngest.

Minutes after the accident, I thought of my great-grandmother, who I had never met. My father once told me that my grandfather had a younger brother who died at the age of three, and that afterwards his mother was never the same, living the rest of her life in the twilight of depression. I was scared that my mother would change; that she might become depressed. Perhaps she would even need to see a psychiatrist. Men in white gowns and white gloves would take her away, never to be seen again.

With the passing of the weeks, she withdrew and sat motionless and unresponsive, crying silently. I tried to speak to her, but she would not answer, as if her spirit were hovering far above us, distant and disconnected. I reached out and held her hand, but she did not hold mine. Why would she not talk or only speak in a whisper?

When I was a boy, she had picked me up, cleaned my cuts and treated my wounds. But the mother I had known was gone, and I did not know if she would ever return.

Before Timothy died, I never saw my parents fight, and I convinced myself they didn't. My memories were of them staying up late at night drinking tea and reading together in the living room. My mother went to extremes to avoid disagreeing with my father in public. But after Timothy died, they argued over trivial things, raising their voices in anger. They retreated from each other's touch, as if they had become brittle. My certainty that they loved each other faltered.

I hated the conflict, but what I feared even more were the terrible silences. They were like ghosts that entered the house and became larger, more real and more terrifying the longer my parents avoided each other. The silences were often so long, I feared my mother and father would get divorced and wouldn't speak to each other again.

That was the worst bit – waiting for the arguments; I never knew exactly when they would come. I don't remember what any of the arguments were about, but I knew why they were fighting – it was always Timothy's death. Speaking only made things worse, compounding their hurt. Our grief is as unique to us as fingerprints, and no two people can ever grieve the same. My parents grieved in their own way, and the space between them filled with the cobwebs of misunderstandings and affronts.

Even David, Peter and I all responded differently. I often wondered if Peter missed Timothy because I so rarely saw him cry. That was until I heard him wail one day when he was on his own in the garden. Peter kept to himself, and even though we were so close in age, he often remained a mystery to me.

* * *

That month, on 7 November 1991, Magic Johnson announced he was HIV+, and everyone in Spain knew about Magic Johnson and Larry Bird. It wasn't just gays or *yonkis* who were getting it any more. A few days later, on 24 November, Freddie Mercury of Queen died of AIDS. It was in all the papers. Every kid in the neighbourhood loved Queen and could sing 'We Will Rock You'; the English was gibberish to them, but the chorus rocked.

AIDS had become a front-page story. AIDS-awareness ads interrupted movies and shows on television. The red ribbon had only appeared a few months earlier at the Oscars, and we started seeing it everywhere. I thought it was unlikely any of the people who wore it knew someone with the disease. They might have cared about celebrities, but I doubted anyone cared for our friends. No one would write about them.

When we came back to Madrid, everyone was getting ill.

My mother's friend Marimar, one of the first women in the centre, came down with severe pneumonia. She was married to Carlos *El Bruto*, a bruiser who got his name because of the frequency with which he started fights and the ease with which he ended them. They lived in the programme and left after a year. It was wonderful to see their family happy and healthy together. They had two daughters, and Marimar started a cleaning business. Marimar loved my mother and had given her a beautiful charcoal print that hung in our living room.

At first Marimar's fevers weakened her and gave her terrible fits of coughing. She entered the hospital with *pneumocystis carinii* and a fungal infection called *candida* that left her partially blind. She could no longer work or even care for her daughters. Her thick black hair was thinning; she was frail and did not look like the woman I had known.

Some people at church said that was what Marimar got for not taking her AIDS medicine, but I didn't blame her. I had seen many people die who took Retrovir, and those who lived often suffered awful side effects. I thought it didn't make any difference whether she took it or not; perhaps she felt the same.

My mother went to the hospital to encourage Marimar, but found her cheerful already, encouraging the woman in the neighbouring bed on the ward. My mother's trips outside the house were rare. At church or with other missionaries, she chafed at the slightest remark. Marimar was one of the few people my mother wanted to see, and I was almost glad she was in the hospital.

When my mother could not visit, Marimar wrote letters from her bed on the hospital stationery:

Hello Mary! How are you?

Mary you are on my heart, and you have helped me so much. You are like a spiritual mother to me and a great friend who has always helped me through all the difficult times I have gone through. But now it is you who is going through great pain and I want to share it with you and tell you that I love you and that you are a great woman with a great ministry. Don't forget that a lot of people need you.

I am here in the hospital and it gives me much time to think and pray and this morning I thought of something I wanted to share with you.

You know that sometimes I already feel as if I had lost my daughters. I see them so distantly and I have such little strength to raise them.

I do not want to make you sad, Mary, but just wanted to cheer you and say that the Lord is the only one who can heal our pain. Mary, let Him comfort you. There are times when I feel I've already lost Clara and Maria, until the Lord gives me new strength, and I think that if I go to be with the Lord, I hope they will be looked after. You know Mary, there are many times when I can't wait to hug my daughters in desperation. Mary, the Lord can console us and we can feel His love in our hearts.

> *My daughters are precious to me. We both have the heart of a mother and God knows it and He has a special love for us.*
> *I know God is with you.*
> *With much love,*
> *M Mar*

(Forgive my handwriting, my pulse is not very good.)

One evening my mother told us about her visit to Marimar in the hospital earlier that day.

'Marimar smiled and was happy when we talked, even though she had needles and tubes going into her body. It's the only time I've felt any comfort – when her grief touched mine. But at the end of our conversation, she cried. She cried when she talked about Clara and María. "It's normal for parents to die before their children. But I do not want to die. At least not now. I'm still young and Clara and María are only eight and four. It's not natural." And do you know, when she told me that I couldn't think what's worse, having your kids die too young or dying before you've had a chance to raise them.'

She left the table. We heard her crying back in her room.

Was there a finite supply of tears, a reservoir somewhere that at last ran dry? Surely it had to end.

My father went back to the room, but the door was locked.

'Mary, open up. Please, can you come back out?' he pleaded.

After a long silence, my father returned to the table.

David, Peter and I sat at the table. We poked the food but didn't eat a bite.

Marimar died a few weeks later. My mother wrote a note so that David, Peter and I could be excused from school and attend her memorial service. At noon we went to Betel's auditorium. Clara and María were at the entrance, weeping. They clutched Carlos's arm and refused to let go.

I struggled to say something to them and choked on my words. There was no point. I would not insult them with cheap, sentimental dreck. Nothing I could say would change anything for Clara and María. All I could marshal was, 'I love you.'

About a week after Marimar died, on a grey winter day, I accompanied my mother to run some errands. It had been seven months since Timothy had died. We walked to the local *farmacia* to buy some cough medicine. Pharmacies were as fortified as banks because addicts held them up for *tranquis* like Valium or Buprex when they couldn't score heroin. The floors had the miasma of disinfectant, and a saleswoman stood behind a thick glass partition while I ordered through a microphone.

As we returned home, my mother asked me, 'Jonathan, how many sleeping pills do you think I'd have to take?'

'What are you talking about? What do you want to do to us?' I said. 'Please, don't you ever say that again.'

We did not speak for the rest of the shopping trip.

I did not want to find her overdosed in her room. Would I have to go through her drawers daily and search for pills when she was out shopping?

With each step, I tried to hide my growing sense of panic. How had we become as broken and hurting as the people we came to help? Was her question the hairline crack in the glass of sanity? Was this the small break before everything shattered?

My mother began corresponding with mothers in the United States who had lost a child. A friend had put her in touch with The Compassionate Friends, an organisation for bereaved parents. She sat back in her room, reading and writing for hours. I did not understand how she could write so much to women she never had met and yet spoke so little to us.

I did not ask what she wrote to her new friends. Did she blame God? Did she blame David for driving? Did she blame my father for letting David drive? If she had been there, she would have seen what a freak accident it was.

My mother had retreated from us and from Betel. Hotel Tepper closed to guests, and she stopped leading the Tuesday evening Bible study for the mothers in Betel. She stopped singing hymns at church. She no longer went to the weekly women's meetings and stopped giving devotionals at the women's centres.

She had crossed the river dividing the living from the dead, and only felt at home among those who had been touched by death. Paqui, a young woman from the drug centre who had lived homeless with her husband under the tunnels of Paseo de la Castellana downtown, sent my mother a letter with a rose. She had suffered a miscarriage and felt she had no one to speak to. That day, my mother invited her over for coffee. I came home from school and found them crying, holding hands in the living room. Deep calls unto deep, and suffering unto suffering.

Pilar and the mothers from church came to see her. From the hallway I saw through the open living-room door that my mother was leaving her life ajar so others could enter. I hoped Pilar could help. Most of the older women from church had children who were on drugs, and many had lost sons to overdoses, AIDS and violence on the streets. In San Blas it was the lot of mothers to suffer. When I was a child, I heard Pilar's story many times, but did not understand. All the details of her story had merged into the story of every other mother.

As a child I had gone with my mother to Pilar's apartment and could not help feeling virtuous, thinking how kind we were for calling on her in her suffering. I had seen the picture of José's first communion on her wall. As I looked back, the visits became faintly embarrassing. How little did I know that we tell each other our stories to know we're not alone.

At Timothy's funeral my father said that he had consoled many parents in San Blas when they had lost a son to violence or an overdose, but he had not fully understood their pain – until the accident.

In years past, when my mother spoke at church, she always spoke without notes, but when she finally spoke one Sunday, she had written every word with the utmost care.

'This has been the hardest year of my life. When Timothy died, part of me died. I will never be the same person I was a year ago. I know that many of you have hurt for me and cried with me. I want to thank you.

'Forgive me for not having communicated much this year. I did not want to be here, nor did I want to be anywhere, not even in the States. For months, I did not even want to be alive. I feared losing my faith, the pain was so great.

'Many of you did not know what to do with me. People couldn't bear to see me, the missionary, in so much pain. But I'm a normal mother with a normal heart. What else could I feel?

'I had to withdraw and isolate myself until I understood what was happening inside of me.'

She shared about how she had written letters to mothers in the United States who had lost children.

'I have learned that life is very fragile. And painful. I have felt pain before, but never like this. One day, perhaps, I can share more of what I have learned. But right now, I can only live one day at a time.'

'There is a time for everything, a time to be born and a time to die, a time to weep and a time to laugh. And for me, it is still a time to weep and a time to mourn, a time to be silent.'

When she finished speaking, Pilar and the older mothers in the front row stood up. Even though the service was not over, they came to the front of the church and embraced her.

No one said anything; they cried and hugged each other.

El jardín de las delicias terrenales

The garden of earthly delights

I T WAS AN odd time to be living in Spain. All around us the country was giddy, standing at the centre of the world. Barcelona hosted the summer Olympic games in 1992. The Dream Team with Michael Jordan and a constellation of NBA stars captivated the global press. Sevilla was home to the futuristic pavilions of the European Expo. *Time, Newsweek* and magazines from all over the world put the 'new Spain' on their front covers. The world could not get enough of the country.

Yet we were still grieving, and by the end of the year more than 3,500 people were expected to die from AIDS in Spain. The newspapers said the number would double every year for the next decade. Hundreds were dying in San Blas.

San Blas was the old Spain, an embarrassing skin that needed to be shed. The city government had erected walls around the Gypsy camp as if it were an infection to be contained. Construction workers bulldozed some of the shacks to make way for the wall, and the Gypsy camp became smaller. The neighbours regularly protested by the *muro de la vergüenza*, the wall of shame, calling for the mayor to lance the boil and raze the entire village.

The problem of heroin did not go away – it just moved. When we arrived in Madrid in 1983, San Blas was the main drug-dealing point of the city. However, as the city government continued the never-ending building projects, the major points of supply shifted further south and west. The neighbourhood of Vallecas sat outside of the circular M-40 that divided Madrid into concentric spheres. Vallecas was home to *Los Pitufos*, the Smurfs, because of the low blue and white Gypsy houses.

When I had entered the Gypsy camp in San Blas as a kid, the trips were an adventure with my father as guide, but when I visited *Los Pitufos*, it became a surreal fantasy.

My father parked alongside the highway that divided the Spanish apartment blocks from the small Gypsy houses. He gave me some Betel flyers with the directions to our main office, and we went out to invite the *yonkis* to the centre.

A lot had changed in the nine years since we first went to the streets of San Blas. My father could still do thirty one-handed push-ups after a Betel devotional to amuse the men in the centre, but the first almost imperceptible shades of grey had crept into his hair and his face had not ignored the passage of time with its furrows and sags. I had turned sixteen and was taller than him. And I no longer gave out flyers for an ice-cream treat.

Even though a bed of bloodstained syringes covered the ground, my father wore sandals in the summertime. He tottered around as if he were in our living room. In fact, I often recognised some addicts who had been in our home in San Blas or stayed in Betel's houses. They recognised us but nodded and scurried off in search of heroin. Helping addicts was like tilting at the windmills of human nature. We had been unable to help them, or perhaps they had been unable to help themselves.

Many *yonkis* were new and I had not seen their faces before. But they knew of my father and Betel; if they ever sought help, we would take them in, no questions asked.

Drug taxis came from every corner of Madrid; all fares paid up front in cash. Most of the cars entering the wasteland of *Los Pitufos* were missing bumpers and had cracked windows, but even chauffeured cars rolled in alongside them. They bought their drugs and left. If you spent enough time there, you saw how the mire swallowed the wealthy like everyone else.

As I walked around with my father, I saw the addicts who had been hooked for a while crowded into the old vehicles as they shot up together or squatted around the cars smoking their heroin, trying to trap the smoke and extend their high, if only for an instant.

When I was a child, I couldn't remember anyone smoking heroin – the high was less intense than injecting – but the fear of AIDS changed the way people used. Some addicts opened new needles each time or cleaned their old ones with bleach. But many could not be bothered.

Rats scurried among the thousands of small plastic bleach bottles that littered the roads and open fields. The government provided free bottles to disinfect and gave out more than 150,000 needles a month, but it was a losing battle against HIV. Even if an addict was using clean needles nine out of ten times, he was still using dirty needles a few times a week.

Nearby was a clinic that gave out thousands of doses of methadone a day. There were none of those when we arrived in Spain. Most addicts, though, were supplementing their habit with amphetamines, coke and cannabis.

The police drove in with their Jeeps if there had been a murder, but otherwise they had no interest. The pushers dealt freely, and the *yonkis* went about their business oblivious to the occasional patrol car of young policemen who looked anxious to leave.

My father and I made our way across a field and met a couple of men from Betel. *Yonkis* welcomed Betel in *Los Pitufos* because the van came bearing gifts. Every day, Eduardo, a leader in Betel, came loaded with cookies, yoghurts, sandwiches and fruit juices. You could always spot those who had lived there for a while. Their ribs showed beneath their tank tops during the summer, and in winter their coats and jackets hung from their bones. Their cheekbones jutted out, showing the jagged edges of their skull.

When Eduardo opened the back of the van, addicts swooped on the food from all directions. They ate like vultures, and then left to find more heroin.

In Madrid, where there were drugs there were Gypsies. Gypsies built their homes along a dirt road at the far end of the camp. They had small shops where besides selling heroin they sold tin foil for smoking it, coffee and snacks.

When addicts did not have enough money to buy a *papelina* of heroin, they resorted to buying *micras*. The doses were too small to have a powerful effect, but it was better than nothing. If they became too weak to steal, they offered themselves as *machacas*. It became their job to sweep the insides of the shacks and stand at the door as lookouts.

Even though I grew up right next to the drug supermarket by the Gypsy camp, things I paid little attention to as a child now struck me as odd. I had hardly considered the hunger and suffering of *yonkis* as a child. Did my father ever get used to it? Did he ever lose a sense of sadness seeing the misery around him?

I looked around and saw him standing by a shack talking animatedly with two *yonkis*. They had aluminium foil folded behind their ears and were getting ready to smoke some heroin together. One of them was tall and skinny; he had a T-shirt hanging over his right shoulder. Days in the sun had deeply tanned his skin. His friend was short with a beard and had time-worn grooves on his face. I had seen my father do this hundreds of times before when I was little. He was still as eager to invite addicts to Betel as when he used to go out with Lindsay and Raúl, perhaps even more so now.

He pleaded with them. 'Why not enter Betel today and give it a chance?'

The tall *yonki* did not like my father's question. 'I'm fine. I don't need help.'

'Have you looked at yourself in the mirror?'

'I don't need anything or anyone.' He looked over at his friend and pointed towards the open field. 'Come on. Let's go. I need to get high.'

'Why do you look so tired? Why does your friend look so hungry?'

His short friend glanced over at my father, '*Sabes . . . Esto, esto no es vida.*' – You know . . . This, this isn't life.

'You know people here die of overdoses all the time. You don't even know if you'll still be around next week.'

They looked away but did not leave.

The tall *yonki* looked my father up and down. 'I've been in Betel before with your *aleluyas* and food past the sell-by date. If it worked, I wouldn't be using any more . . . You run businesses, don't you? Where does the money go?'

'I went to Harvard Business School and gave up everything to be a missionary. I don't get a *peseta*.'

'Right . . . Then you're crazier than I thought.' He looked over at me. 'You shouldn't let your father bring you to this place.'

My father took out a flyer for Betel and handed it to them. 'We'll be by that white van over there. See the one with the dove and a broken needle on it right by the main road? We're leaving in half an hour, but if you want to come, we'll see you there.'

The younger addict asked to smoke his heroin first and then he'd give Betel a try. My father told him to go smoke and then come back. We would be waiting.

'Dad, if he wants to get high, clearly they're not interested in getting off drugs. Why did you tell them we'd wait for them?'

'Trust me, they'll be there,' he said.

Betel had grown over the years, and it was no longer necessary for him to go to the dump. My father could have spent his time overseeing his regional leaders and preaching at church on Sunday morning. But he came looking for lost sheep.

A few years earlier, I'd hated being a missionary kid and eating sardines and lentils, but there was nobility in my parents' quiet work of rescuing those who were hurting. My parents didn't have a penthouse on Park Avenue like some of my father's friends, but they had meaning and purpose in helping others. That was enough.

My father and I waited by the Betel van we used to distribute food. I chatted with the men in Betel, but my father stared off into the distance, lost in his thoughts as he often was at the dinner table.

'Dad, is everything OK?'

I put my hand on his shoulder.

'I should have been a better father. I . . .' Tears were welling up in his eyes. 'I should have driven that day.'

'Don't say that.'

'I miss Timmy . . . I do.'

I awkwardly embraced him. He was probably right, but I wasn't going to say anything about it.

'Jonathan, one day this world will fade away in the light of eternity.' He let go of me and dried his eyes. 'We've got to reach them before they overdose. We've got to . . .'

'Dad, what if there isn't a heaven? What if we never see Timothy again?'

'Do you really believe that?'

'I'm asking.'

'Do you remember when I read Lewis's *The Silver Chair* to you as a boy? Jill and Scrubb and Puddleglum had freed Prince Rilian, the true heir of Narnia, and the Queen of the underworld came back and tried to cast a spell on them. Remember what Puddleglum said about Narnia and Aslan?'

My father quoted the passage:

> *Suppose we have only dreamed, or made up, all those things – trees and grass and sun and moon and stars and Aslan himself. Suppose we have. Then all I can say is that, in that case, the made-up things seem a good deal more important than the real ones. Suppose this black pit of a kingdom of yours is the only world. Well, it strikes me as a pretty poor one . . . I'm on Aslan's side even if there isn't any Aslan to lead it. I'm going to live as like a Narnian as long as I can even if there isn't any Narnia.*

'What if, you ask? Even if it weren't true, I'm a Narnian.'

Once again, I did not know what to say to my father.

I had heard of 'Cafeteria Catholics' whose approach to faith was to take a little of this and a little of that and leave what they didn't like. I was in awe of my parents and their selflessness helping and loving others. That was the part I wanted. I didn't know if I could eat all the other servings – the creation story, the genealogies, the miracles, the afterlife and judgement day – that came with it.

We waited half an hour for the two men to show up. The short man with a beard came, but his friend did not. The tall one said maybe he would enter Betel next week, not now. I never saw him again.

My father and I said goodbye to the men in Betel and drove home. I changed clothes and caught the Metro downtown for my frequent pilgrimage to the Prado and to have coffee, and I always took a book for the subway ride. I shared the Metro and café with the crowds, but in those moments, I felt the quiet, anonymous escape and the sense of being alone that you can only feel in a city.

Madrid's most illustrious museum was a little more than five miles from *Los Pitufos*, but culturally it might as well have been another galaxy. Stray dogs did not bark, motorcycles did not zip around lanes, people did not argue over drug deals.

At the Prado everything was hermetically silent. Careful footsteps shuffled quietly from one painting to the next, and the occasional purring of air conditioning kept the paintings at a constant temperature and humidity. I was relieved to be in the cool retreat from the pounding anvil of the sun outside.

Most visitors flocked to Velázquez's *Las meninas*, Goya's *Las majas* or El Greco's *The Adoration of the Shepherds*, but I went to see the paintings of Hieronymus Bosch. Every Bosch in the Prado was a gem that shone from no matter what angle you looked at it, but the greatest was the triptych *The Garden of Delights*. The garden in the central panel is filled with frolicking nudes, fantastic animals and fruits of every kind. The painting progresses from the original sin of Adam and Eve on the left panel to the torments of hell on the right.

Bosch's painting shows the fall of man and the state of a fallen world. Ghouls, snakes and creatures of his own imagination run wild, devouring sinners. It was such a strange painting and had so little to do with the other ones in the museum. My guess is that he must have been on mushrooms when he painted it.

When I got home, I asked my father, 'Have you ever seen Bosch's *Garden of Delights*?'

'I know it well. I had a poster of *The Garden of Delights* right next to Gustave Doré's illustrations of Dante's *Divine Comedy*. It was on my wall in the commune at Harvard. I used to look at that painting and stare at it for hours on LSD. Those were intense trips.'

It was Dante, the fiercely ambitious, self-taught poet, who wrote of his vision of hell with its fire and ice. Maybe he had epilepsy, maybe he too was on mushrooms. No one knows what caused his visions.

'Life echoes art. *The Garden of Delights* is a painting, but it puts a lot of things in perspective,' my father said.

I could not believe we both liked the same painting, even though we had never spoken of it.

We choose our books and paintings, and they make us.

Carcoma y rasguños

Woodworm and scratches

WORK IN THE centre was an antidote to thoughts of heroin. If you were busy restoring furniture, you did not have time to think about shooting up. My parents said if hard labour in Betel could give *yonkis* a sense of responsibility, perhaps it could sort us out too. When summer came, we had to work with the painters, plumbers or mechanics, and we had to learn a trade.

It had been almost a year since Timothy had died, and that summer I was happy to do manual labour; I did not want to be alone with my thoughts.

David headed off to college while Peter and I stayed behind. Peter worked as a mechanic. Mechanics in Betel were prized above all other tradesmen. A fleet of vehicles transported hundreds of men and women living in the programme in Madrid, ferrying them to work and to the farms every day. The dilapidated wrecks still rattled as they spewed diesel fumes, and they broke down more often than they worked. It was not uncommon to begin journeys with a prayer, asking in all seriousness that the Almighty extend the life of the vehicle by at least one more trip.

When a *yonki* entered the centre, if he knew the slightest thing about cars the central office immediately sent him to the garages. Peter worked and lived with the mechanics in Betel on the farms near the garages and repair pits. They worked constantly, performing miracles by repairing transmissions, engines and carburettors. They leapt in and out of the pits, passing wrenches, joking and telling stories. As a child Peter had taken things apart for amusement, but now at the age of fifteen he was fixing things that mattered. His blue coveralls were dusty, his hands and fingernails blackened from grease, but he beamed with happiness whenever he revived a motor and heard its purr.

Peter was below the legal driving age, but he had already learned to drive vans and trucks. The mechanics baptised him in engine oil, as they did with all apprentices. He had become one of the guys, and I envied how he could relate so easily to others, while I observed the world with detachment.

I was assigned to be an ordinary house painter. The work grew long and repetitive, but there was beauty in taking a grey, smoke-stained apartment and turning it brilliant white, with touches of colour.

A summer's day in Madrid turned the rooms into hothouses, filling them with the pungent fumes of paint. The sweat streamed in rivulets and stung my eyes. By the time lunch came, exhaustion had set in, my muscles ached and I needed a siesta. Unless we were working right next to the centre's offices, we brought along *bocadillos* and cold Cokes. I lay on the cold floor, the heat flowed out of me, and the tiles whispered in my ear as I fell asleep.

The hardest part was not treating the walls for water damage or mixing the paint; making sure the new men were not running off and smoking proved far more difficult.

I worried when I sent them on errands. Were they bumming cigarettes or buying heroin to take back to the farm? One time we found a small cannabis garden on a terrace we were supposed to paint. The situation may have been more fraught than when Satan tempted Jesus in the desert. That set the record for the fastest job we ever did.

The men I painted with had tattoos of everything: Che Guevara, the Rolling Stones, the Virgin Mary and Playboy models. While we painted, Victor, a man on my painting team, taught me how they tattooed themselves with a needle and a ballpoint pen in prison. It hurt like hell, but it did the job.

Victor was my encyclopedia. He had grown up near Torre del Campo. His first memories were of his mother spending hours putting make-up on before she went to mass so the priest wouldn't notice her bruised face. Victor had a Fu Manchu moustache and big scars that interrupted his right eyebrow. It was impossible not to take his word when he talked about knife fights or stays in prison.

When Victor spoke, you saw his mind leave the painting job and I sensed his glee in remembering lurid thrills. He rubbed his hands and sheer enjoyment spread across his face. And then he returned from the reverie to enlighten me.

Victor leaned in, his voice dropping to a whisper. 'You want to know how to make crack?' he asked, glancing over his shoulder. I hesitated, but nodded. He grinned, eyes gleaming. 'It's easy – but you have to be careful. One wrong move and you're in trouble.'

As he described the process, I felt a strange thrill – half fear, half curiosity.

It turned out, he was not much of a dealer; he smoked all the crack he made.

Drugs fascinated me, but I reminded myself that my duty was to steer the conversation back to painting. I feared his mind would leave the painting job and he would never come back, like so many of my friends who left the centre that I saw back on the streets. How could I forget Antonio *El Canario*, who I had worked with once, begging with a McDonald's cup and a toothless grin on Gran Via, asking me for money as I went to watch a movie with kids from school? How could I be so cold to an old friend and not spare him more than a few *pesetas*? But it did not stop me from asking Victor to go on, and I hoped I wouldn't find Victor on the street one day.

As a child, the *yonkis* on the streets aroused my curiosity. What interested me were the telltale signs – the track marks, burned fingers and rotting teeth – the stigmata of their addiction. As a teenager, though, the stories possessed my thoughts. What was it like for heroin to hit the brain? What experience was so intensely pleasurable that it could curse someone to a life on the streets like a stray?

Victor told me that anyone who said that drugs were bad had never tried them.

'It's not drugs; it's the life of drugs that destroys you. Drugs are amazing. Nothing, absolutely nothing, is as good as the first rush of heroin. Every junkie will tell you that because it's true.'

I had to take his word for it.

He told me about the first time he shot up. A friend sucked all the *caballo* into the syringe and tapped it with his index finger to get rid of the air bubbles. He examined Victor's outstretched arm to find a pulsing vein and avoid the muscle.

The first time Victor got a heroin flash was 'like the euphoria of scoring a goal, like winning the lottery, like an orgasm with a girl you actually love, but a thousand times more powerful'. When he shot up, his body melted. His chest floated on the ceiling as the room turned. The sensation slowly faded until he felt wrapped in a tingling warmth. The hunger and pain were gone.

As Victor said, 'With heroin I didn't have to think about my problems any more.'

How could something like that be bad? I envied my father and Raúl. Living life as an obedient, studious, hard-working son, I was cut off from thousands of experiences. Prodigal sons always had the most gripping stories; theirs was the best of both worlds – the thrill of the experience and the comfort of redemption. They understood the addicts in a way I could not.

My father had read St Augustine's *Confessions* to us at the dinner table. He had indulged in temptation and learned enough to write of it, 'Lord, give me chastity and continence, but not yet!'

Perhaps if I tried heroin only once as my own private experiment then I would know what it was like. It might even help me understand the addicts.

I knew who sold heroin, where it was sold, how to prepare it and how to shoot up. The only thing I did not know was the most important thing of all – what it felt like. But what if the *camello* told the people of Betel and my parents? What if one time was not enough? What if I died of an overdose or got the virus?

I was curious, but not an idiot, I told myself. The urge was there, but so was the fear. I stared at the line I dared not cross. The knowledge of heroin would forever elude me. I'd never know the euphoria of shooting up.

Victor had told me that after shooting up, he injected his girlfriend and then they had sex – the most incredible ever – and that became their habit. Soon, though, the needle replaced the sex, but it did not matter. Heroin was better than sex, he said. I had to take his word for that too. I did not know how sex smelled, tasted or felt – although I thought about it often enough.

You can't learn all of life from books, and parents are no help with our deepest urges.

I knew the Christian standards, and I was desperate to fall short of them.

Talk of herpes, syphilis and gonorrhoea in Betel was as normal as talking about chicken pox and colds, but sex itself was rarely mentioned.

I had many friends who had been prostitutes, but I never had a girlfriend. The girls at school were still girls compared to the women in the drug centre.

Puberty and adolescence are hard enough on their own, and harder still with junkies as older brothers and sisters.

One day when I went downtown without my parents, Peter and I went to see a movie together. We told a friend from church to meet us at Gran Via. That was where the buildings stretched higher and bright neon lights exploded in greens, yellows and reds against the evening sky.

When Peter and I arrived at the stop, we stared at the signs. We had no idea one stop could have so many exits on different streets. I waited by the main entrance near a McDonald's by the Gran Via and told Peter he should wait around the corner on Calle de la Montera.

We may have known San Blas, but we did not know downtown. No one came out on La Montera's side unless they meant to. Sex shops lined the street, and the hotels charged for rooms by the hour.

The neon lights flickered overhead as we waited, lost in the crowd. As Peter came out, suddenly a middle-aged woman wearing next to nothing approached him.

'Blond boy, want to buy me a juice?'

'I'm waiting for a friend.'

'Get off the street, kid. You're scaring the customers.'

The women were scantily clad beneath the street lamps. They looked hungry and sick, and you could see the track marks in their arms from a distance. Perhaps one day they might become my friends in Betel. I hoped they would.

They did not look like the naked women in yoghurt commercials who glistened in the shower – the ones who came to my mind at night, under the covers, and at the worst possible moments at school, giving me erections that I tried to hide by holding my books close to my body. They weren't Julia Roberts in *Pretty Woman*. I did not feel a tingling in my chest, and I did not get hard when I looked at them. Their customers looked lonely, loitering across the street as they tried to summon their courage.

I often wondered: did they put the grown men at ease by asking if they wanted a juice? And was the juice worth the squeeze?

When I worked with the men, I almost always took a camera donated to the *rastro*. I fixed it, covered it in black tape and started shooting. My early efforts were amateurish, but I read everything I could and studied the works of Elliott Erwitt, Robert Capa and Henri Cartier-Bresson.

Betel became my subject. I lived in Betel's residences on weekends and photographed the men and their daily lives. Beauty and nobility were in everything – most often where least expected. Through the dim flicker of the tungsten lights, I snapped pictures of men feeding the chickens on our farms. I used a wide-angle lens to capture the bent, tattooed arms of brick-masons repairing the pavement outside the *rastros*.

My photographic trips were an excuse to live with the new addicts and hear their stories. Almost all told me they were HIV+. I could scarcely believe how many said they had stolen their parents' life savings for a few grams of heroin. They could not imagine ever receiving forgiveness. Others spoke about their children they had lost through neglect. And I remembered Victor's words: 'It's not drugs; it's the life of drugs that deadens you and destroys you.'

When the painting business had little work or the second-hand furniture shops were short-staffed, the house leaders reassigned me to *portes*. I helped the men pick up sofas and dressers as donations. Those jobs were easy because we carried everything downstairs. We had gravity on our side. Other times I helped deliver closets to a fifth-floor apartment after the *rastro* had made a sale.

I finally understood why Jambri would not let me help move things when I was a kid. The weight I was holding cut off the circulation to my fingers and tore at my skin. By the third floor, I had to take a minute's break. My shoulders swayed back and forth while I caught my breath, and my whitened fingers slowly turned pink again.

As I paused between floors, I looked at the closet. It had been a mess in the shop, but the men had done a fine job restoring it. They had sanded the wood and varnished it. But as I inspected it more closely, the faint outlines of old scratches beneath became visible. I never noticed it before, but faint patches dotted the surface. It looked like the furniture had woodworm; the grubs had burrowed in the wood.

As a child, when I was at Jambri's *rastro*, I believed that no matter how broken and scarred by scrapes the pieces were when they entered the shop, they could always be restored.

Now, though, I saw that although the scratches and scars grew fainter, they were never gone. The woodworm remained hidden, but the ravages of time could never fully be reversed. How easily we are damaged, and how hard to put back together.

On the first anniversary of Timothy's death, I was painting an apartment. The brush slipped in my hand as I glanced at the clock. It was quarter to eleven, the exact moment we went off the road. My chest tightened. I could still hear the bellowing of steel, the shattering glass, the silence that followed. How could I forget the hands of the minivan's dashboard clock frozen for ever?

The lines of W. H. Auden's 'Funeral Blues' came to mind. I wanted to stop all the clocks, but time is indifferent to our pleas.

A fault line below the surface, the accident remained hidden from others, but we could never escape its faint tremors and vicious aftershocks. It only took something as minor as finally giving away Timothy's toys or finding something of his around the house. Grief hid beneath the surface with that ghastly feeling of numbness.

The only things that distracted my mind were study and work. Work had its way of changing me. No job was dirty or undignified, and there was nobility in hard work. The rollers and brushes produced sores that burst and calloused. My skin grew hardened, resembling the hands of the men around me. And I felt pride in that.

Working with my hands, though, was a luxury. My parents did not say it because they did not need to: my brothers and I would never be manual labourers. We had books on our side. Medicine, law, economics and engineering were acceptable career paths, but not manual labour. I would have to escape through books. They were always a reliable refuge from the pain.

Betel worked at many neighbouring chicken farms, and sometimes Peter left his work with the mechanics to help collect chickens for slaughter. When the summer was almost over, I visited him on one of the farms that the centre looked after. The chicken barns were half a mile long; the rows of tungsten lights that hung from the ceiling extended as far as the eye could see and merged into one in the distance.

Peter and the men went into the farms late at night to chase the chickens and grab them by the feet. The ground was covered in sawdust and chicken droppings that rose as they worked. The men wore rags to protect their noses and mouths. They tied cloths around their arms to protect themselves from the chickens' claws.

What was most striking about the chicken farm was the pungent, overpowering stench of ammonia from the chicken droppings. The first time I entered, I held my breath and ran back to the entrance. I gasped for air, my eyes watered and my nose stung.

The scent mysteriously disappeared after a few minutes and then ... nothing. That was how the body worked: with time it shut out anything uncomfortable.

I hoped it would. And I did my best not to feel.

El olor a lejía

The smell of bleach

'Mary, we'll meet you at Ángel's room. Jonathan and I are going to race.' My mother rolled her eyes, but she was used to my father's antics by now and she took the lift. 'Ready . . . Set . . . *GO!*'

I burst up the stairs, skipping three or four at a time as I leapt and pushed myself against the walls at the turns in the stairwell. My father was right behind, keeping the same quick, almost mechanical pace floor after floor. Three . . . four . . . five . . . By the sixth floor, my sides hurt, and I was short of breath. Only two more floors to go until the infectious diseases ward at Ramón y Cajal. As we rounded the corner of the seventh floor, I swore my father would not beat me as when we raced up the stairwells in the buildings near Torre del Campo. As I reached the landing on the eighth floor ahead of him, the day had arrived. I had finally won.

My mother was by the lifts, waiting for us.

'Stop!' I gasped. 'Let's wait a minute. We can't go in there like this. Do you remember what room number it is?'

'We'll find it,' my father said with always more action than planning.

We caught our breath and then looked for Ángel *Veneno*. People were still calling him Poison, even though he was one of the kindest people I knew.

Veneno was alert and watching television when we found him. We were his only visitors. He looked like he had so many years before when he introduced my father to the *yonkis* in San Blas, but his skin hung on his bones, and the virus was hollowing him out.

Right next to his hospital bed was a photograph of his little son Johnny. Johnny had sandy blond hair and dark brown eyes. Ángel's wife, María, had been a heroin addict as well. She had died of AIDS soon after little Johnny was born. During pregnancy a mother's antibodies to HIV are transferred to the baby. After a year and a half, the children often shed their mother's antibodies, as Raúl's daughter Raquel had, but Johnny had developed his own. He had become HIV+ just like his parents. He stayed at La Paz, the largest children's hospital in Madrid, whenever he was ill. Johnny was talkative when he wanted and enjoyed it when my parents brought Timothy's old GI Joes. But sometimes he turned over in his bed, looking at the wall and refusing to speak to anyone.

Some nurses came into the room, and Ángel introduced my father and mother as his parents. His speech was a little slurred and I feared he might have AIDS-related dementia. I looked at the table next to Ángel's bed. He had a photo of my family with him next to his Bible.

'How are you?' my father asked.

'Fine. I can't lose. I have had more years than I thought, and soon I will get to see my friends who have gone before me.'

'My only regret is you never became a preacher and fisher of men. You would have made a good one.'

'I didn't need to be a preacher. I brought you Raúl. He was a big fish,' Ángel replied.

As a television game show played on in the background of the dimly lit room, my father took out his small pocket Bible. He prayed for Ángel's health and speedy recovery, and for little Johnny, and then read aloud Isaiah 40:30-31.

> *Even the youths shall faint and be weary,*
> *And the young men shall utterly fall;*
> *But they that wait for the Lord shall renew their strength;*
> *They shall mount up with wings as eagles;*
> *They shall run, and not be weary;*
> *They shall walk, and not faint.*

As a child I found it wearisome to listen to my parents read the Psalms and Isaiah at the dinner table, but it was difficult not to be moved by what my father said at Ramón y Cajal. The familiar verses echoed in the memory, the fragments becoming life preservers of hope to hold onto for dear life.

My father always tried to impart hope. Out in the corridors, he prayed for life, and he approached our friends' bedsides with a sense of transcendent awe. The hospital was trapped in the fleeting twilight between life and death, and my father believed hospitals were an anteroom at the doorway to eternity.

As my father continued reading, I excused myself. I did not like hospitals. I hadn't liked them since I first saw Jambri with screws in his arms so many years ago. I felt lightheaded and sat in the hallway and held my head between my legs.

Breathe, breathe, breathe, I told myself. *It's happening again.*

For a moment, I was transported to the dark room with the X-ray machine where I sat alone without Timothy after the accident.

The doctors did little to help Raúl or Jambri, and I was certain one day soon I would sit alone in a hospital room and weep for them. Who was I to encourage Ángel and the addicts in the centre when I could not even handle a brief visit to a hospital?

Hospitals struck me as dreadful places, and not just because they were full of the sick and the dying. The halls and rooms smelled of disinfectant and the cleaning staff were always mopping, but the floors never looked clean. Perhaps it was the dim flicker of the fluorescent bulbs that made everything look sickly. The walls were a drab tan, and I suspected they had been yellowed and darkened by cigarette smoke. Even though 'No Smoking' signs hung everywhere, most doctors and nurses smoked in the hallways and stairwells.

When Raúl or any of my friends from Betel were sick, they went to the Ramón y Cajal because it was the largest hospital in Madrid and had the best care for AIDS patients. The vast building perched on the edge of a northern hill. The main building extended for almost a kilometre, and three enormous towers jutted out from it like giant teeth from a comb, overlooking the nearby highways and apartment blocks. The hospital was an imposing place; it made me never want to get sick. The eighth floor of one wing was the infectious diseases ward, where the doctors put those with tuberculosis, hepatitis and AIDS. That is where we spent our evenings and weekends.

If anyone in Betel was ever in the hospital, my parents went to see them, so they would know they were loved and not forgotten. My father had read Dag Hammarskjöld's *Markings* to us at the dinner table: 'Friendship is solitude delivered from the anguish of loneliness.' Even in the maze of corridors in Ramón y Cajal, our friends should not feel lonely.

While I hated the hospital, I looked forward to seeing my friends. It was too easy to drift into detachment and surrender to grim inevitability. There was absolutely nothing I could do for my friends, but love and friendship are the antidote to helplessness. The visits may not have provided a cure to them or me, but a hug pierced the dark clouds that surrounded us, even if only for an instant.

I never worried about catching anything at the hospital. My friends who were HIV+ had to worry more about me than I did about them. My immune system protected me from most diseases; theirs barely functioned. I was rarely sick, and felt guilty about it.

How often had I taken my days of health for granted without an ounce of gratitude or relief!

Ramón y Cajal was a lifeless place, and I did not understand why my friends had to stay there. The doctors were well-meaning but incapable of doing much, and every time my friends entered the hospital, they ended up getting someone else's infections. The doctors didn't know how to cure my friends, and the drugs only seemed to make them worse. Ramón y Cajal at times felt like the wait before the drop of the guillotine.

How did the nurses and doctors manage to stay sane? Over ten years into the epidemic of AIDS and doctors prescribed intravenous Bactrim and oxygen for *pneumocystis carinii* and Amphotericin for *candida*. Retrovir was the great hope, but many died even though they were taking it. The doctors could treat the symptoms, but they only offered helpless words of encouragement for the syndrome itself, not cures.

The doctors got to know Raúl, Jambri and my other friends from the centre, and the care the doctors showed their patients was uncommon in its generosity. Once when Raúl and Jenny were on vacation near Barcelona with their young girls, Raúl grew sick and came down with a very high fever. Jenny called the director of Betel of Barcelona, and they went straight to the airport to get him on a plane to Madrid, where he took a taxi to Ramón y Cajal. Jenny drove eight hours to Madrid with her two daughters and got home near midnight. She was exhausted and hung up her phone, knowing Raúl was in good hands. When she woke up in the morning and re-connected her phone, she found that Dr Antonio Antela had feared that Raúl might not make it to morning. Dr Antela had called her repeatedly throughout the night and spent all night in Raúl's room by his side, so he would not die alone. Raúl was not just a patient, but a friend. Raúl didn't die and the fevers subsided for a while, but Raúl and Jenny never forgot Dr Antela's care.

My parents spent so much time at Ramón y Cajal that they became friends with Dr Luis Buzón, the head of the infectious diseases ward.

The doctor told my father, 'We have no weapons. We can only accompany our patients and try to slow death down a little.' At times Ramón y Cajal felt more like a crowded hospice than a hospital.

A reporter once asked doctor Buzón how he kept going. He said, '*Tenemos la obligación de vivir.*' – We have a duty to live.

After a few years, Dr Buzón quit to work in public policy and research because he felt burnt out. Losing patients who became friends weighed on him, and he often felt there was no more room for pain in his heart. Medicines did almost nothing, and working in a lab was probably the best thing my father's friend could do. He had been kind and loving to the people from Betel and had the task of working with people with AIDS without even a glimmer of medical hope. Every day he embraced his patients and felt their lives slip through his fingers.

If doctors left medical school with the hope of curing people, how could they ever reconcile themselves to a disease they could not treat, one that forced them to watch patient after patient die?

The old San Blas was sick and dying.

I had known *Majara* on the streets since I was eight years old. He entered Lindsay's apartment when Raúl first invited him to move in but did not stay long. For years after that he had shot up and refused to enter Betel. 'I'm fine,' he had said. 'If I ever wanted to quit, I could do it without a problem.'

Manolo had become a leader in Betel, along with his wife, who worked with the women's program. On the streets his nickname had been *Majara*, but in the centre they called him *Chatarra*, Junk. Strangely, the name was a compliment. He had traded his knife and gun for tools and worked miracles with a blowtorch and scrap metal. He fixed everything around Betel.

One day I went with my mother to visit him in the hospital. Manolo was unrecognisable. He looked so different than he did in the photos by his bed when he was strong and rugged, with his young son and two daughters. Those days were gone.

As he lost weight, his skinny fingers fitted into my hand as mine had into his when I was eight. But I was seventeen, and his grip no longer crushed my hand.

I do not know what came over me as we greeted each other. We shook hands and I held his and did not let go.

'Remember how you used to squeeze until it hurt, and I begged you to stop and how you laughed? What'd you say if I crushed your hand now?'

A look of fear flashed across his eyes. 'I didn't do that.'

'Oh yes you did. I don't forget.'

'I did a lot of things to a lot of people. Some stuff I wish I could forget, and terrible things I don't even remember. I've changed, and I hope you can forgive me.'

He reached out to embrace me. 'We're brothers now.'

We hugged, and I wish I could have taken back what I said.

As we left the hospital, my mother reprimanded me, 'You should have more love and compassion. His father beat him whenever he was drunk, which was every day.'

'But Mom, he was very mean to us.'

'*Majara* may not have been nice to you when you were little, but you must never harden your heart. The answer to suffering is always more love. Always more love.'

My mother's look of disappointment hurt far more than my father's spankings when I was a child.

I felt deeply ashamed.

* * *

Visiting my friends in Ramón y Cajal was a hidden part of our high-school schedule. During the weekdays it was impossible to get time off during the school day, and on afternoons my parents insisted I do my homework. I went to the infectious diseases ward most Saturdays. My mother sometimes wrote get-out-of-school notes, but unlike other students, we were not leaving school to take family trips. We would slip away to attend a funeral or memorial service.

Almost none of the students had any friends who were HIV+. The janitor, Salvador Míguez – or Salva as everyone called him – was a former heroin addict and was HIV+, but he never talked about his health. His brother José had already died of AIDS. Most students did not know because they never asked. I knew he had full-blown AIDS. We had both crossed the river of heroin and AIDS and been touched by death.

Salva was a lanky man with short ink-black hair that he parted in the middle and a carefully groomed pencil moustache. As he suffered from hepatitis and fevers, he lost weight and became even skinnier, and his face became thin with a beak-like nose. He wore thicker shirts and heavier sweaters that drooped over his shoulders. But he cleaned the school every day, even when he was sick, and he always had a new joke he wanted to try out.

'Listen to this one. It is about a Catalan . . .'

'I'm sure I've heard that one before.'

'Come on, give me a chance. You'll like it. As I was saying before you interrupted . . . So this Catalan goes into a public bathroom and sees a *peseta* at the bottom of the toilet and it's not even flushed. He's torn. He wants to grab it, but it's not worth putting his hand in next to some shit for a *peseta*. But he's a smart guy, so he throws a twenty-five-*peseta* coin in. And then he puts his hand in and picks up both coins. He reasoned: for a *peseta* it isn't worth getting your hand dirty, but for twenty-six *pesetas*, that's another question entirely.'

It was just as funny the second time.

As Salva got weaker, even his sense of humour faded. I encouraged him to call in sick and go home to rest. Sometimes he complained to me about working too much, but he never took my advice.

As he told me, 'Working is bad. But not working is even worse.'

One day, he was outside the school about to get into his car. I had not seen him in a few weeks. I ran towards his car. 'Salva, wait! How are you?'

He slowly got out and shut the door. 'I'd like to say I'm fine, but I'm not going to lie to you. The doctors don't think I'll live long, and I don't know the answer either. I've left instructions for part of the money I've saved up to go to Betel. I've had a second chance at life since I've been clean, and I want to give something back.'

He had got clean on his own and hadn't gone to Betel. I didn't know how to respond.

'You sure that's what you want to do?'

'When I die, I want to help others have a second chance too. Tell your parents I admire the work they do. Hope to see you again soon.'

My throat tightened, and I tried not to cry in front of him.

'*Cuidate!*' – Look after yourself! – he called out as I left.

I did not see Salva again. He died a month later, on 19 January 1993.

Few students knew Salva had AIDS before he died. Some teachers knew, but he had not told everyone, and I probably would not have done either. David, Peter and I almost never talked to our fellow students about AIDS. It only ever came up when the great tennis player Arthur Ashe or the ballet dancer Rudolf Nureyev died of AIDS. Celebrities' lives were worthy of discussion, but not our friends. That cut too close. Our lives at school never intersected with our lives in Betel. We carried our experiences like a hidden scar.

How could I put into words what it was like to see so many friends die? I didn't even try.

Raúl drove Peter and me to the funeral. Like so many that we attended, it was simple and solemn. Salva wanted to have it in the park where he once shot up so his old friends could attend. The ground had frozen hard, and the winter wind blew the leafless branches. We braced ourselves against the chill, and I feared Raúl would catch a cold.

As we drove back to San Blas, I warmed my hands against the dashboard's heating vents and hoped the biting winter would end.

Escultor de su propio cerebro

Sculptor of his own mind

R<small>AÚL WAS A</small> natural. He loved the life of a pastor: greeting all the visitors, talking to the old mothers who sat in the front row next to my mother, listening to people's problems and preaching. My father could not have run the drug centres and the church in Madrid without Raúl. And after seven years of working together, he trusted Raúl utterly.

Our home reopened once again as Hotel Tepper, and guests streamed through on their way to distant cities and countries to start new drug rehabs. Betel expanded into almost every province of Spain. At times, it felt impossible to tell where our family ended and Betel began.

Raúl and Jenny came to our home a few times a week for long dinners. They came with the leaders of Betel to talk about the businesses and the latest emergencies. In the summer, we gathered on the patio drinking my mother's Southern iced tea. My parents, Raúl and Jenny talked late into the night as the sun set over the neighbourhood and darkness relieved the labourers of Betel from their toils. Peter and I no longer feigned falling asleep and stayed to listen to their conversations. Jenny kept a watchful eye on Séfora and Raquel who played nearby.

Even though Jenny was HIV+, I was relieved that she was almost never sick, and Raquel had not developed her own antibodies. Raúl had nicknamed Séfora *Wonchu* because of the way she said, 'One, Two . . .' in a Spanish accent. And he called Raquel *Wondy*, which he said was short for wonderful.

Once my father and Raúl were discussing what to do about a *yonki* who had left the centre but spray-painted graffiti on the church. Raúl said, 'If we beat him with an iron rod, that would solve it.'

'That's not Christian,' my father replied, 'nor a good testimony.'

'But it would work.'

No one was beaten with an iron rod. But I could see why people feared Raúl on the streets.

Every few weeks, high fevers interrupted Raúl's work, and Jenny drove him to Ramón y Cajal. Raúl was always in good spirits, no matter how tired he was. I didn't like going to hospitals, but every time I visited him, he did his best to cheer me.

One Sunday afternoon, I walked into his room and saw him sitting in bed. He had an oxygen tank by his side and a table next to it covered in books and tapes. He shuffled his books around, searching for something.

'Where are they, Jonny?' He looked at me with annoyance. 'You've misplaced them. I know it.'

He kept searching frantically, and I worried that this was the first sign of AIDS-related dementia. This couldn't be happening.

'My guns, Jonny. Where are my guns?'

Our friendship was like an old, scuffed leather shoe, perhaps not the prettiest thing to others, but already broken in and comfortable. Our conversations were rarely serious or momentous. Often, we said nothing at all and treasured each other's company in a way only possible for those who have known each other for a long time.

I sat on the side of his bed and we chatted. In hospitals some people only talked about their illness or about Retrovir dosages and the doctor's last visit. But with Raúl, we talked about almost anything else.

The bed next to him sat empty, but the sheets were wrinkled. 'Where's your roommate?'

'Out in the hall. He's gone to talk to his family. He used to shoot up too. I've been talking to him all day. I've got a captive audience here.' Raúl smiled.

I noticed he had a copy of *The Imitation of Christ* by Thomas à Kempis.

'Do you like it? My father read it to us when I was ten.'

'Is that so . . .'

'Yeah. It's interesting. But I haven't read it since. I've got a lot of other books I'm working through.'

'You're smart, but you're a know-it-all . . . I know. I used to teach you Sunday school. In fact, I don't think I ever told you, but when you and your brothers were kids, I asked your father if I could stop teaching you.'

'*What?* Why?'

'You were a little know-it-all who had swallowed a dictionary. You knew the Bible inside out, and it was miserable teaching you. I was learning all the Bible stories and was excited by what I found, and I'd come to class, and you'd pick me apart when I made a mistake. You told me you were bored. You even offered to teach the class once.'

I had no idea how often I'd veered over the line from precociousness into sheer obnoxiousness to others. How often had I done that to people without thinking?

No. From then on, I'd make Raúl proud. I would not learn to show off, but to learn for learning's sake.

Raúl reminded me of one of the lessons from *The Imitation of Christ*: 'It should be a man's task, to overcome himself, and every day to be stronger than himself.'

He rearranged the books on his bedside table and got up. 'Come on. Let's get some fresh air.'

We walked out to the hallway near the stairs where sunlight streamed in through the windows.

'I wasted my time with girlfriends and drugs and dropped out of school,' he said. 'Be humble. Like your dad and mom. They know a lot, but they wear their learning lightly. Never be an annoying know-it-all. Promise me that you will be wise and not a smart aleck.'

'I promise.'

'By the way, do you remember Ramón, from the Sunday school?'

'Of course.'

'He died last week in Vitoria . . .'

I didn't know how sick he was.

We said goodbye, and I took the lifts to the ground floor. At the entrance, I stopped at the steps and looked up at a quote above the doorways. The hospital was named after the neuroscientist Santiago Ramón y Cajal, the first Spaniard to win a Nobel Prize in medicine for establishing the neuron as the basic unit of nervous structure. He sketched striking drawings of the root-like neurons he saw under the microscope.

I had not paid close attention to his words before. '*Todo hombre puede ser, si se lo propone, escultor de su propio cerebro.*' It was written in bold, luminous letters:

EVERY MAN CAN BE THE SCULPTOR
OF HIS OWN MIND,
IF HE SETS HIMSELF THE TASK.

The gold leaf stood out against the white lintel, and light reflected off every letter.

I stood soaking it in for minutes, transfixed.

Could I make my mind whatever I wanted? Was the quote an exaggeration? It didn't matter. It had to be true. It was *going* to be true.

On that day, the universe was broadcasting a tune on a frequency that only I could hear. It came as an epiphany, one of the great experiences of life.

My father had heard from God on a bridge near Harvard, but in that moment on the steps of Ramón y Cajal, at last I heard my own call. I would step to my own music.

I passed through the doorway into a changed world.

Homer, Seneca, Dante, C. S. Lewis and T. S. Eliot had joined us for breakfast and dinner. Once again books presented themselves as friends. And it did not matter what time I read, the writers came and revealed their ideas, speaking patiently until I learned their words by heart. Across time their friendship was a comfort.

My reading was not to find answers; there were none for why some people died and others didn't. That was pointless. Those questions were best stored away in the recesses of the mind and never touched. No. Reading was the means of escape and a way to order my own little world.

On our walks to school, Timothy and I had talked about going to Harvard and getting an apartment in Boston. After his death, I had put the thought out of my mind, but once again I resolved to chase our dream. Timothy's picture rested on my desk, an ever-present reminder of our quest and the burden of memory.

I was going to have to teach myself. Our missionary school lacked the resources for anything but rudimentary science labs, rarely had maths teachers, and the library contained about as many books as my parents had at home. The teachers did their best with little; what was remarkable was not that the school failed in some areas, but that it succeeded at all.

David had collected maths books to teach himself and worked on his proofs for fun. He had dreamed of going to Princeton, the Mecca for mathematicians, where John Nash developed game theory and Andrew Wiles solved Fermat's theorem.

Princeton rejected him. David's graduating class only had seven students. How could Princeton take seriously the application of someone who came from a missionary school that provided no trigonometry but offered courses on Christian living? Instead, he went to the University of North Carolina at Chapel Hill, an old state school where my mother went to university.

It was a little over a year after Timothy died, and David was on his own. He was under eighteen, still a minor, and my mother had to go and sign all his papers as guardian when he enrolled.

Every week I looked forward to receiving David's aerograms with his small, precise handwriting, letting me know about the advanced classes he was taking. University was a world where professors wrote their own books, discovered new compounds and developed original proofs. Far away, in colonial red-brick buildings and Tudor Gothic halls, a new universe was waiting for me.

Some students from our missionary school went to colleges with hardly illustrious names like Blue Hills Bible College. I felt I'd die of shame if I had to go to a place like that. No, today's missionary kids were not like the ones I had read about in books. Henry Luce grew up in Beijing and founded *Time* magazine after graduating from Yale; Edwin Reischauer played in the streets of Tokyo as a child and became a Harvard professor and American ambassador to Japan. Episcopalian and Presbyterian missionaries were lettered people. Today's missionaries, my father said, were not of the same mettle.

If Peter and I wanted to learn, we would have to teach ourselves. Nothing could stop us. Curiosity is like a flower, shooting up through the stones. It will find a way to sunlight.

In a world I did not control, where my parents had decided everything for me since I was a child, learning was the golden ticket to deciding my own fate.

David became our accomplice, stealing learning from any source possible. He sent me his textbooks and any books I requested. I absorbed economics, and with David's help, I worked my way through course books, John Maynard Keynes's *The General Theory*, Milton Friedman and Anna Schwartz's *A Monetary History of the United States*, and many others.

At the dinner table, my father drew graphs and symbols on the napkins. He made the complex simple and showed that ideas I thought were plain had hidden intricacies. How had he learned it all if he had spent his time taking LSD on a commune and reading poetry at Cambridge and Harvard? Perhaps you *could* do drugs and not destroy your mind.

What David could not send, Peter and I found by rummaging through book sales. Jambri and the men at the *rastros* saved the good ones for me. Some books were honest as mirrors, showing you as you were, and others changed you even as you read them. It did not matter how old the books were, for even if the pages were faded and the spine worn, I still received their message. Each book had its own character, its own scent and feel when I held it to my nose and pressed my thumbs against the covers. Even the lightest books had a special weight in my hands. Had the musty pages spoken the same way to other readers? I wanted each moment to last.

As I held Aristotle's *Poetics*, I had to put it down every page to ponder the ideas, chew on them and digest them. Why must the hero have a tragic flaw that is the source of his own undoing? Oedipus unknowingly ruins his own life and that of everyone around him. What were my parents' or Raúl's flaws? Were all our great acts to end in tragedy?

The only consolation in Aristotle's writing was in the *katharsis*. Aristotle argued that *katharsis* as 'purification' is the aim of tragedy. Suffering was harrowing but maybe it had meaning and nobility in it. As we write the stories of our lives, perhaps the task is to find love and beauty in the brokenness.

As a child I had the same appetite for books as for playing *fútbol* and daydreaming, but now reading had taken the place of almost everything else. Words without experience were empty, but with time they acquired meaning.

Most people read books once and discard them, but those who love reading savour books again and again. Great books were meaty, and they always gave more nourishment on a second and third reading.

Learning was the ultimate escape. With David's help and his books, I taught myself everything he had studied in his first year at university. Using Ebbings's *General Chemistry* – a book thick enough to stop any door – I memorised the periodic table and drew molecules that grew across the page in spidery outlines.

Hardy was my favourite. In *Jude the Obscure*, Jude learned Latin and Greek on his own by candlelight. Jude was a humble brickmason, but he dreamed of attending the university of Christminster, a transparent allusion to Oxford with its otherworldly Gothic spires. Jude worked with his hands, carving the facades, making Latin inscriptions in the stone. He chiselled away at Christminster but was locked out of the world of learning. I identified with Jude's yearning for knowledge and a better life. Unlike Jude, I didn't want to chip away at the towers of learning; I wanted to be inside.

I read book after book but forgot much and in the end, I felt my knowledge was nothing more solid than the dregs of whatever I had last read. But the accretions hardened and grew over time. It was a start.

Soon, I'd be joining David and leaving high school behind. I was counting the days to going off to university, and I marked them off on my calendar as if counting down the days of Advent.

After dinner, I worked in the living room, and my mother and I drank tea while we read and listened to classical music. Aaron Copland was our favourite. Tears welled up in our eyes as we listened to his *Billy the Kid* suite and the melancholic, beautiful music after Billy's mother died. The piece had a wistful yearning and spoke more powerfully than words. Copland himself once wrote, 'The music of poetry must forever escape me, no doubt, but the poetry of music is always with me.'

When we had saved enough money, we'd go to hear the RTVE orchestra play Stravinsky, Mahler, and above all Tchaikovsky, who was her favourite. At first, we were both learning about classical music together, but as the months passed, we invented a game to see how long it took to guess the piece on the classical radio. Some pieces we intuited within seconds, and others took up to a minute. Even in the harder snippets, there were always clues and composer's fingerprints in the orchestration and the counterpoint.

While my father was on his trips visiting distant Betel centres around Spain, we shared fragments of our reading like trinkets. My mother would read from her latest book.

'Listen to this: "She preferred imaginary heroes to real ones, because when tired of them, the former could be shut up in the tin kitchen till called for, and the latter were less manageable." Sometimes I wish your father were a little more manageable!'

'Where's that from?'

'Louisa May Alcott's *Little Women*.'

The amused relief of my mother's laughter was something I had not heard for so long.

My father had a quote by Robert Browning above his desk: 'Ah, but a man's reach should exceed his grasp, Or what's a heaven for?' He was still Odysseus, off chasing adventures of starting new centres, and my mother, like Penelope, kept the home from falling apart.

Late at night, I worked in the study. One night, my mother came in, her eyes squinting in the dim light.

'Don't you think you've read enough for tonight?'

'I'll finish soon. Just another hour.'

She left quietly. As I read, she returned with a cup of tea. She reached out and held my hand.

'The books will still be here in the morning.'

Missionary education at times felt as dated and constricting as a corset. The more I read, the more questions I had. Whether it was memorising Bible verses by rote or debating the finer points of Calvinism and Arminianism, the discussions at school were as useful as a medieval disputation. Did man have free will or not? And if God had predestined those who would be saved, how could anyone be damned for not believing? It was in those moments that doubts grew like weeds, spoiling faith's well-tended garden.

Timothy died without reason, suddenly, violently. I had already lost many friends to AIDS at Ramón y Cajal, and the hour of the taking for Raúl and Jambri would come soon as well. Happiness was the exception and pain a certainty, but how could I reconcile all of that with a loving, omniscient and all-powerful God?

As C. S. Lewis wrote after his wife died, 'The conclusion I dread is not, "So there's no God after all," but "So this is what God's really like. Deceive yourself no longer."' But ceasing to believe was a real danger to me.

How could I think that, though? Surely my parents would reject me if I ever told them I did not believe in their God, the God of our breakfast-table devotionals. They had almost infinite love for the *yonkis*, but would they have any love for me if I rejected the family's beliefs?

The worst part would not be rejecting my parents or brothers or Raúl and Jambri. The unbearable part would be rejecting myself. I wrapped my entire identity in layer upon layer of belief, offering Christian love to outcasts and trying to live as Jesus had.

Education can be a bittersweet experience. For all the joy of discovery, sometimes I wished I were a house painter and had skipped school when I was twelve. I would know how to read, but I might not be troubled by questions of belief.

Curiosity is the ultimate rebellion. King Solomon wrote, 'For in much wisdom is much grief: and he that increases knowledge increases sorrow.' If only my parents had not taught me how to think, I would not have had the tools to take my own beliefs apart piece by piece and to saw off the branch I was sitting on.

Who needed stories of the parting of the Red Sea or the multiplication of loaves and fish when my friends were sick? Not once had I witnessed a miracle. I followed a God who was never to be seen and always to be obeyed.

Jesus healed the lepers and raised the dead. He spat into the mud and rubbed it into the blind man's eyes to heal him. But the Bible stories all seemed like a sick joke when the men and women in the centre were dying with no healing in sight.

And what a waste for Raúl to have AIDS! The man who saved so many could not save himself. And yet he still believed. God in His supposed benevolent omniscience allowed him to be sick. How did Raúl live with it?

Raúl once said in a sermon that the most beautiful story anyone can tell is the story of his own life. Raúl did not only say that right after getting off drugs and before finding out he was HIV+. He said it afterwards, after he had lost many friends to overdoses, violence and AIDS, after he had found out that he was HIV+.

If Raúl understood and lived with faith in a sick, dying world, maybe I could too. But I didn't know how.

Bailamos porque no podemos volar

We dance because we cannot fly

IT WAS OBVIOUS Raúl was sick. Raúl had been *El Tocho* in the neighbourhood. He was never fat or chubby, just strong and well-fed, and he had always had a handsome round face. But his fevers made him lose weight. The thick, broad-shouldered man I met when I was eight years old was getting thinner and thinner. He was gaunt, and even though he bought smaller and smaller clothes, his belt struggled to hold his trousers up and his shirts draped over his shoulders. When he came to church, he brought a cushion to place on the wooden chairs. AIDS had withered him into skin and bones.

He had as much appetite as ever in the early days of his sickness. When he was in Ramón y Cajal, he would send Jenny on secret missions to bring him doughnuts and chorizo *bocadillos* when he felt the nurses did not bring enough food, but he did not gain weight. Years earlier, when he became ill with tuberculosis of the intestine, he lost a third of his weight but regained most of it. Those days were over.

But I refused to accept reality. I would find a way to arrest the advance of the disease.

One day it occurred to me to give Raúl the protein and calorie shakes I used after lifting weights. I was proud of my idea. If they made me stronger and helped me gain weight, at least they would do a little for him. And maybe even a little would mean a lot.

After a few weeks, he came for dinner at our house with Jenny, Séfora and Raquel. I offered him some more protein drinks. 'Thanks, but I won't drink them. Please don't give them to me again.'

'Why not? What's wrong?'

'They're not as bad as the monkey brains I ate in Africa or your parents' Thanksgiving meals. But they just make me go to the bathroom. My body can't absorb the calories and proteins any more.'

'They don't help even a little?'

'It's no use, Jonny.'

I wasn't the only one who cared about his weight. Some old ladies in the church had far more interest than tact, and they asked how he was feeling incessantly. Raúl was too gracious to get angry or avoid the women, but the distant, pitying whispers bothered him. He hated having his weight scrutinised under a public microscope.

On one occasion, Raúl told me, '*Parece que ya quieren echarme tierra.*' – It seems they already want to throw dirt on me.

'They should leave and find another church,' I said.

'Jesus came to save the lost, Jonny. We must love them. They are certainly lost.'

When Raúl preached a powerful sermon, many members of the congregation wanted to speak to him after the service. They felt that God had spoken directly to them through his words. A young Mexican missionary who had arrived in Madrid approached Raúl after the sermon. The young man coughed, instinctively withdrawing his hand to cover his mouth while his chest heaved. He then rubbed his hand on his jeans and extended it towards Raúl.

'You don't have to shake my hand,' Raúl said.

He smiled and put his hand on the young missionary's shoulder. Never had I seen someone so gracefully decline a handshake.

Other times, when listeners praised his sermons, he would smile and say, 'You're not the first to tell me how well I've done. The devil already told me that to inflate my pride.'

Raúl was noble, but was I beatifying him prematurely in my own mind? Was my unspoken worry about his health as wrong as that of the old ladies who asked him too often how he was doing?

When we were kids Raúl said we would become the first Americans to play for Real Madrid. There was no chance of that happening. Summers were no longer devoted to playing *fútbol* until the sun set, but we still went with Raúl to the Bernabéu to see *El Madrid* play against Barcelona.

One Saturday evening we bought tickets to see the most anticipated game of the league. Raúl drove Peter and me downtown, and parked half a mile from the stadium. We made our way by foot and slipped into the crowds that swarmed like platelets through the arteries of the avenues surrounding the stadium. The *Ultra Sur* dressed in Madrid's colours and packed the pavements in every direction. I glanced over at Raúl, trying to make sure people in the throng were not knocking into him.

The police lined the streets with their shields and truncheons. Officers moved about on horses, and between the legs of one of them I made out a white sheet on the ground. An arm protruded from the side wearing the wrong colours, and the sheet slowly became bloodstained. I stopped to stare, but felt a bony hand grab my collar.

'Keep on moving,' Raúl said as he pushed me.

The game was a draw but all I thought about during the game was the white sheet. There were matters of life and death; *fútbol*, though, was not one of them.

I did my best to conjure the feelings of joy I usually felt visiting the Bernabéu, but they were gone.

And a verse came to mind from First Corinthians: 'When I was a child, I spoke as a child, I understood as a child, I thought as a child: but when I became a man, I put away childish things.'

Whenever Raúl was not sick, he preached. Growing up as a preacher's kid, I had listened to sermons on almost every passage of the Bible. I was a jaded listener. In a few months, I would go to college. As a child I focused on the stories of David and Goliath or Daniel and the lions' den. Now, at seventeen I sat back and made mental notes, critiquing structure, content and rhetoric, as I graded preachers' performances.

Sermons were like chess games where I stayed steps ahead of the speaker, and the clumsy preachers always telegraphed their moves in advance and had nothing fresh to say. It was hard to find new ideas in sermons, but when Raúl shared from the Bible, he brought life to passages I had read a hundred times. He preached like my father: calmly and clearly, without ever raising his voice. Raúl had an effortless, intuitive understanding of cadence and parallelism of phrase. He had never finished school and grew up in the maze by Torre del Campo, yet he grasped the many rhetorical devices that seminarians can strain for all their lives and never develop.

Years earlier, when Raúl stood up behind the podium, he had been an imposing physical presence. As he lost weight, he grew tired speaking and found it difficult to stand for long. But he still wanted to preach, so the men in the centre removed the lectern and brought a soft comfortable armchair for him. They lowered the microphone stand, and he sat in his armchair and spoke.

Perhaps it was only stubbornness that kept him going, but I did not know courage and long-suffering until Raúl preached.

He began his sermon, 'I apologise I haven't spoken at church recently. I have been in the hospital. It is good to be back.'

'I can complain about my health and sickness, but I was reading Second Corinthians this week, and I was moved by what the Apostle Paul wrote: "My grace is sufficient for thee: for my strength is made perfect in weakness."

'We don't know what the Apostle Paul suffered from, but he was clearly sick. "Most gladly therefore will I rather glory in my infirmities, that the power of Christ may rest upon me. Therefore, I take pleasure in infirmities, in reproaches, in necessities, in persecutions, in distresses for Christ's sake: for when I am weak, then am I strong."'

Raúl paused. The congregation was hushed.

'I can't say I'm glorying in my sickness. There is nothing wonderful about what I've got, but now I understand what finding grace and strength in weakness means. Pain is the great teacher.'

Seeing Raúl preach was humbling. When he spoke, feet did not move. People did not cough. No one got up to go to the bathroom. Everyone hung on his words. The gospel of Matthew said that Jesus spoke with authority, not like the Pharisees, but I did not understand the verse until Raúl preached that day.

As he read from Matthew 6:19–21, the moment etched itself on my memory. His frequent dry coughs punctuated the verses:

Do not lay up for yourselves treasures upon the earth, where moth and rust consume, and where thieves break through and steal: but lay up for yourselves treasures in heaven, where neither moth nor rust doth consume, and where thieves do not break through nor steal: for where thy treasure is, there will thy heart be also.

To his listeners heaven might have been an empty idea, but to Raúl heaven was even more real than the world he inhabited. Nothing physical could endanger the part of him that ultimately mattered. His spirit was unbroken.

As I sat at the back of the church and listened to him speak that morning, I believed.

The sermons in Betel had become weightier over the years. In the early days violence and overdoses had taken friends, but those losses were rare and random.

Death had never been far from us; it had only felt that way through childish or wilful ignorance, a powerful sort of denial. AIDS changed everything, reminding us that the hour of death was close. Most addicts were infected or sick, and every visit to the hospital served as a reminder of how short life was. My father and Raúl would have failed as ministers if their sermons had not spoken of death and eternal hope.

Strangely, as the sermons became more solemn, the music became more boisterous.

One summer, Betel held a camp meeting and dozens of centres from all over Spain gathered with the many different churches. Betel had gathered more than a thousand recovering addicts. The service started under a large circus tent that had been pitched in a dirt field. The music swelled like a river, and men and women clapped their hands furiously. People danced between the aisles and the dust rose in the air like poor man's incense. Others stayed by their chairs, closed their eyes and raised their tattooed arms in surrender to God. Like an outsider looking in, I did not feel their joy, but I could not deny it was real. I stood at the front and scanned the vast congregation with a sense of growing embarrassment.

Some visitors who were used to a more conservative style of worship could scarcely conceal their horror at the unrestrained jubilation of the ex-*yonkis* dancing. They approached Raúl and begged him to control the unruly crowd.

Raúl ascended the makeshift stage at one end of the circus tent and took a microphone in his hand. The dust still hung in the air, but every voice quieted.

'Some people have asked me why we dance at a church service. I'll tell you why we dance. No one would have given a *peseta* for us on the streets. We were once worthless and broken. But now we have been restored and are whole. Once we were sad, but now we're joyful. You ask why we dance? I'll tell you why we dance. We dance because we cannot fly.'

The exhilaration of the summer camp never failed to raise everyone's spirits. But when camp was over, the circus tent came down like a deflated hope. The men folded the chairs and packed everything to return to the farms and used-furniture shops. It was then that reality reasserted itself.

After the camp, my father told us that Trini, one of Betel's leaders, was dying. She had barged into our lives years before. She went to Betel's offices one Saturday evening, banging and screaming on the door. The neighbours yelled at her to shut up, but that angered her even more. She was drunk, and no amount of reasoning could make her shut up or go away. The police arrived but had better things to do on a Saturday night than lock her up for disturbing the peace.

My mother was in the middle of cooking dinner, and my father was preparing his Sunday sermon, as he always did on Saturday nights. I volunteered to take her out to one of the women's houses. A Betel pastor drove by the church, and we picked her up.

A hazard of running a drug centre is that all too often while our family was sitting down to a warm dinner or when we were trying to sleep, an addict showed up and banged on the door of the church and demanded to enter the centre. The easy thing to do would be to tell them to come back during the opening hours. But for my parents, running a drug rehab was not a job but a calling from God, with no nine-to-five shifts.

Trini was short with curly hair and was brimming with a nervous energy. From a few feet away, I smelled the beer on her clothes.

'It's about time you showed up,' she complained. 'I fuckin' thought you were never going to come. Where were you? I was banging for fucking hours.'

I slowly reached out my hand and spoke softly to calm her: 'I'm Jonathan and my father runs the drug centre. What's your name?'

'My name is Trini.'

'Trini. We don't have many rules in the centre, but one of them is no cursing.'

She lowered her head and extended her hand and shook mine. 'Well, I'm sorry. You know, I respect you tremendously for what you're doing. I really do. I'm glad you came to get me. So no complaints here.'

The sudden change in her was startling.

'We're here to help any way we can.'

I held her arm and helped her into the car. I had to push her inside to keep her from careening onto the pavement. She fell into the back seat and sighed. 'Sorry 'bout the cursing. I promise I won't do it again. You have my word on that. It's a fucking awful habit.'

I said nothing more. People were still giving *collejas* in Betel. She'd learn.

Trini went through withdrawal, recovered and became a leader in one of the women's residences. After two years in Betel she married Tomás, another leader in the centre and former addict. They worked with Lindsay and Myk in Valencia. The image of a drunk, high, cussing girl was stuck in my mind, and it was beautiful to see her transformed. She was loud and pushy, but she was also caring and gracious.

Trini was HIV+, like almost all heroin addicts in Betel. Such a high number of *yonkis* were that I assumed everyone was.

Often friends appeared to be healthy, but they entered the hospital with a fever or some other problem and died within a few days. A few years earlier, a Dutch television crew had interviewed Trini. They asked her where God was in all the suffering. Trini thought that merely surviving was a gift from God, 'The last few years are a gift and don't belong to me.'

She came back to Madrid from Valencia. At first, I thought she'd returned for medical care. Ramón y Cajal was the best place for AIDS patients, even though the doctors could do little to help them. But the truth is she had got badly drunk and could not be a leader until she recovered. Much of recovery was not an arc that bent towards perfection but a zig zag that stumbled from failure to forgiveness and grace.

Betel offered second – even third and fourth – chances, but the HIV virus gave none. When her borrowed time ended, Trini's health deteriorated quickly.

Trini's defences were gone, and her body could not protect itself. Over the previous months, she'd had pneumonia, tuberculosis, abscesses in the stomach, cancer in her uterus, blindness in one eye and Kaposi's sarcoma. I had seen a lot over the previous years, but nothing like that. Finally, Trini had a brain haemorrhage, and the doctors gave her days to live.

When I visited Trini at Ramón y Cajal, she was losing her hair, and the little she had left was short and thin. She lapsed in and out of consciousness. When she talked, she whispered and was short of breath. Her liver was failing and her flushed complexion had faded. The yellow pall of hepatitis had taken over. She was a crushed husk of her former self, her once soft, round face now impossibly thin, her eyes set in hollows.

My parents, Raúl and many of the leaders came to visit her and surrounded her bed. There was no right thing to say, and we stood silently by her husband Tomás as she approached eternity. Tears rolled slowly down my face, as I watched his rounded, fleshy fingers hold her bony hand on which her wedding ring now appeared oversized.

I stood at the back of the crowded room as my father prayed for her and read Ezekiel chapter 37 from his little black Bible:

The hand of the Lord was upon me, and the Lord carried me out in a spirit, and set me down in the midst of the valley, and it was full of bones; and He caused me to pass by them round about, and, behold, there were very many in the open valley; and, lo, they were very dry. And He said unto me: 'Son of man, can these bones live?' And I answered: 'O Lord God, Thou knowest.' Then He said unto me: 'Prophesy over these bones, and say unto them: O ye dry bones, hear the word of the Lord: Thus saith the Lord God unto these bones: Behold, I will cause breath to enter into you, and you shall live. And I will lay sinews upon you, and will bring up flesh upon you, and cover you with skin, and put breath in you, and you shall live; and you will know that I am the Lord.'

Then my father prayed, 'Lord, we ask that you blow new life into our dry bones. Give us life and strength. Restore Trini and pour out your love upon her today.'

Trini bleated, 'Ay, ay, ay,' and mumbled garbled sentences pleading for help. When we spoke to her, she stared off into space, unaware we were all present.

I stepped out of the hospital room. I sat against the wall by the brown vinyl chairs in the corridor and started crying.

As I was crying, Raúl came out of Trini's room. He stooped and put his hand on my shoulder. Then he dried my tears with his hand. He took my hand and helped me back up on my feet.

'I don't think I can do this any more,' I told him.

As we walked back to the room, Raúl struggled for words, 'I am not afraid to die. I can handle getting sick . . .'

Tears welled up in his eyes. He was *El Tocho*, the tough guy in the neighbourhood, and I had only seen him cry once before, when Timothy died.

'But what I can't bear is seeing Jenny or my daughters suffer. I don't know when, but I know I'm going to die . . .' His voiced trailed away.

I didn't want to hear him talk about it. I embraced him.

We stood in the hospital hallway; he hugged me as we wept.

'Jonny, look after my daughters.'

I had just turned eighteen and did not know how to take care of them.

'I promise.'

Trini died a few days later. Her family arranged a traditional Catholic funeral near her hometown. My parents, Peter, Raúl and I drove a long way to the cemetery to bury her. The midday sun burned bright, and all the Spanish mothers dressed in black from head to toe. They hid their bloodshot eyes beneath black sunglasses. They fanned themselves in the heat while the village priest commended her soul to eternity.

When the gravediggers threw dirt on the coffin, Trini's relatives wailed loudly and wildly, paying no attention to the priest. I had seen many people cry, but never anyone mourn so uncontrollably. We had all wept at Timothy's funeral, but nothing like that.

Raúl looked over at me, 'We are not like those who have no faith. We have an eternal hope, and one day we'll see God face to face.'

I craved Raúl's certainty.

Si no nos rendimos, venceremos

If we don't surrender, we will overcome

Man has places in his poor heart which do not yet exist,
and suffering enters so that they might have existence.
Léon Bloy, *Pilgrim of the Absolute*

RAÚL RUMMAGED THROUGH his closet as he grasped for something. He found a bag full of long-sleeved shirts. He took them out one by one and handed them to me. 'Take these. They don't fit any more.'

One shirt was his favourite, a checked green one that he wore often when he preached.

'Are you sure you want me to have *this* one?'

'Go ahead. I want you to have it.' He handed me the shirts and pulled out a dark green cloth cap that he wore in the winter.

'This as well?'

'Take it. You'll need it. It'll get much colder there than here.' In two weeks, I would go to university in the United States and be away for the next four years. 'Take them. I won't be needing them.'

Raúl understood the situation much better than me. I could not refuse him.

While I had my growth spurts in adolescence, Raúl had lost weight and become smaller. As his waistline and shoulders shrank,

I got his hand-me-downs. At first he had to buy new clothes every half-year, and as he lost more and more weight, his wardrobe changes became even more frequent. I was proud to receive Raúl's shirts and touched he would give them to me. Yet I did not want to take them – I would have given anything to see him strong once again.

As my father had written to American churches in his newsletter of Jambri, Raúl and other Betel leaders who were working despite their condition, 'What can one say about men like these? To the natural man's eye, they are thin and frail, but to those who can see, they are giants.'

When I had to write my university application essays and discuss the person who had most influenced me, I wrote about Raúl. Raúl had none of the advantages that I had had. My brothers and I had grown up in San Blas, but we had my mother and father and lived in a world of books, isolated on an island of our own imaginations in the company of T. S. Eliot, Shakespeare and the Apostle Paul. Raúl still made curious spelling mistakes when he wrote, confusing Bs and Vs in Spanish, but he had taught himself theology and apologetics and spoke with eloquence. However, it was his strength and serenity in the face of death that I admired most.

The thoughts played out in my mind as I had tea with Raúl and Jenny in their living room. I tried to build up the courage to tell him how much he meant to me, to tell him the things I wished I had told Timothy when he was still alive. To say goodbyes when they were still possible. But I said nothing that mattered. It would have been too final.

I left Raúl and Jenny's apartment and descended the hill towards the heart of San Blas. Eleven years had passed since we arrived in the neighbourhood, but it felt like many more. I was seven when we arrived, but now I felt old. The streets of San Blas had changed. Cranes were laying foundations for new apartment blocks in the open fields. The billboards by the construction sites showed pictures of beautiful red-brick buildings covered with gleaming windows and large balconies.

In the distance I tried to make out what was left of the Gypsy camp. The government had already cleared many of the dwellings. Powerful bulldozers belched diesel fumes and roared as they razed the shacks. The makeshift homes offered little resistance. For years the camp had been a part of the neighbourhood, and when it disappeared San Blas would never be the same.

The Gypsies were not sentimental about their eviction. Most had already loaded their belongings into their new vans and left. Some stood around as if watching a spectacle, throwing stones at journalists. A few residents, though, clung to their doorways and, amid shrieks and tears, fought the police. The officers wore latex gloves as they wielded batons and removed the Gypsies. Mothers and fathers from San Blas cheered and cried for joy.

Los Focos, the prefabricated houses at the north end of the camp, were still standing, but they were going to disappear as well. Signs near the construction site announced that there would be a *centro commercial* for the neighbourhood. It would have shops of every kind, as well as a cinema with many screens, and car parks.

Everything would change, I told myself. When we arrived in San Blas in 1983, I listened to the short-wave radio every day with my father for the latest news about the United States and the Soviet Union. In 1994, though, stories from Bosnia and Rwanda filled the airwaves. The Berlin Wall had fallen, apartheid had ended, and progress was unstoppable. The world was changing; why should San Blas be any different?

The neighbourhood would not look the same when I came back from university, but it did not matter. Could San Blas ever be the same without the people?

The only place you could still find the old neighbourhoods of Madrid was on film. The *cine kinki* movie genre chronicled heroin addiction and violence in the early 1980s. If you watched *Deprisa, Deprisa* or *Colegas*, you could get a sense of Madrid at a unique time and place. Many of the actors were kids from the streets, and some were even from San Blas. They shared the same fate too. *El Torete* and Sonia Martínez died of AIDS. José Antonio Valdelomar died of an overdose in Carabanchel jail. *El Pirri* even died of an overdose by the Gypsy camp on Carretera de Vicálvaro near our home where we used to find the addicts overdosed.

That was the way with overdoses. The only ones that ended up in the papers were of celebrities like River Phoenix, who had died outside the Viper Room on Sunset Boulevard a few months earlier. But if you weren't famous, no one cared.

The older generation of addicts I had known as a child were dying. For San Blas the virus was devastating; many of its youth became part of 'the almost lost generation'. Few of the men and women I'd met while handing out tracts in Parque El Paraíso were still alive. The people, not the buildings, were the neighbourhood.

Graduation from our missionary school was a strange end to an education. For years my life had been divided between two worlds. At school David, Peter and I had laboured in our studies, sung in choir, played our instruments in the band, excelled in sports, and led the student government. We had won every prize and award the school could give. David had won a scholarship and fellowships at university, and I hoped I would as well.

San Blas and Betel had been our life, but our studies would become a greater part of who we were, while San Blas would recede. We had never talked about our studies or our hopes to go to Harvard or Princeton with the people of Betel. I feared countless books separated me from my brothers and sisters in Betel, permanently exiling me to another world. Too many books had opened up between us. Few of the ex-*yonkis* had gone to high school and none to university. The word university itself was a meaningless abstraction to them because they had never seen one.

No one from Betel came to my graduation; I had not invited them. The ceremony would be in English, and I did not want them to feel out of place.

For weeks before graduation, I ran home from school to see whether Harvard had accepted me. My mother said if a thick packet arrived, I had been accepted, and if not, it was a rejection.

After the thin letter arrived, I tore down my Harvard posters, and I burned them. What a fool to have such dreams!

The University of North Carolina at Chapel Hill would be my university. I was not good enough for Harvard, I thought, but I was too good for Chapel Hill. At least I could be close to David.

I didn't feel like much of a student, and I wasn't much of a trumpet player either.

Before Timothy died, the only music I cared for was jazz, but I couldn't listen to it any more. It was too joyful, too full of life. It was simply too much. I gave away all my tapes and only kept *Milestones*. Perhaps I'd listen to it again one day, but I could not imagine when, if ever.

I sold my trumpet at a music shop in the city for far less than it meant to me. For years I had played my horn every day for hours and polished it with great care. But I could not have become Dizzy even if I had wanted to. And even if I could have been Dizzy, I am not sure it would have been worth it without Bird, the other half of my heartbeat. Miles needed Coltrane, Herbie Hancock needed Wayne Shorter, and Wynton Marsalis needed his brother Branford. Jazz was only jazz if it was a lively dialogue.

As a graduation gift, my father took me to see drug rehabs. It was what we did as a family.

Betel had opened a centre in Naples, and we were going to Italy. I was surprised to hear that Jambri was in Italy. His health was not good, and when he lived in Spain he was in and out of the hospital with a grim, mechanical regularity. Jambri's centre in Cuenca was growing, but he wanted a new challenge. His doctors advised against going anywhere in his condition, but he refused to wait for death in Madrid.

Jambri had dropped out of school when he was twelve, but he found he had a gift for languages. Years earlier he had written to Lindsay, 'I know that to be a missionary you have to have studied and I'm not smart, but what I've got is a little bit of love and I know that with that God could do something.'

In Italy, Mari Carmen had never seen so him so happy since they got married. He hired a tutor for the men in the centre and took away all their books and music in Spanish and locked them away in a cupboard. He bought Italian books, magazines and tapes for everyone instead. Jambri studied Italian day and night and within a few months he was fluent. And he set up a *mercatino* like his old *rastro* on Calle Esfinge.

Jambri had fallen in love with Naples. But it wasn't the bay that extended in a never-ending arc or the brightly coloured *palazzi* in the hills he loved. Behind the natural beauty of Naples was a noisy, anarchic city that heaved with life. Chaos had a colour and smell in Naples. In Piazza Garibaldi, the square near the railway station, addicts looked for a fix, *spacciatori* sold heroin, and women waited for hourly customers. What was once a beautiful square had become a bus station and parking lot. The families that ran the *Camorra* in Naples lived there. Most people who arrive take one look at Piazza Garibaldi and catch the next train or bus out of the city. But Naples was Jambri's kind of place.

When I was in high school in Madrid, I wrote to Jambri and we sent each other letters and postcards. He invited me to visit him, and I wanted to see his *rastro* and the men's home in Naples. He told me he would help teach me Italian, and I was keen to go.

The day before my father and I had to go back to Madrid, Jambri insisted on taking us to Pompeii. We drove to the entrance and marched up the winding stairs towards the Marina Gate. It faced away from Vesuvius and towards the sea. I walked ahead of my father and Jambri, taking photographs of everything. Vesuvius is irascible and once flooded Pompeii and Herculaneum with lava. In the museum I saw the plaster figures crouching, shrieking as they died from poisonous gas and hot ash. Just like Jambri had told me, Pompeii was a ghost town, a city preserved without its people.

My father and Jambri walked slowly and talked about Betel's businesses, about the new men in the programme, and about plans to open more centres in Italy. I wandered ahead towards the forum, the centre of life in Pompeii. I searched and could not find my father or Jambri. I retraced my steps and looked to the left. They were in the basilica, looking at the columns.

Why were they so slow? I walked around far ahead of my father and Jambri and made my way to the coliseum of Pompeii. But as Jambri, my father and I left the amphitheatre, my father caught my attention and switched into English.

My parents almost never spoke English around Spaniards.

'I know you're excited to see everything, but our friend is not feeling well. He's tired and should go home and get some rest. We've done enough sightseeing.'

I walked over to Jambri. 'I'm sorry for making you walk around all of Pompeii today. We can go whenever you want.'

'I was hoping I wouldn't get too tired, but I need to stop walking. I need some rest. I'm feeling feverish.'

'I didn't want to drag you here today. We could have come on our own.'

'Jonathan, you didn't bring me here. I *took* you here. You won't see anything like this in San Blas.'

* * *

Saying goodbye to my family at Madrid airport was but a brief, painful parting; we would see each other again at Christmas and in the summer holidays. But would I see Raúl and Jenny and all my friends in Betel again?

I could come home in the years ahead, but it would never truly be the same. You cannot turn back the days to the hours of youth and health. Home is not even a place; it is a fleeting state of mind – of innocence – you can never go back to. You can never truly go home.

I didn't want to leave San Blas. Four years at university in the United States would be too long. There would be no Indian summer, no reprieve from death for my friends. With no cure for AIDS, the sharp scythe of time would cut them all down.

I had read enough books and articles to know that a cure for HIV would not be found. The moment scientists found a cure, the virus would change itself and attack with greater ferocity than before. I had no hope that the racing progress of science would make it chronic but treatable, like diabetes. It was pointless to delude myself. I merely hoped that scientists might find something to treat the symptoms and keep death at bay for a few more years – long enough for me to see them again.

'I'll carry them for you,' David said as he took my suitcases. He led my mother and me down the long corridor searching for my dorm room. The room was empty, and the faded walls were bare. I would have to fill them with the subway maps of Madrid and the postcards of *The Garden of Delights* from the Prado I had brought to remind me of home. Better yet, I wouldn't stay; I would move off campus and live with David as soon as I figured out how.

My mother took us to the underground Ratskeller, her favourite restaurant, and told us about her time at Chapel Hill. She spoke in the same reverent tone that my father did when he recalled his days at Cambridge and Harvard. Would I ever do the same about Chapel Hill? I doubted it.

'Do you have any final words of advice as a mom?' I asked.

'I have none. In fact, you shouldn't need my advice.'

'What? No advice?'

'You know our values and right and wrong. If you need me to tell you what to do now, I haven't done a good job as a mother, have I?'

She always had so much to say with so few words.

'I know you wanted to go to Harvard, but don't ever let circumstances that cannot be changed get under your skin. Things are going to work out for you. The best is always yet to come.'

When I said goodbye to her after lunch, she held back her tears, as she had when she left Wilmington in 1983. I think she hoped to return to Wilmington to live one day. Perhaps she thought being a missionary would be like being in the army and doing a few tours before coming home to Main Street for Fourth of July fireworks. I don't think she bargained on a one-way ticket to foreign lands, a permanent exile, far from her family for the rest of her life. Old missionaries are generally forgotten, their hearts buried abroad before they can make it home. Her life was in Madrid now, and I don't know if she ever admitted to herself that her dream had died.

I hugged my mother, and it all became real.

David led the way and showed me the campus he had come to know so well over the past two years.

As we walked the streets and red-brick paths beneath the ancient oaks, Chapel Hill was an idyllic contrast to Madrid. San Blas was a noisy, frenetic neighbourhood of a quarter of a million people. Chapel Hill was a bucolic town of thirty thousand. Franklin Street was the only main street, and nearly all businesses closed at five o'clock.

In the parks of San Blas, grandparents, parents, children, alcoholics and drug addicts mingled. In Chapel Hill there were no children, parents or old people. As far as I could tell, a dull sea of happy young men and women tasted liberty away from home at last. They were like excited electrons, breaking free from parental bonds.

Many of them wore T-shirts with Greek fraternity letters. Did they even know the difference between Koine and classical Attic Greek? Had they read Aristotle or Sophocles?

The university sat on a gentle hill and on Franklin Street quaint shops filled the many red-brick buildings. Historic houses and charming cottages hid away down quiet lanes. Every corner of the town was green, and hickories, cedars and pines lined the streets. I didn't know that because I recognised the varieties of trees or shrubs – there were few in San Blas – but because one of the university orientation booklets told me so. And it meant nothing to me.

In Spain I had never become a Spaniard; I always felt too much of an alien, too proudly American. The feeling of strangeness was natural. But in the United States, which was supposed to be my home, being an American felt like an ill-fitting suit that I wanted to put back on the hanger before even trying it. Perhaps it would change over time, and I would grow into it. I never knew how American I was until I was in Madrid, nor how Spanish I was until I left. I felt half-American, half-Spanish, yet if you scratched and sniffed, I was neither.

The university orientation included the usual introductions to academic life and presentations on the student union, and I skipped most of them. But a final mandatory meeting was a student health presentation.

A vivacious, pretty blonde girl arrived and handed out latex gloves to everyone in the room. She then took out a thick marker and coloured a large, blood-red dot on her palm. She encouraged everyone to shake each other's hands. And each time that she shook someone's hand the dot spread to the next person's white glove. What started with one person quickly spread to the entire room, and soon everyone had the red dot.

'OK, everyone, y'all have AIDS now! This is how it spreads. It only takes one person to get everyone sick.'

The students laughed and amused themselves with the illustration.

The same light-headedness that I had felt at Ramón y Cajal returned, and I needed to leave the room. I took off the latex glove and walked to the doorway. The blonde girl pursued me with her anodyne smile.

'You can't leave yet. It's not over. AIDS is a very real threat to student health and this session is important. You could help save yourself and others if you stay and listen,' she said.

I made my way to the door and did not respond.

'I said, you can't leave. This is a required session.'

She had a bag of red bows to give everyone at the end. They were the bows celebrities wore when they collected their Oscars.

Had any of the kids at Chapel Hill ever known anyone who was HIV+? Had they ever visited anyone in the hospital who had gone blind from cytomegalovirus or developed AIDS-related dementia? I didn't think so.

Fuck her and her red ribbons.

I left the building and sat outside on the steps of the student union. I wiped away my tears with my hairy forearms.

Fuck her.

As the weeks passed, the town became a strange fairy tale – impeccably manicured lawns, colourful leaves floating in the autumn breeze, rain-slicked walkways that reflected lamplights – but also a world I could not escape.

San Blas was 6,400 miles away, and my only link back was the phone. At weekends, I took my blue address book where the name and number of everyone in Betel was carefully noted and biked over to David's apartment. Together we called my parents, Raúl and Jenny, and friends in Betel. Over the dry, crackling lines their distant, disembodied voices spoke to us. Those expensive transatlantic phone calls were always too brief.

Winter arrived and the first snows fell. Late at night when I returned from the library, the campus was empty, and I followed the brick walkways beneath the trees. I stopped not far from the oldest university building and looked up at a bronze statue of a young soldier. The silvery street lamps cast their light, and the shadows of branches fell on him. He stood alone, broken and defeated after four years of fighting, returning home to a world he did not recognise.

I took out Raúl's green cap, put it on to keep me warm, and pedalled back to my room through the snow.

The first year at Chapel Hill passed quickly. Days were dosed in coffee cups and measured by piles of books. I never went to parties and never joined a fraternity. I never attended a basketball game, even though I knew that Michael Jordan played at Chapel Hill. I didn't care.

I had nothing in common with anyone. I didn't know how odd my childhood was until academic advisors and students started asking me questions about where I was from and what my parents did for work. Dentists, doctors, teachers and lawyers were acceptable professionals. But missionaries who work with heroin addicts were too weird. Answers only led to the inevitable questions, 'Did you feel safe growing up around heroin addicts?' and 'Did you ever question your parents' judgement?'

My parents might be strange, but there was nobility in the struggle to help others. Of course we were the other side of normal, but as to whether they had messed up my life, only time could tell. Maybe I was unaware of my own maladjustment, the patient who cannot diagnose himself. But I would not dwell on it.

The only person I felt I had much in common with was a Moroccan who had grown up in Barcelona, gone to a French high school, and spoke six languages. He didn't know what culture he belonged to, and I didn't either. We were strange mongrels, cultural mutts. At least we had that in common.

I had grown accustomed to being lonely, an outsider, different. The old routine didn't bother me. I could count my friends on one hand. They were all friends David had made and introduced me to. David and I had each other, and we had the library. That was all I needed.

The university was a maze I learned to navigate. My parents had no money to give me, so I bought my college textbooks, read them and took mental notes. If you returned them within two weeks, you could get a refund. And so I did. It saved me hundreds of dollars. Until that moment I did not know how much David had sacrificed to give me his textbooks without asking for anything in return.

The Davis Library was the third largest in the country after the Library of Congress and Harvard. More than two million books lined the shelves, and I stared in wonder. Eight floors that were each bigger than a few football fields held an endless labyrinth of books that led to new realms of knowledge. Like clues in a treasure hunt, I followed their trail. Each book created new hungers that could only be fed by other books. And I wished there were more hours in the day to read. What a vast difference there was between learning and getting a degree!

It was late on Friday and the library was almost empty. Most students were at fraternity parties or out on Franklin Street. I put my headphones on and unlocked my bike to head back to the apartment David and I had moved into. I turned the dial of my pocket radio to find the college station. Dad and Mom had Dylan and Baez, but at college I found Counting Crows, the Goo Goo Dolls, Nirvana and Nine Inch Nails. It wasn't beauty and nobility like my parents sought, but the poetry of pain felt more relevant and much more real.

Mom, Dad and Peter would be visiting for a week, and we cleaned our apartment and looked forward to all being together again as we had been in Madrid.

Peter graduated a year after me; he went to the United States Military Academy at West Point. He was only eighteen, and when my parents, David and I said goodbye to him on his first day at the academy over the summer, he joked and smiled until the last minute. But I sensed the terror before they shaved his head. The place took kids and turned them into a long grey line of officers, but first it put them through 'Hell Week'.

At the end of the summer, I did not register the news that Raúl had entered Ramón y Cajal again. It happened so often. He came down with fevers easily and had always got better and returned home. Foolishly, in my own particular strain of denial, I thought the pattern would continue for ever.

Raúl went into the hospital with an intense fever and pneumonia. His lungs quickly filled with fluid, and the doctors gave him oxygen to help his strained breathing. The pneumonia was more severe than normal, and fluids continued building between his lungs and the ribcage. The doctors tried to insert a drain to relieve the pressure, but they punctured his lungs. Raúl was in distress as his pneumonia got worse.

The doctors wrapped him in layers of morphine to kill the pain. They told Jenny his situation was grave. Raúl slipped in and out of consciousness. He asked if people had moved the furniture in his room. He had not been in such a state of delirium since doing heroin.

My parents were in the United States visiting the churches that supported them, as they did every four years.

My father called Raúl, but he got no response. He called Carlos, one of the first addicts who had been in the apartment with Raúl when Betel started. Carlos took his mobile phone to Ramón y Cajal and handed it to Raúl.

My father told me, 'He is drawing near to eternity. I asked Raúl how he was doing, and he is in agony. He could not bear the pain any more and said he is ready to depart. But his spirit was still strong. I told him I loved him, and he said he always loved me. He said, "Remember Jenny. Remember my daughters."'

My father bought a ticket to fly back to Madrid to be with Raúl. I wanted to go as well and hated remaining in Chapel Hill, so far away from San Blas and Ramón y Cajal. But my parents only had enough money for one ticket.

As I sat at my desk, I looked out of the window. The sunlight fell on the tangled ivy and leaves. The shadows shifted and the afternoon slipped away, but I could not study for my classes.

All I wanted was to go to Ramón y Cajal, walk up to the inscription that I stopped to read at every visit, race up the steps to the infectious diseases ward, and find Raúl's room.

Jenny stayed by Raúl's side. She read to him and sang, wondering all the while whether he was listening.

One day as she was softly singing a hymn from her youth in New Zealand to him, Raúl took off his oxygen mask and said, 'Jenny, I think I'm dying now.'

'Don't say that.'

'It's true. I swear angels were singing,' he said. He smiled at Jenny with a glint of mischief in his eyes and put his oxygen mask back on.

All the ex-*yonkis* who were now directors of Betel came to Madrid to be with him. As the leaders streamed into his room, some of them stayed for a day and went back to help run the centres, but others did not leave his side. Raúl received them in his room. He struggled to speak, but as they said goodbye and left the room, he pointed to the ceiling and said, 'See you in heaven.'

Raúl had been in the hospital a little over a week when his health deteriorated rapidly. The doctors increased his morphine doses, and the leaders of Betel kept vigil in the room.

As Raúl drifted in and out of consciousness, he took off his oxygen mask and with great difficulty spoke to the Betel leaders in the room.

'*Si no nos rendimos, venceremos.*' – If we do not surrender, we will conquer.

He died an hour later, on 1 September 1995. He was thirty-seven years old.

My father had not yet caught his flight to Madrid. Jenny called the apartment that David and I shared. I picked up the phone, and I asked her how Raúl was.

'Raúl died, Jonny.'

I choked on my words. 'I love you all. I loved Raúl very much.'

'And Raúl loved you. He loved all of you.'

I handed the phone to my father and went to the hallway. I sat against the wall with my knees pulled up against my chest and wept.

I had lost my older brother. My brother, my brother! Why?

When Timothy died, Raúl had flown from Spain to the United States to be with us and speak at the funeral. Now my father made the reverse journey to speak at Raúl's memorial service. He flew alone, and I stayed at Chapel Hill with my mother, David and Peter.

I turned on the radio to a song. It was Joan Osborne's 'One of Us?' In the song, she said, if God had a name, what would it be and would you call it to His face? What would you ask Him if you could? I knew what I'd ask God. I didn't think He'd have a good answer.

If God knew my heart, surely He could read my mind.

I still read my Bible, prayed, and attended church. I spoke to God, but I didn't know if He spoke back any more as He did to my parents when I was a kid.

The week Raúl died, Peter went on leave from West Point. When he flew down to Chapel Hill, we were relieved to see him. He had lost weight in the stomach and gained muscle in the neck and shoulders. He had almost no hair, and David gave him a *colleja* on his exposed neck.

'You know Raúl would have done that to you . . .' David said with a smile.

I would have tried too, but Peter was thicker than me and was no longer my little brother.

Never had I felt such a strange emotional twilight, a mixture of sadness and happiness that was neither day nor night. And I cried as I laughed and felt guilty. We talked and struggled to make sense of it all. At dinner Peter took out a book he was reading and shared the words of Dietrich Bonhoeffer, a German Lutheran pastor who was hanged for opposing Hitler. Before his execution, he wrote:

Joy is rich in fears:
Sorrow has its sweetness.
Undistinguishable from each other
They approach us from eternity,
Equally potent in their power and terror.

My father had read it to us at the dinner table, but I had not understood it until then. Life is brief, and death itself made life more vivid and precious.

Raúl had told Jenny he wanted a joyful memorial service to commemorate his life and affirm his belief in heaven. I had to wait for my father to bring back a tape recording of the service to hear it. I held the tape anxiously, eager to hear what people had said about Raúl.

My father spoke. Raúl was many things: a desperate addict on the street, a transformed young man who had left heroin behind and was eager to help his friends, a leader in the men's residences, an eloquent preacher, a caring minister, a close friend, a loving husband to Jenny and a doting father to Séfora and Raquel.

Most of all, though, my father remembered Raúl as a son and an older brother to David, Peter, Timothy and me. We adored him as children, and the love only grew over the years.

'Do you not know that a prince and a great man has fallen?' my father asked as he quoted from King David's eulogy at the death of General Abner.

'Who could fill Raúl's place? Who could stand in the breach as he did?' Raul was unique in his charisma, his joy and his profound humanity.

As my father looked around the church, dozens of men and women who shot up with Raúl in San Blas surrounded him. Manolo *Chatarra*, Ángel *Veneno*, Paco, Carlos – all entered the centre and stayed because of Raúl.

Lindsay spoke after my father did. He had been with Raúl from the first days in the apartment and had stood by his bedside when he died. Lindsay had begun as the teacher and had become the student. Lindsay told Raúl before he died that they were like King David and Jonathan, and 'the soul of Jonathan was knit with the soul of David, and Jonathan loved him as his own soul'.

My father and Lindsay had helped Raúl change his life when he was a *yonki*, but he changed theirs more than they did his.

One by one the leaders of Betel came forward to speak about Raúl. In the early days, Raúl had been their 'shadow'. When they wanted to leave the programme, he had shown them love and encouragement. Raúl was the first addict in Betel, and in a way he *was* Betel to everyone.

As I listened to the tape, I could not believe Manuel *El Vasco* had made it to Raúl's memorial service. The last time I had seen him, he was skeletal.

Manuel spoke of how he resented the *collejas* and washing dishes for months as punishment for cursing, but Raúl was rubbing off his rough edges.

The small acts of kindness, even strange ones, were the things that people most remembered. Raúl could have called him One Eye, like some men did, but he simply called him *El Vasco* because he was Basque. And he was grateful that Raúl's nicknames were always the ones that stuck.

I hoped that wherever there was a heaven, Raúl and all the men and women in Betel were home together, like in the old days on the farm, preparing *paellas* and playing *fútbol* and keeping each other company. A childish thought, but a real one nevertheless.

A few weeks later, Manuel *El Vasco* finally succumbed after fighting AIDS for years.

The news of death came often in the months after Raúl's funeral. It came over the rasping and hissing of international phone lines. Manolo *Chatarra* died a month and a day later. Then Ángel *Veneno*. Then his son Johnny. And so many more.

The deaths kept coming in, call after call. The news fell like drops, and the patter increased until it became a storm, washing away everything I knew.

Fra i dannati di Cotugno

Among the damned of Cotugno

I SLID THE KEY in and opened my mailbox with anticipation. It had been weeks since the last letter from Jambri. He wrote long notes and sent postcards of Naples. I pinned them on the bulletin board over my desk for inspiration.

When I was at Chapel Hill, Jambri and I wrote letters to each other in Spanish and Italian. Jambri's Spanish had childish spelling mistakes, but he wrote Italian with no spelling errors. He loved the language, and he transmitted that love to me.

He sent me books and reading recommendations. I devoured Dante's *Divina Commedia*, Boccaccio's *Decamerone* and Ariosto's *Orlando Furioso* in the original. What he could not send, I found for a few dollars at used bookshops in Chapel Hill. They were musty copies printed in Italy in the 1920s, and the pages looked like they had never been opened and the books had been waiting patiently for someone to discover them. I followed as Virgil beckoned Dante in Canto I of *Inferno*:

segui, e io sarò tua guida,
e trarrotti di qui per luogo etterno,

Follow me, and I will be your guide,
And lead you through the eternal place,

And so began my journey through circles of hell and heaven.

Dante too had been an exile, banished from Florence, cast into a *selva oscura*, a dark wood, far from home. He was a poor autodidact, a self-taught scholar. Books and dreams were his comfort, and I felt a connection with him across the centuries.

My father had read *The Divine Comedy* to us at the dinner table, but what a world of difference it made to read it in Italian. The Jewish writer Hayim Bialik once wrote, 'He who reads the Bible in translation is like a man who kisses his bride through a veil.' I did not know what he meant until I read Dante in Italian. No translation could ever capture the magic and beauty of Dante's prose, and his writing felt like a lucky find in my hands.

Books were my companions because at Chapel Hill I was a complete disaster socially. If I was good at one thing, it was reading and teaching myself. And I failed to appreciate or even learn from my fellow students. What a vast gap between knowledge and wisdom! I was no more responsible for my odd, schizophrenic childhood than they were for their normal ones, yet I placed the burden upon them to understand me. It is easier to blame others than to accept our shortcomings and grow. And so I retreated further into my shell.

I missed Betel and volunteered at the homeless shelter to look after the men overnight. I volunteered to translate for Mexican migrants at the community clinic. Alcoholics and the poor I understood, but not students my age.

I would not fail again. If I couldn't fit in, the only option was to stand out. I was on track to write two honours theses in my senior year. One was not enough. And I had not forgotten the shame of home-schooling because of exchange rate moves in the 1980s. Everything could be mined for raw materials. An old *National Geographic* inspired me to learn Ladino, a fifteenth-century dialect of Spanish mixed with Hebrew. Who knew that reading the Old Spanish in *El Poema de mio Cid* with Jambri would ever be useful?

I got scholarships and fellowships every year like shiny baubles; I collected them out of financial need, but mainly out of a self-imposed burden to make Timothy proud. I tried to live for two and did not want our dreams to die.

One morning I checked my mailbox before I went to the library. A package in Manila paper and bubble wrap was waiting for me with a stamp from Naples. I anxiously opened it.

A small pocket Bible in Italian with gold-leafed letters on the cover slid out. I held the fresh black leather cover to my nose, then felt its uneven surface with my thumb and delicately sliced open its pages with my fingertips.

I wanted to be worthy of the gift. The little Bible accompanied me everywhere, and to improve my Italian I read page after page – in my room, in the coffee houses on Chapel Hill's main street, in the quad between classes.

My parents had read the Bible to me and my brothers every day at breakfast and dinner pontifications, so I had much of it memorised. Finding a verse for any occasion was almost a theological party trick. I did not need to carry around a dictionary for the tough words in Jambri's Bible. The verses were etched in my brain.

My method worked wonderfully for passages such as Psalm 23, Jambri's favourite Psalm, '*Il signore è il mio pastore, nulla mi mancherà.*' – The Lord is my shepherd, I shall not want. But plenty of times I scratched my head reading it. The book of Leviticus was the worst, '*Potete mangiare di ogni animale che ha lo zoccolo spaccato e il piede diviso che rumina.*' – You may eat from every animal that has hoofs and is cloven-footed and chews the cud. My system had its limitations, and I never found a chance to use my Levitical vocabulary.

Whenever I got a chance, I went to the library to watch old, grainy black-and-white films by Vittorio de Sica and Federico

Fellini. But my favourite movie was *Cinema Paradiso*, a new work by the Sicilian director Giuseppe Tornatore. The heart of the story was an eager apprentice's childhood friendship with an old man. The young boy nagged the projectionist for something to do. During the flicker of films, they shared their work, their lunches and their lives. And I wrote letters to Jambri with all the new words and expressions.

I had no idea how sick Jambri was. His letters never gave a hint of what he was going through. He had every right to self-pity but was never given to it.

Jambri had been sick in Spain, but his health deteriorated when he got to Naples. By the time he sent me the Bible, he was living in Cotugno Hospital, the hospital for infectious diseases in Naples. He became friends with all the doctors and patients on his ward. One day the nurses accidentally forgot to give Jambri lunch, and his roommate, a man connected to the *Camorra*, let the doctors know that there would be 'consequences' if something like that ever happened again. From then on, Jambri did not miss a meal.

I received the little black Bible on 2 April 1995. A few days earlier, on 21 March, *Il Mattino*, the main newspaper of Naples, had published a story about AIDS patients in Cotugno Hospital. A photograph of Jambri covered a third of the page. He appeared disturbingly thin in his pyjamas as he lay with his little mobile phone resting by his side. The headline above read, 'Among the Damned of Cotugno: This Is How the Sick with AIDS Die.'

The article recounted how the doctors and nurses were reluctant to work with HIV+ patients, how they did not have enough medicine to dispense. It was better to die quickly than waste away under the disinterested rounds of doctors. The journalist said that the article was meant to tell the plight of AIDS patients, but the headline did Jambri no good.

The article could not have painted a more misleading picture. Even though Jambri was confined to his room in the hospital, he kept his *telefonino* at his side and coordinated the work schedules for the shop. The leaders in Betel came in once a day to visit him and give him an account of what was going on in the centre. Jambri was sick but not damned, and if he was going to die, he would keep on running his *mercatino* and the men's residences for as long as he could.

After the article came out things were never the same again for Jambri, Mari Carmen and Isacco, his son who had been born right after they arrived in Italy. Women in the neighbourhood stopped talking to Mari Carmen and they even crossed to the other side of the street when she approached. When she took Isacco to play in the park near their home, mothers grabbed their children by the arm and led them away.

Rather than fight it, the men in Betel helped Jambri and Mari Carmen move to another neighbourhood.

My father visited Jambri in Cotugno. When he arrived, a general doctors' strike had closed most of the hospital, but my father bribed the guards to let him sneak into the building.

As he walked the empty corridors, my father saw the courtyard. The doctors, nurses and patients had thrown twisted bed frames, torn mattresses with protruding springs, soiled hospital sheets, and unwashed gowns out the windows. Blood covered the walls, and toilet paper streamed onto the ground from the bathroom windows. The only clean rooms were those kept tidy by visiting family members who guarded their dying sons and daughters. Because of a shortage of nurses, a transvestite patient with broad shoulders and long bleached blond hair had volunteered to give Jambri injections. In a coquettish voice he would say, 'Darling, don't you worry. I was a junkie. I *know* how to find veins.'

My father was amazed by Jambri's stories. An African patient lived in the next room over. During the day, when he had enough energy, he would walk over to Jambri's room and they would chat.

One night the man woke Jambri. He thanked Jambri for his friendship and said goodbye. A few minutes later, sirens blared in the street, and he heard yelling in the corridors. Red and blue lights swirled on the walls and ceiling of his room. His friend had jumped out the window.

'He had lost hope,' Jambri told my father. 'I'll never lose hope.'

The conditions of the hospital appalled my father. Ramón y Cajal was not the cheeriest of places, but it was a paradise in comparison with Cotugno. My father offered to bring Jambri back to Madrid. There at least he could preach on Sundays and rest during the week.

Jambri was incredulous. 'What's the difference? I can have fevers in Spain just as I can have them in Italy. I'll stay in Italy and work.'

One never knows when one is going to die with AIDS, but in January 1996, the doctors were sure that Jambri had only a week to live and told him to prepare for his death. Jambri did not want to burden Mari Carmen with repatriating his body to Spain, so he returned to Madrid.

Jambri did not die in a week, and he was right about having fevers in Madrid as easily as he had them in Italy. In Madrid he went in and out of the hospital. Mari Carmen learned to look after his oxygen supply and give him his pills and injections. He hated not working or running a *rastro*. He detested how his oxygen machine tied him down.

It was on a trip home at the end of summer that I saw Jambri at church. He was sitting on a cushioned chair in the front row with Mari Carmen and Isacco.

My throat tightened and I could barely speak.

'How are you?'

I put my arm around his shoulders.

He spoke softly and deliberately with his ever-so-slight lisp. 'Not well. Being sick is horrible. There isn't anything good about it. I have not been well for a long time. The doctors gave me a week to live months ago, and time is running out. But I can't change a thing about my health.'

He paused to catch his breath.

'There's nothing good about the disease, but my spirit is strong. I know I'm going to die, and I'm ready.'

He coughed and quoted from the Apostle Paul's letter to his young disciple Timothy, 'For I am now ready to be offered, and the time of my departure is at hand. I have fought a good fight, I have finished my course, I have kept the faith.'

I could not find the words to say anything and did my best not to cry.

Jambri held my hand like when I was nine, not because I was still a child but because he had become my older brother.

'One day your parents are going to tell you I've died. Don't be sad for me. I will be alive. My spirit cannot die.'

Jambri spoke about Naples and about his time in the hospital, and I learned the things he had not told me in his letters. We switched from Spanish to Italian, and he corrected me on occasion. I told him about all the Italian books and all the movies I had devoured. He encouraged me to continue learning Italian and never to give up my studies.

The church had filled, and the service was about to start. The singing began and after it was done, Jambri walked to the pulpit. Just as Raúl had done, Jambri waited for men in the centre to move the pulpit so he could preach sitting.

Jambri apologised that his speech was slow and for his dry cough; he was fighting a 100-degree fever. His doctor had told him to rest, but Jambri said he was going to preach even if someone had to prop him up. And for the next half-hour, he spoke eloquently.

As I listened to Jambri preach, I was struck by his words. He told the congregation that in the hospital, he had suffered alone in his room. One night, Jambri was on the verge of giving up, and he feared he would become like his African neighbour. He had to fight with every ounce of strength he had.

Jambri could not change his condition, but he conquered it by leaving no room for bitterness or unhappiness. He said, 'Everything material can be taken away from us, but only our joy can never be taken away.'

After the church service, we said goodbye. I promised him I would keep up my Italian and that I would write to him as soon as I got back to Chapel Hill.

As I was leaving, Jambri told me that his greatest sadness about dying was for his son Isacco. Jambri would have enjoyed seeing his son grow up, 'Sometimes I think life is too short.'

I was only a few years older than Isacco when Jambri and I first met.

Jambri and I never got a chance to write to each other again. The day I returned to Chapel Hill, my father called to let me know that Jambri had died. My parents visited him before he passed away. He was lucid until the end.

My father took his pocket Bible to the hospital, and Jambri asked him to read Psalm 23, his favourite Psalm. Jambri was short of breath and struggled to recite each word, but as my father read, he gathered his strength and whispered slowly:

The Lord is my shepherd; I shall not want.
He makes me to lie down in green pastures;
He leads me beside the still waters.
He restores my soul;
He guides me in straight paths for His name's sake.
Even though I walk through the valley of the shadow of death,

> *I will fear no evil, for You are with me;*
> *Your rod and Your staff, they comfort me.*
> *You prepare a table before me in the presence of my enemies;*
> *You have anointed my head with oil; my cup runs over.*
> *Surely goodness and mercy shall follow me all the days of my life;*
> *And I will dwell in the house of the Lord for ever.*

Jambri closed his eyes to sleep. He died ten minutes later. It was 14 August 1996, barely a week before his thirty-fourth birthday.

I thought a lot about San Blas after Jambri's death. When Jambri was in the hospital, he told one of his friends in the centre that all of Betel was going to heaven. Raúl, Trini, Manolo *Chatarra*, Ángel *Veneno*, little Jonny and many others we loved had died. Sometimes both parents died, leaving children orphaned. Everyone Jambri had shot up with was either dead or dying. Jambri's friends were my friends; they were dying, and my neighbourhood was dying with them.

When I was a child Jambri said he would never forget me because he could not get rid of me. I just kept coming back.

Now that I was twenty, it was the memory of Jambri that I could not get rid of. It was his smile and his thin face that kept coming back.

L'amor che move 'l sole e l'altre stelle

The love that moves the sun and the other stars

Culture may even be described simply as that which makes life worth living.
          T. S. Eliot, Notes Towards a Definition of Culture

AS THE INTERNET spread in the mid 1990s, my parents joined millions of others online. We no longer needed to rely on letters, beautifully folded aerograms and expensive phone calls. Over the screechy sound of dial-up modems, we instantaneously sent and received updates.

My mother kept us up to date with news of our friends through her emails. She had sent her boys out to the world as men, and as she told me, her job of teaching us the right values and to educate ourselves was done. But her work as a mother was never done. The men and women in Betel had become her children. She was like Sarah, the matriarch, and I often pictured her putting Abraham in his place. Her many children were much more friends, confidants and even co-conspirators in girlish levity. She wrote of how she'd take Paqui and others to McDonald's downtown for caramel sundaes as a treat after the weekly women's meetings.

I asked her if she regretted only having boys, and she said, 'I'm so used to you boys that I don't know what I would have done with a daughter.' And yet so many young women had become daughters to her.

Her emails connected us to home, but faster news did not always mean better news.

Scientists had discovered a cocktail of drugs – highly active antiretroviral therapy – that suppressed the virus and prolonged life. The first Spanish patients got it in late 1995, shortly after those in the US. There was no cure or effective vaccine against the virus. Everyone infected with HIV will carry that virus until the day they die, even if they die from something else. But the cocktail worked to stop AIDS in its tracks. The combination of drugs was so powerful it was even called 'the Lazarus effect', as it rolled the tombstone away and brought skeletal figures back to life.

While the cocktail of drugs was an unbelievable, almost magical cure, it did not mean that everyone was safe. Not everyone got it immediately or even took it, and some were too far gone for it to make a difference. It would take time for the deaths to completely stop. Deaths became less frequent, but they were no less cruel.

My mother and father often sent short, hurried emails informing me of the latest news. Esperanza had been in the women's Bible study group with my mother.

> *Just got a call from Javi. Esperanza died at home. They let her go home last Friday although they had been giving her the cocktail. That will really affect everyone here. Oh God, give us grace.*
> *Much love,*
> *Mom*

And news of old friends from the Barajas farm in the early days.

> *Last night Pedro went to be with the Lord after fighting courageously to be as long on this earth as he could with his family and*

Betel. We are going with a van-load of people at 12:00 midday today to the tanatorio and then have a special meeting at 6:00 at the Betel Valencia church. We will return to Madrid tonight. The funeral will be tomorrow morning, but we all want to be together today.

My mother was the correspondent who knitted our family together across the ocean with her email threads of anecdotes, encouragement and even the news of losing those we had loved for so long. She interspersed the updates with mentions of my father's travels to distant drug rehabs and notes on which Tchaikovsky pieces she had been listening to. It felt at times that we were still together, drinking our tea, reading books and listening to his Serenade for Strings in C major.

I had saved the addresses and phone numbers of my friends in my little blue address book. The names of loved ones who had died filled its pages. When I received the news, I'd look through it. But I could not bring myself to cross the names out.

One day, when I was procrastinating, I read an article online in *El País* that said that forty thousand Spaniards had died of AIDS since the first case appeared fifteen years earlier in Spain in 1981. I took my address book and started counting my friends who'd died of AIDS, uncertain of what the number would be. I stopped counting at twenty-five and I wasn't halfway through the book. These were the names of friends vanished and gone. Shame overwhelmed me. They were not statistics; they were my friends, and I loved them.

For years, I had cried every night, remembering Timothy. And now that my friends were dying, I was looking at address books and counting names, doing sums. Did I not feel? Did I not care?

I emailed my mother and asked if our hearts become hard with suffering. She replied:

I was thinking myself over the weekend that I have not cried about Estrella and her health, as much as I love her. And then as I read your email, I cried. Yes, you will cry again. Many times when I think I am going to cry, I don't; and when I think I won't, I do. We are funny creatures, we humans.

Only she could say so much with so few words.

Our hearts do not have to become hard. Losing friends does not get easier with repetition, and suffering does not diminish with practice. Death still hurts, but as my father wrote in his newsletter a few years before, 'AIDS breaks your heart. It makes you compassionate and softens you.'

As I went about my studies at university, the news of deaths slowed to a trickle, and then there were no more.

Like the sun rising in the morning, there was not a single moment when darkness turned to light, but the mist vanished, and we looked out on a brighter world where AIDS was no longer a mortal threat. Parents in Betel would live to see their children grow up. Almost all of my HIV+ friends could finally feel the breeze on their skin and the sun on their faces and know they might grow old like everyone else.

AIDS had become as boring and treatable as diabetes. Science had conquered it.

Life at Chapel Hill went on after Jambri and Raúl died, but everything else felt trivial. I missed them and wanted to disappear and leave all that I was doing. But the thought of doing nothing, of marinating in my grief and self-pity, as I so often did, was even more awful.

The only way I knew how to escape was through books. They had always been my retreat. And I sought refuge in the cloisters of libraries and bookshops. The stacks surrounded me like jagged ramparts, keeping the world outside away. My parents' books at home had been a bridge to another world, but on my own I stacked them high as if building a wall in my room, unsure of what I was even keeping in or out at that stage.

C. S. Lewis had been our guide at dinners, as my parents read from his books during my father's pontifications. I had seen the new film *Shadowlands*, which was based on his life as a don at Oxford University. In the film, Lewis says, 'We read to know we're not alone.' How strangely true it was! I did not relate to students around me and sought solace and company in my books, the ongoing conversation with dead writers and imaginary characters.

The hauntingly beautiful cinematography of Oxford's spires in *Shadowlands* inspired me.

Just as I had put maps of Harvard on my wall in high school and invested so much of my imagination, maps of Oxford University adorned my wall at Chapel Hill. I memorised the city's streets, tiled photos together of its Gothic colleges and knew their names by heart. I pinned my dreams to a cheap cork board, and hoped this time would be different. It was not Cambridge, as my father wanted. I was following my own North Star.

Yet I was my father's son. His presence guided me still. 'Look, here comes the dreamer.'

What I needed most of all was something to strive towards. Studies and activities filled my time as they had in high school – the more the better. I convinced myself I had to take my exams, perform in plays, work at homeless shelters, teach English to migrant workers – anything except idle time alone with my thoughts.

Fellowships and scholarships became my obsession. My father had sailed on the Queen Elizabeth to Southampton with Rhodes and Marshall scholars when he went to Cambridge. He said that no scholarship was more prestigious than the Rhodes. Notable scholars include Nobel Prize winners, politicians like President

Bill Clinton and Senator William Fulbright, secretaries of state like Dean Rusk, Supreme Court Justices Byron White and David Souter, and countless household names.

The odds were almost impossible. In 1997, the year before, a few thousand students across America applied to be their university's nominees, but only thirty-two could become Rhodes scholars. It wasn't hard to do the maths: 1 per cent chance of success and 99 per cent chance of failure.

Those odds were impossible: why even try?

And I remembered, 'Ah, but a man's reach should exceed his grasp, Or what's a heaven for?'

Writing an essay for the Rhodes application is a daunting endeavour. As I sat at my desk with Timothy and Raúl's photos staring at me, I felt completely lost for what to write. The first rule of writing is to write about what you know, and all I could write about was San Blas. I got excellent grades and wrote two honours theses – many of the applicants had. I had been adopted by a few renowned professors who took me under their wings – every candidate would have great letters of recommendation. I was obsessed with classical music and art – there was little unique about that.

A childhood growing up in San Blas, though, that was like a flawed stamp, spoiled by the printer. To some people it was useless and ugly, but to a collector its flaws made it rare and valuable. Or so I tried to convince myself.

I refused to wear San Blas as some cheap, pathetic, phony badge of honour and thought of not writing about it for fear that I would not do it justice. But if one thing shaped my ambitions, fears and hopes, it was my parents' work. Everything else flowed from there. For so long, I thought San Blas and the world of learning could never meet, but how wrong I was. College is a chance to reinvent yourself, but it is rediscovering your roots that holds the truth.

Un chaval de San Blas. A kid from San Blas. That's what I was. I loved my parents, Betel and my experiences working and even learning in San Blas. That was my home. Take away all that, and I had little left to write about. And so, I wrote:

> *Over the years I have spent months living and working in our centres. The recovered addicts are my brothers and sisters, and it is with sadness and joy that I have been with them as they have worked to help others – often until their last breath, as too many have died of AIDS.*
>
> *My parents often told me and my brothers, 'To whom much is given, much is required,' and it is a lesson that has not escaped us. We did not have much, but we took advantage of every opportunity we got. When my older brother went off to college, he sent me all his used books. With his college textbooks, I taught myself economics, history, chemistry and many other subjects. In my senior year I took ten Advanced Placement tests and was awarded almost two years of credits entering college.*

I hoped it would be the right amount of modesty with a little bit of humble bragging. It could be forgiven as it was for a good cause, I thought.

A friendly professor did not want me to get my hopes up, lest they be disappointed, and informed me my odds were not good. I was an oddball, and the university had more than twenty-five applications for a few nominations.

To my astonishment Chapel Hill nominated me and the Rhodes selection committee for North Carolina invited me for interviews. The odds had improved only marginally. First, I'd have to get North Carolina's nomination, and then get to the regional final.

The Rhodes selection process is a well-choreographed dance. The night before the final interviews about a dozen candidates and a handful of judges gather informally, milling about a room, chatting casually over soft drinks. The young nominees are already accomplished Goldwater scholars, Truman scholars, star athletes with perfect GPAs and weirdos with special abilities. I did not envy the judges' task.

Like errant moose in their yearly mating season, the candidates and judges wander in circles, awkwardly sniffing each other out. The young students know they are closely watched, while the judges pretend they are not taking stock of everyone. The next morning the candidates endure a barrage of questions in front of a committee of judges. Then the deliberations last a few hours. Knowing the routine in advance made it no less fearsome for the candidates.

My interview early in the morning was oddly unremarkable. The judges asked me many questions about history, foreign policy and politics and barely discussed my essay. That was not good.

I had no idea what the judges were thinking. Did they like me? Were they merely being polite? After twenty minutes of answering questions, I had no more idea of my odds than when the interview began.

The committee thanked me and sent me away.

I went away to get a coffee, trying not to look at my watch. At least I had given it a shot.

The judges said that they would announce the finalists at three o'clock. All the candidates gathered outside the deliberation room. Everyone was too tense to make small talk.

Before the clock struck three, a judge stepped out from the room, 'Is Jonathan here?' I raised my hand. 'Can you please come back for final questions?'

What was happening?

The head judge asked, 'Your essay discusses your family's drug centre and your interest in foreign policy. If you had to choose between working with addicts as your parents do or becoming secretary of state, what would you choose?'

I still do not know where my answer came from, but it arrived in a flash.

'Well, I'm only twenty-one. In an ideal world I'd live long enough to do both, but if I had to choose, I'd follow my parents. British history is my speciality, and a figure that comes to mind is Lord Castlereagh, who was foreign secretary for over a decade. Besides Lord Palmerston, he was probably the greatest British diplomat of the nineteenth century. He was the main British negotiator behind the Quadruple Alliance, the Treaty of Paris and the Congress of Vienna. He oversaw the resumption of ties with the United States after the Treaty of Ghent in 1813. By any measure, he was an exceptional diplomat. Yet, despite all his successes, he developed a paranoia and deep unhappiness and committed suicide in 1822.'

The judges sat in silence.

'My parents have a plaque in their study with the words of Jesus: "What does it profit a man if he gains the whole world and loses his soul?" I could be like Lord Castlereagh, achieving everything I wanted as a statesman, and still lose my soul. If forced to choose, I would choose to be like my parents.'

I was sure I had blown my chances. Rhodes scholars were distinguished secretaries of state; they did not work with grubby heroin addicts. I'd sacrificed whatever slim chance I had with that answer.

I wanted to go for a walk, but they asked us all to stand by.

A few minutes later the judges came out and announced North Carolina's two nominees. What a relief! I was one of them.

I felt an immense but fleeting sense of reprieve from the pressure. A judge wished me luck but told me not to get too excited. The state interviews were easy compared to what we would face at the final interviews. The finals would be a pitched battle.

At the final held in Davidson College, North Carolina, on the night of the informal drinks, one judge stood out among them all: Professor Benjamin Dunlap, a professor at Wofford College in South Carolina, soft-spoken but impressive. After he studied at Oxford as a Rhodes scholar, he received a doctorate from Harvard. He was a man of the world and he had lectured in Asia as a Fulbright scholar, and in his spare time wrote poems, essays, opera *libretti* and novels. 'He's the film critic from public TV,' someone whispered to me as he passed.

Was there anything Professor Dunlap had not done or did not know?

Over soft drinks and dry snacks, we had failed to answer his questions correctly. He had already weighed us and found us wanting. We all believed before we went into the interviews that he was going to tear us to shreds. He told us he had placed the scholarships in a cupboard and asked us not to touch them. We were evenly divided as to whether he was a mad genius or just a genius.

My interview was at nine in the morning, and I was grateful they had not called me earlier. In my hotel room, I read Jambri's little Italian Bible and held it like a talisman. I did not have faith figured out, but I could hold on to the parts that were beautiful, and I hoped that was good enough.

Professor Darryl Gless, a Rhodes scholar who taught Shakespeare at Chapel Hill and had studied at Oxford with President Clinton, told me before I left, 'If you win, it's not your doing; if you lose, it's not your fault.' Everyone who reaches the interview stages is accomplished; it is often luck that makes the outcome.

Professor Gless was right. The other finalists were supremely intimidating, like a top-ranked cadet at the Naval Academy who was captain of the rugby team, a polyglot who spoke a dozen languages, and others whose skills I dreaded discovering.

As we waited to be called by the judges, a young woman from Harvard informed all the other finalists that the selection process was deeply unfair to Harvard statistically. All Harvard students were superstars, yet the president of Harvard made few nominations, unlike second-rate universities that nominated many big fish in small ponds.

'You may be right. But you made it this far. You're here, and we're all here now. If you fail, you'll have no one to blame,' I said.

Six judges sat on the panel; most of them were older Rhodes scholars. Usually they are university professors, accomplished lawyers, celebrated political figures and journalists. They were well known in their fields. The idea of an interrogation by them is enough to unnerve any candidate.

As I walked in, I remembered the quote at the entrance to the Gypsy camp in San Blas, 'Abandon all hope, you who enter.'

The first to fire questions at me was Professor Dunlap, who asked, 'If you can speak Italian, and your father read books such as *The Divine Comedy* to you when you were growing up, please translate a passage and tell me who wrote it and where it is from.'

He quoted from memory:

Guido, i' vorrei che tu e Lapo ed io
Fossimo presi per incantamento
E messi in un vasel, ch'ad ogni vento
Per mare andasse al voler vostro e mio.

At first I stumbled because I could not understand every word of the Italian through his lilting Southern accent, so I asked him to repeat it. The judges leaned forward in their seats. They scented blood.

Even after repeating it, I did not catch everything with his Southern accent. 'One more time, please.'

The judges had to think I was a fraud.

'It is a quote from Dante Alighieri's *Divine Comedy*.'

For an instant, I wanted to be taken from the interview, but I did my best. I translated it:

Guido, I wish that you and Lapo and I,
Were taken by enchantment and
Placed in a vessel that with each wind
Would travel on the sea wherever our hearts desire.

Even though my translation was correct, the lines were from Dante's *Rime* and not *The Divine Comedy*.

Professor Dunlap asked me, 'Who was Guido?'

'Guido Guinizelli.'

'Wrong.' I was not doing well. 'But who was Guinizelli?'

'He was the creator of the *dolce stil nuovo* and the main influence on Dante's style.'

'Good answer. The right Guido is Guido Cavalcanti. Who was he and who was his father?'

'Guido was Dante's best friend and his father was Cavalcante Cavalcanti.'

'In the sixth Canto of the *Inferno*, Dante addresses Cavalcanti as *voi*. What is particular about that?'

'*Voi* is the archaic formal address. Dante used it as a sign of respect for the father of his dear friend.'

'Where else is it used in the *Divine Comedy*?'

'Brunetto Latini was addressed as *voi* in Canto XV.'

'Why was Brunetto Latini in hell? What was his sin?'

'He was *un violento contro natura*, a sodomite.'

He sat back, 'After a series of answers like that, I have no more questions.'

It was a long way from Neapolitan slang, but Jambri would have been pleased.

The other judges smiled as well. I had made it through the gauntlet of Professor Dunlap's questions. If I could make it through that, no other questions that morning were going to unnerve me. I was fascinated by so many well-informed, interesting people. It reminded me of answering questions, jousting with my father at the dinner table.

The pace picked up, and the other judges fired away questions, ranging from the bureaucratic reform of the State Department to specific decisions by the Supreme Court concerning freedom of speech to questions regarding British political reform movements in the nineteenth century.

A British historian who was the provost of the College of William and Mary concluded the interview. She asked, 'What motivated you to ask your brother to send you his college textbooks? That's an odd thing to do.'

'Whenever I visited my friends who were dying of AIDS at Ramón y Cajal Hospital, I saw the quote "Every man can be the sculptor of his own mind if he sets himself the task" above the entrance. I paused to take it in. Santiago Ramón y Cajal was the first Spaniard to win the Nobel Prize in sciences. His words have been my guiding light. I want to be the sculptor of my own mind. I don't want to chip away at the walls of learning like Jude the Obscure. I want to be inside and study at Oxford.'

The committee thanked me for my time answering questions and excused me. I went for a walk.

It didn't matter if I won or not. For the first time, I didn't feel like an oddball. Or at least, I felt at home with oddballs like Professor Dunlap.

The deliberations took only a few hours, but they felt interminable.

Finally, the judges emerged from the room; I had been chosen as a Rhodes scholar.

I was elated to be selected but feared I would not live up to the expectations placed upon me. As one of the older scholars had told me, 'A Rhodes scholar is a young man with a bright future *behind* him.'

It was late in the afternoon Spanish time, and the first thing I did was make a collect phone call to Madrid. My parents were waiting by the phone. 'Mom, Dad, I won! Tell all the people in Betel I got the Rhodes. I'm going to Oxford.'

'Jonathan, all the pontifications paid off in the end, didn't they? I'm sorry Mom and I ruined your life . . . It's not Cambridge, but I'm proud of you.'

'Elliott, knock it off.' My mother giggled. I couldn't remember the last time she was so happy. 'Don't listen to your father. You're your own man.'

'We're so proud of you. You've surpassed me academically, and I couldn't be happier. We'll tell all the men in Betel . . .' my father promised.

With that, the connection mysteriously dropped. I did not know if the line had gone dead or if they were already calling the people in Betel. It didn't matter.

I said goodbye to the other candidates and thanked the judges. Professor Dunlap approached me and smiled. 'I thought you'd do well.'

'But you were the hardest . . .'

With a mischievous grin, he said, 'It only looks that way from the outside. It was my role to give you a chance to dazzle or fail spectacularly. You did the rest.'

I practically leapt off the steps of the college building and pumped my fists to touch the sky. I yelped and hollered and cranked up the music in the car as I sped back to Chapel Hill to celebrate with David.

In that instant, winning the Rhodes gave me a rush – a surge of complete, utter euphoria unlike anything I had ever felt. *This must be what it feels like shooting up. This. This is the feeling I've been searching for.*

My mother was right. The best is always yet to come.

David and I shared a beer at Chapel Hill. We raised a glass for Timothy.

That night I barely slept.

For so long studying had been a way of forgetting. Yet now that I had found success, all I could do was remember those I loved.

For years I had read books and had become so engrossed in them that little else mattered. Perhaps I had hoped my mind would be like a blackboard and by writing and rewriting over it, the sadness that had etched itself would blur and be wiped away for ever. I had tried to live for two, but had only lived half a life.

When I had visited Raúl in the hospital he never failed to cheer me up and dry my tears. Even in the misery and squalor of Cotugno, Jambri had decided to be joyful. He knew he would die young, but he chose joy. I too would have to learn to choose.

Raúl, Jambri and Timothy had died, but their presence lingered like a boat's wake, growing ever fainter but ever wider.

I knew they wanted me to be happy. They always had. It was I who had refused.

Just like Dante wished to be taken by enchantment with his friends Guido and Lapo, I wished I could have called Timothy, Jambri and Raúl and shared the moment with them.

I thought of Timothy and would have given anything to share the excitement with him. We never went to Harvard or shared the apartment in Boston or played at the Village Vanguard, but I hoped that somewhere he was proud of me.

Jambri would have been amused to know how useful all his letters, books and the little black Bible had been. He had no idea how much his encouragement meant to me. He gave me his friendship, opened Italian culture from Dante to Neapolitan slang, and made my world much larger than I ever could have hoped.

Raúl would have seen how I sculpted my mind as Santiago Ramón y Cajal had written. The bold, luminous letters still guided me. I had learned for learning's sake. The joy was always in the discovery, not in the prize.

My father was right. Books shaped me.

We are the sculptors of our own minds; we are the authors of our own lives and we become the stories we tell ourselves. That's what I had told myself for years and came to believe.

How wrong I was!

We do not do it alone or bootstrap ourselves. My parents read to me at the dinner table every night, and David selflessly gave me all his college books. My friends gave me love and encouragement. My professors at Chapel Hill adopted me, and even friendly strangers like Professor Dunlap saw a spark in me and gave me a chance. I couldn't have done it without them. No. We don't do it alone. It is our family and friends who give us the tools to become ourselves. Our friends show up when we need them. And even when they are gone, we hear their familiar voices speaking, encouraging, and guiding us.

I was lost for words. As I lay in bed, I thought of a few of the last lines from the *Divine Comedy*, when Dante himself was overwhelmed:

a l'alta fantasia qui mancò possa;
già volgeva il mio disio e 'l velle,
sì come rota ch'igualmente è mossa,
l'amor che move 'l sole e l'altre stelle.

Here powers failed my high imagination:
Now my will and my desire were turned,
Like a wheel in perfect motion,
By the love that moves the sun and the other stars.

As my mother said, the answer is always more love. It is the love of family, of friends, and even the love of learning that changes the world around us and, most importantly, transforms us. It is love that makes us who we are and makes us whole.

I put aside any self-pity and despair that had weighed me down for so many years. Unburdened at last, I felt a lightness of spirit.

I went to the closet and found the cassette of Miles Davis's *Milestones* at the bottom of my suitcase. I slid it into the tape player. For the first time in years, I played jazz again.

The syncopated rhythms flooded the room in Davis and Coltrane's animated musical dialogue, *Ta, ta, Ta, ta. Ta, ta, Ta, ta, Taaa* ... I tapped my feet and felt surprised by sheer joy as the notes soared.

Timothy was right. You couldn't listen to *Milestones* without being happy to be alive.

Epílogo

Epilogue

I F YOU VISIT San Blas today, everything has changed. The Gypsy camp disappeared years ago. In San Blas there are no longer make-shift shacks, no more tubs and pipes for sale along Carretera de Vicálvaro. The M-40, a six-lane ring road, now cuts across the open fields between San Blas and the neighbouring town of Vicálvaro. There is nothing to remind me that they ever lived there.

The dump behind our old apartment on Calle Butrón is now full of new buildings and public parks that, although they all look the same, do not have the squat, claustrophobic feel of the older buildings.

A few ageing parents of the first men in our drug centre still live near what used to be Torre del Campo, but the world they inhabited is gone. The old four-storey red-brick buildings are now covered in bright stucco. The dirt lots between the buildings are now parks. Parque El Paraíso has fewer addicts shooting up. It could not be further from the place where I once grew up.

Drugs don't simply disappear. The drug supermarkets moved on from *Los Focos* in San Blas to La Celsa, then to *Los Pitufos*, then to *Las Barranquillas*. The bulldozers keep following them.

AIDS faded away as a mortal threat in the late 1990s, as the cocktail of drugs brought the virus under control. The 'Lazarus effect' was real. Almost all the early generation in Betel died, but those who came in a few years later have all survived. Many of the Betel leaders are HIV+, but they're alive and working helping others.

Betel has gone from a small group of men living together in a crowded apartment to a large organisation with offices and residences in cities around the world. The centre's international headquarters sits on a hill in the neighbourhood of Carabanchel in the west of Madrid, the opposite side of the city from where Betel began. Carabanchel was also home to one of the largest prisons in Spain. Jambri spent five years there for robbing banks, and many of my other friends did time there too.

Today Betel takes care of more than two thousand recovering addicts in residential programmes in more than twenty countries around the world. Over the last forty years, it has helped more than two hundred thousand addicts. The church and headquarters in Madrid is massive and always full. I find it hard to believe it all started in my parents' living room.

The programme is completely free. Betel operates hundreds of small businesses, all run by former addicts working side by side. They are like stones that a river drags out to sea. Living and working together they bump up against each other for hundreds of miles on their way to the shore, wearing away the rough edges. Most of them never graduated from school, but they make sure that everything runs smoothly. They make it happen.

The story of Betel is extraordinary, but my parents almost never gave interviews or sought attention. They thought it was unseemly and not Christ-like.

My mother and father had reason to be proud of all they accomplished over the decades, but not because of the size of the building or the numbers of addicts in the centres. My parents did not set out to create a large organisation, seek political influence, or fight any culture wars. They set out to show compassion to one addict at a time.

My father is seventy-nine and still runs Betel; the centre is his life. The old lion wants to work helping others to the day he dies.

My mother had a major brain surgery in 2009 to remove a large tumour. The night before her operation, the surgeon told us what he would do and how he would saw her skull and cut out her tumour. He told us, 'Your mother will likely not be the same person after the operation. She'll have to recover her skills and may need to learn to read and write again.'

We ignored him. We were optimists, we were fighters, and she was going to get better.

If anything, the doctor understated her problems. My mother had derived so much joy from reading novels and books and writing to her family and friends all her life. From one day to the next, she had to learn to read, write and speak again.

My mother struggled to read more than a few words, and even writing her name took much effort. Her speech was clipped and short, and she struggled to say everyday words. Her mental faculties were not at all impaired, as any conversation with her showed that she not only followed everything everyone was saying, but if you were patient and let her speak, she was her old self and could still offer wise insights and advice.

Every day my father and mother worked on her handwriting and reading. Before the operation, she read *Emma*, *War and Peace* and books of poetry. Afterwards, she could barely read glossy magazines.

My mother was a strong woman who had suffered more than most can bear in life, and I thought she was more than a match for her troubles. Despite all the grief she had faced, she was the one who gave strength to others.

After her operation, her brain struggled to recover its old state. She would lie on the sofa and did not want to go out and see people. When she did venture out, she greeted everyone with a smile and a wave, not showing any signs of her pain.

My father took her to doctors, who within a few minutes put her on anti-depressants and anti-anxiety medication. The psychiatrist told us that taking pills would be a temporary step, they would help her, and she would go back to her old happy self.

My mother would get antsy if she had too much coffee. I can't imagine how anti-depressants made her feel. As soon as she started on them, she complained that she felt like she was crawling out of her skin. Those are her words, not mine. As with almost all medicines, one 'cure' led to side effects, which required further medication.

Moments of panic alternated with states of calm. As her panic attacks and shaking got worse, she started speaking of suicide. This was completely out of character for her. She tried to take too many pills, but they made her vomit and wouldn't have killed her. She tried other methods, but they were more a desperate cry for help than any well-thought-out plan. My father and her friends were always around to look after her. We thought we had the odds on our side.

My mother took her life in 2012. She jumped from the rooftop of Betel's headquarters. I knew that she wanted to kill herself, but I did not think it would happen that way. A few days before she died, she told me she did not want to worry us with caring for her. She thought she was doing something noble, like an elder wandering off alone into the snowstorm to avoid burdening the tribe. She had given me life, and I was incapable of keeping her from leaving mine.

My mother suffered a great deal, and now she is suffering no more.

I hope people will remember what a wonderful woman she was all her life. I never met a kinder, gentler, more selfless person.

More than 1,500 people came to her memorial service, and thousands more watched the service live as it streamed on the internet. People I didn't even know hugged me, and through the tears, told me she had changed their lives. A young man who was a stranger embraced me and wept. He said, 'I didn't know her well, but I know that she gave me back my parents.'

Before my mother had her brain tumour, she wrote to me about a memoir she had read: 'Last night I finished reading it. It seemed a little anticlimactic. And there was no hope in the end. Jonathan, your book is going to be so much better because there will be so much hope all throughout the book. That's what Betel is all about.' That was my mother, always transmitting hope to others. If there is any love and kindness in this memoir and in me still, it comes from her.

When I was a child, I thought my father had all the answers and was stronger than everyone. I believed my mother had infinite grace and could bear the burdens of the world and bend but never break. Now I know they were not perfect, yet their weaknesses made them more human and all the more admirable in my eyes.

My parents were not saints – I don't believe in them – but they are heroes to me. They were people who practised love and empathy daily. Arthur Ashe, the great tennis player who died of AIDS in 1993, put it best: 'True heroism is remarkably sober, very undramatic. It is not the urge to surpass all others at whatever cost, but the urge to serve others at whatever cost.'

When we were at the breakfast table, my mother and father often repeated the words of John Wesley to us: 'Do all the good you can, by all the means you can, in all the ways you can, in all the places you can, at all the times you can, to all the people you can, as long as ever you can.' They lived by those words.

San Blas is not the same and the centre has grown more than I could have ever dreamed it would, but some things do not change.

Mari Carmen once told me that Jambri threw away almost all of his clothes as he lost weight over the years, but he never threw away the green T-shirt I gave him. He liked it so much he even got her to sew up all the little holes he put in it by wearing it too much. I still have Raúl's green checked shirt and cap, and I too sew up the holes.

The old San Blas died years ago, and it died many times over with each friend that passed away.

I often asked myself where God was when my friends were dying in San Blas and Ramón y Cajal. My family and I went to the hospital to encourage Raúl, Jambri, Manolo, Ángel, Marimar and others, but it was our friends who encouraged us. We came to raise their spirits, but they lifted ours.

I like to think that my friends were refractions and reflections of goodness. It was their joy amid suffering that shone brightly and ennobled them and everyone around them. Their happiness was not something that came easily; it came from a choice that they made again and again. It was ultimately a choice that I had to learn to make.

For years, I had tried to evade grief, to muffle the drums of suffering. But we cannot escape loss, sickness or death. The sadness of losing those we love is the other side of the coin. As C. S. Lewis wrote in *A Grief Observed*, 'The pain I feel now is the happiness I had before. That's the deal.' Every great love story will eventually become one of loss. If we do not love, we will not suffer. We cannot have it any other way.

Suffering itself is meaningless. It is our response to it that gives it meaning, and it is not an easy task to thread the needle of suffering. The answer to suffering is always more love. We can love those who are hurting, and when we are grieving, we can treasure and remember those who have passed.

I now understand what Raúl meant when he said, 'AIDS has been positive.' Losing loved ones is heartbreaking, and I do not wish death on anyone. But with the added perspective of time, death has made me aware of the preciousness of life, the importance of family and friends, and the overwhelming power of love and memory.

As I look back on my life, I feel lucky in so many ways. Shattering tragedies have marked my life, but I was always surrounded by a loving family and community. True misfortune and trauma are for those who suffer and are not surrounded by love.

Raúl once said that the most beautiful story anyone can tell is the story of his own life. I do not know if my story is beautiful, but it is the only one I have. Some writers make a fetish of their suffering and wear it like a medal. Others treat memoirs like letters in a bottle, hoping to send the pain out to sea, never to be seen again. I wrote this book because words keep time from bleaching the colours out of memories, the fading snapshots of the past. I wanted to tell my friends' stories. I hope the memory of my friends might be a blessing to others.

The story of my family and of Betel is of fixing broken things and loving those who are hurting. It is in the brokenness that we find redemption, turning pain into beauty.

My parents did not know what they were getting themselves into when they moved to our neighbourhood. They wanted to go to Spain, but never set out specifically to live in San Blas. If we had settled anywhere else, life would have been unimaginably different. San Blas was not the worst neighbourhood I have ever seen. It was a *barrio* in transformation, at a unique time and place, a world where ordinary people lived uneventful lives and tried to eke out a living day after day.

Sometimes when I think back on the neighbourhood, it all feels like a dream so different from my world today. My parents set out to change San Blas, but they could not have known how stepping into its closed world would change everything in ours.

In college David majored in mathematics, graduating with highest honours. He wrote a thesis of great originality in analytical geometry on fractals and space-filling curves. Fractals are beautiful angular patterns based on equations that endlessly repeat themselves, forming smooth, fluid shapes resembling waves, leaves and plants. There is order in the randomness and uncertainty in the order. If you change a small part of the initial equation, a fractal alters its shape in unpredictable ways, drawing something unexpected.

The pattern of my life would look nothing like it is now if my parents had settled somewhere else. Today, it is hard for me to see what other patterns might have looked like – and I would not want to imagine what they might have been. If given the chance to trade away the sadness, I'm not sure I would. Without my parents' calling, I never would have grown up in San Blas and my life would be all the poorer.

San Blas has changed, and it has changed me over the years. The men and women in the centre who were recovering from heroin addiction became part of me. No matter how far away from San Blas I might live or what I might do, my friends from the *barrio* stay with me.

My brothers no longer live in Madrid, but we go back as often as we can. We all graduated together the same day from Oxford. Many of the Betel directors came to visit, and I showed Raúl's daughters around my college. David works with me running Prevatt Capital, a fund that bears my mother's maiden name. All of the supply and demand curves and formulae my father wrote on the back of napkins at dinner had an influence. Peter was a student chaplain at St Aldate's, Oxford, and now pastors a church in Florida. We are bound by the unbreakable bonds of brotherhood.

This story ends not with death but with the breath of life. Raúl's daughters have grown up happy and well and now have children, and Jenny has retired after working with Betel for decades and lives close to them. My brothers have children of their own, and my wife and I have a boy, our first child. He is a human hurricane of curiosity.

My brothers and I feigned falling asleep at the dinner table, but the lessons my father and mother imparted will forever be with us. I remember my father's reading of Eliot's 'Little Gidding' from his *Four Quartets*, and the idea of the end of our exploring is to arrive where we start. I know that every time I return to San Blas, I rediscover myself. However, it is not that well-known quote, now almost a cliché, that stands out most. A few lines later, Eliot quotes the English writer and mystical theologian Julian of Norwich. She wrote:

And all shall be well and
All manner of things shall be well

When Timothy died, I thought that nothing would ever again be well. The thought repeated itself throughout the years every time a friend died. And I believed I could never be happy. Now I know that we do have a choice. We have to make it. We have a duty to live.

Life goes on, and surely as sorrow follows happiness, tragedy holds within itself the possibility of joy.

Agradecimientos

Acknowledgements

I would like to thank Dr Thomas L. Webber for providing the inspiration to write this book. If I had not stumbled upon *Flying Over 96th Street: Memoir of an East Harlem White Boy* at a bookstore on the Upper West Side of Manhattan, I never would have written a page. Dr Webber wrote eloquently about growing up as an outsider in East Harlem because of the Christian calling of his parents. His coming-of-age story is elegiac, moving and deeply empathetic. He was unfailingly gracious and provided many suggestions, but most importantly, he made me question every aspect of what I wrote and encouraged me to avoid easy writing and be unflinchingly honest.

Humans file memories away imperfectly, and when we call them up – especially from many years ago – we reconstitute them according to patterns we have learned from books and movies. Each time we dredge up a memory, we distort it a bit more in the direction we prefer. To compound the problem, we look at the past through the lens of the present. Even if memories could be recorded perfectly, we all view the same events from different angles and no two recollections could ever be the same.

I spoke to many friends and characters in the story, and their recollections were often slightly different from mine. Any imperfections in the story are entirely my own doing.

J.R.R. Tolkien wrote, 'Good stories deserve a little embellishment,' but I tried to double and triple check everything I could to tell the story as it happened.

I want to thank those who helped eliminate the distortions of my own memory: my parents, my brothers, Jenny Scantlebury, Lindsay and Myk McKenzie, Kent and Mary Alice Martin, Mari Carmen González, Juan Carlos Matesanz, all the older mothers in Betel, Melinda Fish, Merry Davey, Rose Anne Thornburg and Professor Benjamin Dunlap. They let me rummage through their files, photographs and newspaper clippings and withstood many interviews and emails. They helped fan the dying embers of memory.

Thanks to Peter Tepper, Steve Roberts, Pepe Verdú, Carlos Gutiérrez and Priscila McKenzie for helping me hunt for tapes, pictures, documentaries and articles to double check dates, facts and statements. Thanks to them, many quotes from characters come straight from their letters, diaries, emails and recorded sermons. Some chapters, for example, the accident and the year after it, came in part from notes I wrote when I was fifteen.

Despite my best efforts, I'm sure if I could have interviewed Raúl and Jambri, they would have set me straight on a few points.

I changed some names in the story to protect people's privacy, but I have tried to record things as accurately as memory allows.

Dialogues have been recreated imperfectly (no one's memory is *that* good), but I have tried to capture the spirit of the conversations as I remember them. And yet in many cases, I can recall things verbatim years later, like my father telling me after Timothy died, 'From now on, you have to live life one day at a time,' or when Raúl hugged me after Timothy died and said, '*Os quiero, os quiero, os quiero,*' and how he told me to look after his daughters at Ramón y Cajal with the words, '*Cuida de mis hijas.*' There are some things you never forget.

My friends have been a source of encouragement as I wrote. I am in their debt for their criticism and kindness. James Mumford, *il miglior fabbro*, taught me much about writing and kindly read many drafts. Special thanks are due to Turi Munthe, Daniel Swift, Gordon Weetman, Gemma Sieff, Trisha Telep, Keir McGuinness, Peregrine Cust, Joseph Luzzi, Charles Beckett, Patrick Gray, Andrew Rosen, Dr Darryl Gless, Dr David Halperin, Grace Kao, Jeff Kulkarni, David Mignon, Jack Kirkland, Amanda Branson-Gill, Simon and Tiffany Ponsonby, Daniel Rosen and Joanna Rivard.

I wrote the memoir in the evenings from 2005 to 2008, but never got around to editing it. My work always seemed to get in the way, but thanks to Andy Brown for encouraging me to finish the project and get it published.

My literary agent Matthew Hamilton in the UK believed in the book and brought it to publication. My literary agent Sam Hiyate in the US is a wonderful friend and agent. Thanks to both for believing in the manuscript.

Thanks to Andreas Campomar, my editor at Little, Brown, for his sensitive, thoughtful editing. Thanks to Holly Blood for her help and great care editing, proofreading, and bringing the manuscript to publication.

Thanks to Jenny and her daughters and Mari Carmen and Isacco for allowing me to write Raúl and Jambri's stories.

Thanks to Lindsay and Myk McKenzie. They helped start Betel with my parents, and their act of love and courage has changed the lives of thousands.

The men and women of Betel have given me their love and friendship over the years; they are my brothers and sisters. This is their story as much as mine.

Thanks to my wife, Stacey, for putting up with all of my quirks and obsessions, including finishing this book.

Thanks are due above all to my parents. Without them, there is no story.

My brothers Peter and David have been *mis colegas* all these years from the streets of San Blas to Oxford. How I wish Timothy could have been with us for the whole journey!

Fotografías

Photographs

Tepper family before arriving in Spain, 1983
Mary, Peter, David, Jonathan, Timothy and Elliott

Elliott and Jonathan handing out pamphlets, 1984. Luis Mendoza is the addict; he entered the centre and was the first to die of AIDS.

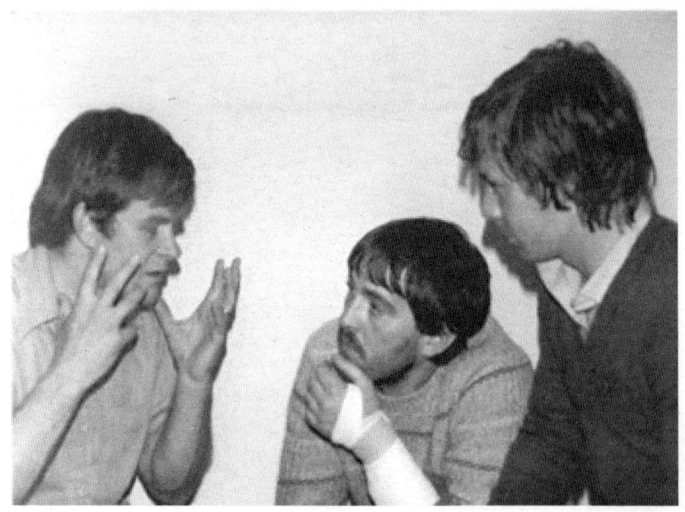

Elliott, Raúl and Ángel *Veneno* in Raúl's first visit to our home

David, Jonathan and Peter (left to right)

Ramón, Elliott, Peter, Mary, David, Jonathan,
Myk, Lindsay and Timothy, 1986

Lunch on the farm, 1986

Betel's first *rastro*

Jambri (left) on the farm

Peter, Jonathan, Timothy and David (left to right)
at Santiago Bernabéu

Raúl (bottom) and the men and women in Betel, 1987. Luis Mendoza is on the far left. Almost all died within a few years of this photograph.

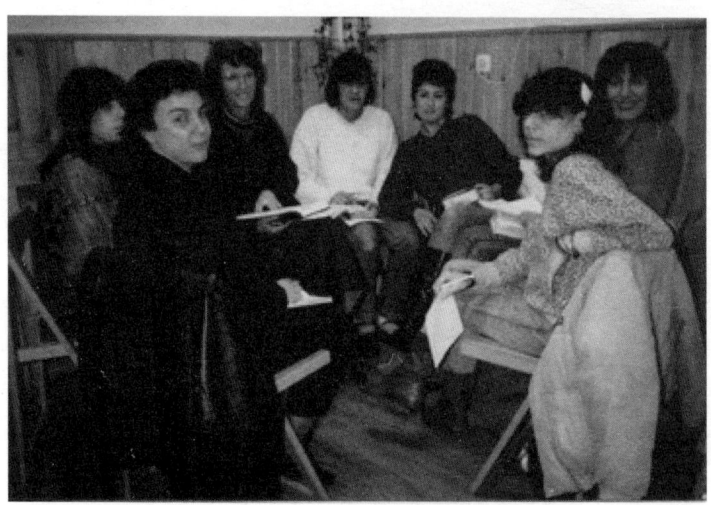

Mary (third from left) with early women's addicts Bible study. Marimar is on the far right.

Betel church, 1986

Betel church after repairs, 1988

Rebuilding Mejorada

Lunch at Mejorada

Elliott, 1985

Raúl, 1986

Jambri, Raúl and Jenny, 1988

Mary, Timothy, Peter and Jonathan, 1988. Home-schooling

Mary and Timothy, vacation, 1989

Timothy at nine years old, 1990

Peter, Mary, David, Timothy, Elliott and Jonathan (left to right), 1991

Betel men working on the chicken farm, 1993

Ramón y Cajal Hospital, with the face of Santiago Ramón y Cajal (1852–1934)

Raúl and Jonathan, 1992

Raúl, 1992

Jenny and Raúl, 1995

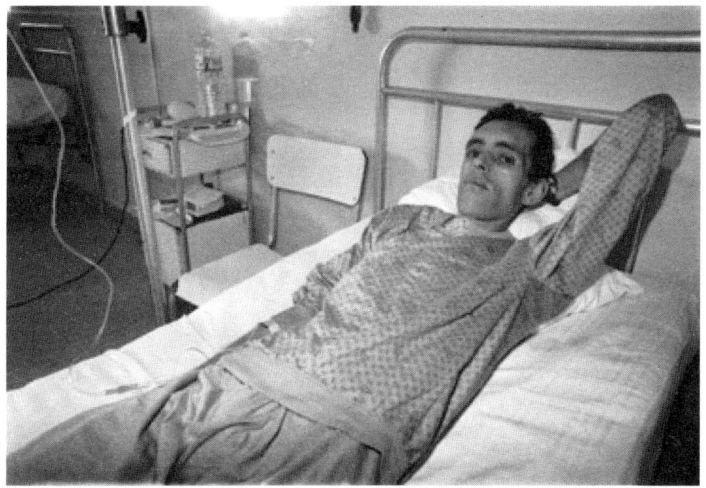

Jambri in Cotugno, 1995

Jambri preaching, 1995

Mary and Jonathan, 1998

David, Elliott, Jonathan, Mary and Peter at Oxford graduation

Peter, Jonathan and David (left to right), San Blas, 1986

Peter, Jonathan and David (left to right), Oxford graduation

Elliott and Mary Tepper, 2009

Sobre el autor

About the author

Jonathan Tepper is the chief investment officer at Prevatt Capital. Jonathan was the founder of Variant Perception, which provides research to asset managers. Formerly, he was an analyst at SAC Capital and a vice president on the proprietary trading desk at Bank of America. Along the way, with his friend Turi Munthe, they founded Demotix, a citizen-journalism website and photo agency. They sold Demotix in 2012 to Corbis, a company owned then by Bill Gates. Jonathan is the author of a few financial books. He is a Rhodes scholar and graduated with highest honours in history and honours in economics from the University of North Carolina at Chapel Hill and has an MLitt from the University of Oxford.